The Muslim Speaker Toolkit

Compiled References from Quran & Sunnah

Copyright © 2018. Asad Zaman. All rights reserved.

Whoever purified it has succeeded

Table of Contents

Foreword 6
   Chosen By Allah! 8
Essential Muslim Qualities 10
   Mercy (رحمة) 11
   Innate Nature (فِطْرة) 15
   Humility (تَواضُع) 17
   Purification (تَزْكِية) 20
   Reason (عَقْلانية) 24
   Hope (أَمَل) 27
   Integrity (إسْتِقامة) 29
   Patience (صَبْر) 31
   Reliance (تَوَكُّل) 34
   Forgiveness (مَغْفِرة) 37
   Repentance (تَوْبَة) 40
   Etiquette of Disagreement (أَدَبُ الخِلاف) 44
   A Word Portrait Of The Messenger of Allah (*peace be upon him*) 48
Characteristics Of The Complete Muslim 50
   Pure Belief (سَلامَةُ العَقِيدَة) 52
   Correct Worship (صِحَّةُ العِبَادة) 54
   Good Character & Conduct (حُسْنُ الخُلُق) 59
   Enlightened Intellect (ثقافة الفِكْر) 65
   Healthy Body (قُوَّةُ الجِسْم) 68
   Capable Of Earning A Living (القُدْرَةُ على الكَسْب) 71
   Organized (تَنْظِيمُ الشُؤُون) 75
   Mindful Of The Importance Of Time (الحِرْصُ على الوَقْت) 77
   Self-Restrained (مُجَاهَدةُ النَّفْس) 80
   Beneficial To Others (النَّفْعُ لِلْغَيْر) 83
   Examples Of Complete Muslims 86
Leadership Qualities & Concepts 87
   Trust (أَمَانَة) 88
   Stewardship (خِلافَة) 92
   Altruism (إيثَار) 97
   Courage (شَجَاعَة) 101
   Consultation (شُورَى) 105
   Juristic Effort (إجْتِهَاد) 107
   Asceticism (زُهْد) 110
   Humor (خِفَّةُ الظِلّ) 113
   An Exemplary Leadership 116
Characteristics of the Islamic Movement 117

- Godliness (رَبَّانية) 119
- Cooperation & Teamwork (جَمَاعَة) 123
- Comprehensiveness (شُمُولِيَة) 126
- Constructive (بِنَاء) 129
- Universality (عَالَمِيَة) 132
- Gradualism (تَدَرُّج) 133
- Balance & Moderation (تَوَازُنٌ وَ وَسَطِيَة) 137
- Realism (وَاقِعِيَة) 141

Key Ingredients Of Successful Teams 142
- Proactiveness (إِيجَابِيَة) 144
- Justice (عَدَالَة) 148
- Personal Development (تَرْبِيَة) 151
- A Classical Approach To Tarbiyah 155
- Diversity (تَنَوُّع) 158
- Commitment (إِلْتِزَام) 161

Dimensions Of Commitment 163
- Understanding (فَهْم) 164
- The Twenty Principles of Understanding 167
- Sincerity (إِخْلَاص) 173
- Activism (عَمَل) 175
- Struggle (الجِهَاد) 179
- Sacrifice (تَضْحِيَة) 182
- Obedience (طَاعَة) 185
- Perseverance (ثَبَات) 188
- Dedication (تَجَرُّد) 191
- Fraternity (أُخُوَّة) 193
- Confidence in Leadership (الثِّقَةُ فِي القِيَادَة) 196

Do they not reflect upon the Quran?

Foreword

All praise belongs to Allah, the Lord of the worlds. Salutations and peace upon our beloved master, Muhammad (peace be upon him) and upon his companions and their followers upon the path of righteousness.

This book began as talking points for various discussions I have facilitated, or lectures and sermons I have delivered. Several people have suggested that I compile them for ease of access.

In this book, I compiled quotes from the Quran and Hadith by topic and added a few quotes from classical Islamic texts. I have kept my thoughts on each topic to a minimum because the Quran and Hadith are more eloquent than anything I have to add. This book is intended to be used to facilitate a discussion on a specific topic. It can also be used as an outline for public speeches or Friday sermons.

I thank the brothers and sisters who have encouraged and helped me with this work. I ask Allah to reward them immensely.

I apologize for the obvious shortcomings in this work. I hope the reader is able to benefit from this work and I humbly ask you to remember me in your dua.

My Lord, indeed you have given me some abilities and have taught me the understanding of some things. Creater of the heavens and the earth, You are my source of strength, cause me to die among those who have submitted to You and resurrect me among the righteous.

Asad Zaman
Rabi ul Akhir 1439
January 2018

Indeed in the Messenger of Allah is an ideal example for you

Chosen By Allah!

Honorable indeed is the one chosen by Allah the Exalted! An exclusive community of people who love Him, answer His call, worship Him, and strive with all their effort to please Him alone.

وَجَٰهِدُوا۟ فِى ٱللَّهِ حَقَّ جِهَادِهِۦ ۚ هُوَ ٱجْتَبَىٰكُمْ وَمَا جَعَلَ عَلَيْكُمْ فِى ٱلدِّينِ مِنْ حَرَجٍ ۚ مِّلَّةَ أَبِيكُمْ إِبْرَٰهِيمَ ۚ هُوَ سَمَّىٰكُمُ ٱلْمُسْلِمِينَ مِن قَبْلُ وَفِى هَٰذَا لِيَكُونَ ٱلرَّسُولُ شَهِيدًا عَلَيْكُمْ وَتَكُونُوا۟ شُهَدَآءَ عَلَى ٱلنَّاسِ ۚ فَأَقِيمُوا۟ ٱلصَّلَوٰةَ وَءَاتُوا۟ ٱلزَّكَوٰةَ وَٱعْتَصِمُوا۟ بِٱللَّهِ هُوَ مَوْلَىٰكُمْ ۖ فَنِعْمَ ٱلْمَوْلَىٰ وَنِعْمَ ٱلنَّصِيرُ ﴿٧٨﴾
(القرآن ٢٢:٧٨)

And strive hard in the way of Allah, as is due to Him. He has chosen you and has not laid upon you hardship in the religion. The faith of your father, Ibrahim. Allah named you "Muslims" both before and in this (Revelation) that the Messenger may be a witness over you and you may be witnesses over the people. So establish prayer and give charity and hold fast to Allah. He is your Protector. An excellent Protector and an excellent Helper! (Quran 22:78)

يَٰٓأَيُّهَا ٱلَّذِينَ ءَامَنُوا۟ ٱسْتَجِيبُوا۟ لِلَّهِ وَلِلرَّسُولِ إِذَا دَعَاكُمْ لِمَا يُحْيِيكُمْ ۖ وَٱعْلَمُوٓا۟ أَنَّ ٱللَّهَ يَحُولُ بَيْنَ ٱلْمَرْءِ وَقَلْبِهِۦ وَأَنَّهُۥٓ إِلَيْهِ تُحْشَرُونَ ﴿٢٤﴾
(القرآن ٢٤:٨)

O believers! Answer the call of Allah and His Messenger when he calls you to that which gives you life; and know that Allah intervenes between man and his heart, and that to Him you shall be gathered. (Quran 8:24)

$$\text{إِنَّ ٱللَّهَ ٱشْتَرَىٰ مِنَ ٱلْمُؤْمِنِينَ أَنفُسَهُمْ وَأَمْوَٰلَهُم بِأَنَّ لَهُمُ ٱلْجَنَّةَ}$$
(القرآن ٩:١١١)

Surely Allah has purchased from the believers their persons and their property in exchange for paradise. (Quran 9:111)

Essential Muslim Qualities

Muslims should possess the attributes beloved of Allah the Exalted. These praiseworthy attributes are highlighted in various places in the Quran. We try to acquire the qualities whenever we come across them being praised by Allah the Exalted.

إِنَّ ٱلْمُسْلِمِينَ وَٱلْمُسْلِمَـٰتِ وَٱلْمُؤْمِنِينَ وَٱلْمُؤْمِنَـٰتِ وَٱلْقَـٰنِتِينَ وَٱلْقَـٰنِتَـٰتِ وَٱلصَّـٰدِقِينَ وَٱلصَّـٰدِقَـٰتِ وَٱلصَّـٰبِرِينَ وَٱلصَّـٰبِرَٰتِ وَٱلْخَـٰشِعِينَ وَٱلْخَـٰشِعَـٰتِ وَٱلْمُتَصَدِّقِينَ وَٱلْمُتَصَدِّقَـٰتِ وَٱلصَّـٰٓئِمِينَ وَٱلصَّـٰٓئِمَـٰتِ وَٱلْحَـٰفِظِينَ فُرُوجَهُمْ وَٱلْحَـٰفِظَـٰتِ وَٱلذَّٰكِرِينَ ٱللَّهَ كَثِيرًا وَٱلذَّٰكِرَٰتِ أَعَدَّ ٱللَّهُ لَهُم مَّغْفِرَةً وَأَجْرًا عَظِيمًا ۝ (القرآن ٣٣:٣٥)

Indeed, the submitting men and the submitting women,
& the believing men and the believing women,
& the obedient men and the obedient women,
& the truthful men and the truthful women,
& the patient men and the patient women,
& the humble men and the humble women,
& the charitable men and the charitable women,
& the fasting men and the fasting women,
& the men who guard their chastity and the women who do so
& the men who remember Allah often and the women who do so
for them Allah has prepared forgiveness and a great reward. (Quran 33:35)

Mercy (رحمة)

Our Lord is The Most Merciful, and urges us to be merciful. The first Hadith taught to the students of Hadith, is the "Hadith of mercy" listed below. It is also called "the first continuously transmitted chain of hadith" (*musalsalat al awwaliyya*). This is done to emphasize that one of the main purposes of all learning is to make the Muslim more merciful.

Mercy lives in the heart and in the soul of the Muslim. But it is not merely internal. This mercy inside the Muslim compels external action. Among the effects of mercy are pardoning those who wrong us, feeding the hungry, helping the weak, clothing the naked, tending to the refugee, and assisting the poor.

عَنْ عَبْدِ اللَّهِ بْنِ عَمْرٍو، قَالَ قَالَ رَسُولُ اللَّهِ صلى الله عليه وسلم "الرَّاحِمُونَ يَرْحَمُهُمُ الرَّحْمَنُ ارْحَمُوا مَنْ فِي الأَرْضِ يَرْحَمْكُمْ مَنْ فِي السَّمَاءِ" (رواه الترمذي — حسن)

Abdullah bin Amr narrated: The Messenger of Allah (peace be upon him) said: *"Those who are merciful will be shown mercy by the Most Merciful. Be merciful to those on the earth and the One in the heavens will have mercy upon you."* (Tirmidhi - Hassan)

كَتَبَ رَبُّكُمْ عَلَىٰ نَفْسِهِ ٱلرَّحْمَةَ (القرآن ٦:٥٤)

Your Lord has decreed upon Himself mercy. (Quran 6:54)

$$\text{فَبِمَا رَحْمَةٍ مِّنَ ٱللَّهِ لِنتَ لَهُمْ ۖ وَلَوْ كُنتَ فَظًّا غَلِيظَ ٱلْقَلْبِ لَٱنفَضُّوا۟ مِنْ حَوْلِكَ ۖ}$$ (القرآن ١٥٩:٣)

And by the Mercy of Allah, you dealt with them gently. And had you been severe and harsh-hearted, they would have fled from you. (Quran 3:159)

$$\text{نَبِّئْ عِبَادِى أَنِّى أَنَا ٱلْغَفُورُ ٱلرَّحِيمُ}$$ (القرآن ١٥:٤٩)

Inform My servants that it is I who am the Forgiving, the Merciful. (Quran 15:49)

عَنْ أَبِي هُرَيْرَةَ ـ رضى الله عنه ـ قَالَ قَالَ رَسُولُ اللهِ صلى الله عليه وسلم "لَمَّا قَضَى اللهُ الْخَلْقَ كَتَبَ فِي كِتَابِهِ، فَهُوَ عِنْدَهُ فَوْقَ الْعَرْشِ إِنَّ رَحْمَتِي غَلَبَتْ غَضَبِي" (متفق عليه)

Narrated Abu Huraira: The Messenger of Allah (peace be upon him) said: "When Allah decreed the creation, He wrote in His book which is with Him on His throne, 'My mercy has overcome My anger.'" (Bukhari, Muslim – Sahih)

$$\text{قُلْ يَـٰعِبَادِىَ ٱلَّذِينَ أَسْرَفُوا۟ عَلَىٰٓ أَنفُسِهِمْ لَا تَقْنَطُوا۟ مِن رَّحْمَةِ ٱللَّهِ ۚ إِنَّ ٱللَّهَ يَغْفِرُ ٱلذُّنُوبَ جَمِيعًا ۚ إِنَّهُۥ هُوَ ٱلْغَفُورُ ٱلرَّحِيمُ}$$ (القرآن ٣٩:٥٣)

Say, "O My servants who have wronged themselves, do not despair of the mercy of Allah. Indeed, Allah forgives all sins. Indeed, it is He who is the Forgiving, the Merciful." (Quran 39:53)

عَنْ جَرِيرِ بْنَ عَبْدِ اللَّهِ، عَنِ النَّبِيِّ صلى الله عليه وسلم قَالَ "مَنْ لَا يَرْحَمْ لَا يُرْحَمْ" (متفق عليه)

Jarir bin Abdullah reported: The Prophet (peace be upon him) said, "He who does not show mercy to others, will not be shown mercy." (Bukhari, Muslim - Sahih)

وَرَحْمَتِى وَسِعَتْ كُلَّ شَىْءٍ ۚ فَسَأَكْتُبُهَا لِلَّذِينَ يَتَّقُونَ وَيُؤْتُونَ ٱلزَّكَوٰةَ وَٱلَّذِينَ هُم بِـَٔايَـٰتِنَا يُؤْمِنُونَ ۝ (القرآن ٧:١٥٦)

My mercy encompasses all things. So I will decree it [especially] for those who fear Me and give zakat and those who believe in Our verses. (Quran 7:156)

عَنْ أَبِي هُرَيْرَةَ، قَالَ سَمِعْتُ رَسُولَ اللَّهِ صلى الله عليه وسلم يَقُولُ "جَعَلَ اللَّهُ الرَّحْمَةَ مِائَةَ جُزْءٍ، فَأَمْسَكَ عِنْدَهُ تِسْعَةً وَتِسْعِينَ جُزْءًا، وَأَنْزَلَ فِي الأَرْضِ جُزْءًا وَاحِدًا، فَمِنْ ذَلِكَ الْجُزْءِ يَتَرَاحَمُ الْخَلْقُ، حَتَّى تَرْفَعَ الْفَرَسُ حَافِرَهَا عَنْ وَلَدِهَا خَشْيَةَ أَنْ تُصِيبَهُ" (متفق عليه)

Narrated Abu Huraira: I heard The Messenger of Allah (peace be upon him) saying: "Allah has divided mercy into one hundred parts, and He kept ninety-nine parts with Himself and sent down one part on the earth, and because of that one part, His creatures are merciful to each other including even the mare carefully lifts her hoof away from her baby, so that she would not trample on it." (Bukhari, Muslim – Sahih)

إِنَّ رَحْمَتَ ٱللَّهِ قَرِيبٌ مِّنَ ٱلْمُحْسِنِينَ ۝ (القرآن ٧:٥٦)

Indeed, the mercy of Allah is near to the doers of good. (Quran 7:56)

$$\text{وَمَآ أَرْسَلْنَٰكَ إِلَّا رَحْمَةً لِّلْعَٰلَمِينَ} \;﴿١٠٧﴾\; (\text{القرآن ٢١:١٠٧})$$

And We did not send you (O Muhammad) except as a mercy for all creation. (Quran 21:107)

$$\text{ثُمَّ كَانَ مِنَ ٱلَّذِينَ ءَامَنُوا۟ وَتَوَاصَوْا۟ بِٱلصَّبْرِ وَتَوَاصَوْا۟ بِٱلْمَرْحَمَةِ} \;﴿١٧﴾\; (\text{القرآن ٩٠:١٧})$$

Thereafter he was among those who believed and urged perseverance and patience, and promoted compassion. (Quran 90:17)

Innate Nature (فِطْرة)

Humans are created on an innate nature of monotheism that compels us to seek out and worship our Creator, the Exalted, the Most High.

If not for external influences, our default template, the template of our father Adam (upon him be peace), would lead us to the natural religion designed for humans by the Creator of humans.

In fact all of the creation of Allah the Exalted have been endowed by their Creator with a default template. Thus everything in the universe performs the task assigned to it by their Creator, the Endower of their nature.

ٱلْحَمْدُ لِلَّهِ فَاطِرِ ٱلسَّمَـٰوَٰتِ وَٱلْأَرْضِ جَاعِلِ ٱلْمَلَـٰٓئِكَةِ رُسُلًا أُو۟لِىٓ أَجْنِحَةٍ مَّثْنَىٰ وَثُلَـٰثَ وَرُبَـٰعَ ۚ يَزِيدُ فِى ٱلْخَلْقِ مَا يَشَآءُ ۚ إِنَّ ٱللَّهَ عَلَىٰ كُلِّ شَىْءٍ قَدِيرٌ

(القرآن ٣٥:١)

All praise is due to Allah, Who gave their inherent nature to the heavens and the earth, who made the angels messengers with wings, two or three or four. He increases in creation what He wills. Indeed, Allah is over all things competent. (Quran 35:1)

عَنْ أَبِي هُرَيْرَةَ - رضي الله عنه - قَالَ قَالَ النَّبِيُّ صلى الله عليه وسلم "كُلُّ مَوْلُودٍ يُولَدُ عَلَى الْفِطْرَةِ، فَأَبَوَاهُ يُهَوِّدَانِهِ أَوْ يُنَصِّرَانِهِ أَوْ يُمَجِّسَانِهِ، كَمَثَلِ الْبَهِيمَةِ تُنْتَجُ الْبَهِيمَةَ، هَلْ تَرَى فِيهَا جَدْعَاءَ" (متفق عليه)

Narrated Abu Huraira: The Prophet (peace be upon him) said, "Each child is born in a state of 'innate nature', but his parents make him a Jew or a Christian or a Magian. It is like the way an animal gives birth to a normal offspring. Do you find it mutilated?" (Bukhari, Muslim - Sahih)

عنْ أبي مُعاوية، ـ قَالَ قَالَ النَّبِيُّ صلى الله عليه وسلم "لَيْسَ مِنْ مَوْلُودٍ يُولَدُ إِلاَّ عَلَى هَذِهِ الْفِطْرَةِ حَتَّى يُعَبِّرَ عَنْهُ لِسَانُهُ " (صحيح مسلم)

Narrated Abu Muawiya: The Prophet (peace be upon him) said,"Every child is not born except on this innate nature until he expresses himself with his tongue." (Muslim - Sahih)

فَأَقِمْ وَجْهَكَ لِلدِّينِ حَنِيفًا ۚ فِطْرَتَ ٱللَّهِ ٱلَّتِى فَطَرَ ٱلنَّاسَ عَلَيْهَا ۚ لَا تَبْدِيلَ لِخَلْقِ ٱللَّهِ ۚ ذَٰلِكَ ٱلدِّينُ ٱلْقَيِّمُ وَلَـٰكِنَّ أَكْثَرَ ٱلنَّاسِ لَا يَعْلَمُونَ ۝ (القرآن ٣٠:٣٠)

So direct your face toward the religion, inclining to upright state. The innate nature within which Allah has created all people. No change should there be in the creation of Allah. That is the correct religion, but most of the people do not know. (Quran 30:30)

وَمَا خَلَقْتُ ٱلْجِنَّ وَٱلْإِنسَ إِلَّا لِيَعْبُدُونِ ۝ (القرآن ٥١:٥٦)

And I did not create the jinn and mankind except to worship Me. (Quran 51:56)

وَأَوْحَىٰ رَبُّكَ إِلَى ٱلنَّحْلِ أَنِ ٱتَّخِذِى مِنَ ٱلْجِبَالِ بُيُوتًا وَمِنَ ٱلشَّجَرِ وَمِمَّا يَعْرِشُونَ ۝ (القرآن ١٦:٦٨)

And your Lord inspired to the bee, "Take for yourself among the mountains, houses, and among the trees and (in) that which they construct. (Quran 16:68)

Humility (تَواضُع)

Among the lost values of the earlier generations of our scholars and teachers is humility. We live in an age where humility is misunderstood and despised. Since no one can enter Paradise without humility, it is essential for us to nurture it within ourselves.

وَعِبَادُ ٱلرَّحْمَنِ ٱلَّذِينَ يَمْشُونَ عَلَى ٱلْأَرْضِ هَوْنًا وَإِذَا خَاطَبَهُمُ ٱلْجَٰهِلُونَ قَالُوا۟ سَلَٰمًا ۝ (القرآن ٢٥:٦٣)

The servants of the Most Merciful are those who walk on the earth in humility and when the ignorant speak to them, they say words of peace. (Quran 25:63)

عَنْ أَبِي هُرَيْرَةَ، أَنَّ رَسُولَ اللَّهِ صلى الله عليه وسلم قَالَ "مَا نَقَصَتْ صَدَقَةٌ مِنْ مَالٍ وَمَا زَادَ اللَّهُ رَجُلاً بِعَفْوٍ إِلاَّ عِزًّا وَمَا تَوَاضَعَ أَحَدٌ لِلَّهِ إِلاَّ رَفَعَهُ اللَّهُ" (رواه الترمذي ومسلم – صحيح)

Abu Hurairah narrated: The Messenger of Allah (peace be upon him) said, "Charity does not diminish wealth, Allah does not increase a man in anything for his pardoning others except in honor, and none humbles himself for Allah except Allah elevates him." (Tirmidhi, Muslim - Sahih)

عن عِيَاضِ بنِ حِمَارٍ رضي الله عنه قال: قال رسول الله صلى الله عليه وسلم : "إنَّ اللهَ تعالى أوحى إلَيَّ أن تواضعوا حتى لا يبغي أحد على أحد، ولا يفخر أحد على أحد" (صحيح مسلم)

Iyad bin Himar said: The Messenger of Allah (peace be upon him) said, "Verily, Allah has revealed to me that you should adopt humility. So that no one may wrong another and no one may be disdainful and haughty towards another." (Muslim - Sahih)

$$\text{وَبَشِّرِ ٱلْمُخْبِتِينَ ۝ (القرآن ٣٤:٢٢)}$$

And give good tidings to the humble. (Quran 22:34)

$$\text{وَلَا تُصَعِّرْ خَدَّكَ لِلنَّاسِ وَلَا تَمْشِ فِي ٱلْأَرْضِ مَرَحًا ۖ إِنَّ ٱللَّهَ لَا يُحِبُّ كُلَّ مُخْتَالٍ فَخُورٍ ۝ (القرآن ١٨:٣١)}$$

Do not turn your face away from people in contempt, nor go about in the land arrogantly. Indeed, Allah does not love the self-deluded and boastful. (Quran 31:18)

$$\text{لَا جَرَمَ أَنَّ ٱللَّهَ يَعْلَمُ مَا يُسِرُّونَ وَمَا يُعْلِنُونَ ۚ إِنَّهُ لَا يُحِبُّ ٱلْمُسْتَكْبِرِينَ ۝ (القرآن ١٦:٢٣)}$$

Assuredly, Allah knows what they conceal and what they declare. Indeed, He does not like the arrogant. (Quran 16:23)

عَنْ عَبْدِ اللَّهِ بْنِ مَسْعُودٍ، عَنِ النَّبِيِّ صلى الله عليه وسلم قَالَ "لاَ يَدْخُلُ الْجَنَّةَ مَنْ كَانَ فِي قَلْبِهِ مِثْقَالُ ذَرَّةٍ مِنْ كِبْرٍ" قَالَ رَجُلٌ إِنَّ الرَّجُلَ يُحِبُّ أَنْ يَكُونَ ثَوْبُهُ حَسَنًا وَنَعْلُهُ حَسَنَةً . قَالَ "إِنَّ اللَّهَ جَمِيلٌ يُحِبُّ الْجَمَالَ الْكِبْرُ بَطَرُ الْحَقِّ وَغَمْطُ النَّاسِ" (صحيح مسلم)

Abdullah bin Masud reported: The Messenger of Allah (peace be upon him) said, "Anyone with a mustard seed weight of pride in his heart shall not enter Paradise." Someone said: "Verily a person loves that his dress should be good, and his shoes should be good." He (peace be upon him) remarked: "Indeed, Allah is Graceful and He loves grace. Pride is disdaining the truth and contempt for people." (Muslim - Sahih)

ٱلَّذِينَ يَجْتَنِبُونَ كَبَٰٓئِرَ ٱلْإِثْمِ وَٱلْفَوَٰحِشَ إِلَّا ٱللَّمَمَ ۚ إِنَّ رَبَّكَ وَٰسِعُ ٱلْمَغْفِرَةِ ۚ هُوَ أَعْلَمُ بِكُمْ إِذْ أَنشَأَكُم مِّنَ ٱلْأَرْضِ وَإِذْ أَنتُمْ أَجِنَّةٌ فِى بُطُونِ أُمَّهَٰتِكُمْ ۖ فَلَا تُزَكُّوٓا۟ أَنفُسَكُمْ ۖ هُوَ أَعْلَمُ بِمَنِ ٱتَّقَىٰٓ ۝ (القرآن ٣٢:٥٣)

Those who avoid the major sins and immoralities, except the small sins. Indeed, your Lord is vast in forgiveness. He was most knowing of you when He produced you from the earth and when you were fetuses in the wombs of your mothers. So do not claim yourselves to be pure; He is most knowing of who is mindful of Him. (Quran 53:32)

Purification (تَزْكِية)

Paradise has been prepared for those who purify themselves and their soul. Purification means abandoning a life of ignorance and wretchedness and leading a life with a purpose guided by Divine wisdom.

قَدْ أَفْلَحَ مَن تَزَكَّىٰ ۝ وَذَكَرَ ٱسْمَ رَبِّهِۦ فَصَلَّىٰ ۝ (القرآن ٨٧: ١٤-١٥)

Indeed is successful, he who purifies himself, and remembers the name of his Lord, then prays. (Quran 87:14-15)

أَلَمْ يَأْنِ لِلَّذِينَ ءَامَنُوٓاْ أَن تَخْشَعَ قُلُوبُهُمْ لِذِكْرِ ٱللَّهِ (القرآن ٥٧:١٦)

Is not the time ripe for the hearts of those who believe to submit to God's reminder? (Quran 57:16)

عَنْ عَبْدِ اللَّهِ بْنِ عَمْرٍو، قَالَ قِيلَ لِرَسُولِ اللَّهِ ـ صلى الله عليه وسلم ـ أَىُّ النَّاسِ أَفْضَلُ قَالَ "كُلُّ مَخْمُومِ الْقَلْبِ صَدُوقِ اللِّسَانِ" . قَالُوا صَدُوقُ اللِّسَانِ نَعْرِفُهُ فَمَا مَخْمُومُ الْقَلْبِ قَالَ "هُوَ التَّقِيُّ النَّقِيُّ لاَ إِثْمَ فِيهِ وَلاَ بَغْىَ وَلاَ غِلَّ وَلاَ حَسَدَ" (رواه ابن ماجه – صحيح)

Narrated Abdullah bin Amr: it was said to The Messenger of Allah (peace be upon him): "Which of the people is best?" He said: "Everyone who is pure of heart and sincere in speech.' They said: 'Sincere in speech, we know what this is, but what is pure of heart?' He said: 'It is (the heart) that is pious and pure, with no sin, injustice, rancor or envy in it." (Ibn Majah - Sahih)

وَيَسْـَٔلُونَكَ عَنِ ٱلرُّوحِ ۖ قُلِ ٱلرُّوحُ مِنْ أَمْرِ رَبِّى وَمَآ أُوتِيتُم مِّنَ ٱلْعِلْمِ إِلَّا قَلِيلًا ۝ (القرآن ١٧:٨٥)

And they ask you, about the spirit. Say, "The spirit is of the affair of my Lord. And humanity has not been given of knowledge except a little." (Quran 17:85)

وَنَفْسٍ وَمَا سَوَّىٰهَا ۝ فَأَلْهَمَهَا فُجُورَهَا وَتَقْوَىٰهَا ۝ قَدْ أَفْلَحَ مَن زَكَّىٰهَا ۝ وَقَدْ خَابَ مَن دَسَّىٰهَا ۝ (القرآن ٩١: ٨-١٠)

By the soul and He who proportioned it, and inspired it with discernment of wickedness and righteousness; He has succeeded who purifies it, and he has failed who corrupts it. (Quran 91:8-10)

عَنْ جَابِرٍ، قَالَ سَمِعْتُ رَسُولَ اللهِ ـ صلى الله عليه وسلم ـ يَقُولُ "لاَ يَمُوتَنَّ أَحَدٌ مِنْكُمْ إِلاَّ وَهُوَ يُحْسِنُ الظَّنَّ بِاللهِ." (رواه ابن ماجه — صحيح)

Narrated Jabir: I heard The Messenger of Allah (peace be upon him) say: "No one of you should die except thinking positively of Allah." (Ibn Majah - Sahih)

وَثِيَابَكَ فَطَهِّرْ ۝ وَٱلرُّجْزَ فَٱهْجُرْ ۝ (القرآن ٧٤: ٤-٥)

Purify your garments and shun uncleanness. (Quran 74:4-5)

قُل لِّلْمُؤْمِنِينَ يَغُضُّوا۟ مِنْ أَبْصَـٰرِهِمْ وَيَحْفَظُوا۟ فُرُوجَهُمْ ۚ ذَٰلِكَ أَزْكَىٰ لَهُمْ ۗ إِنَّ ٱللَّهَ خَبِيرٌۢ بِمَا يَصْنَعُونَ ۝ (القرآن ٢٤:٣٠)

Tell the believing men to lower their gaze and guard their chastity. That is purer for them. Indeed, Allah is aware of what they do. (Quran 24:30)

إِنَّ ٱللَّهَ يُحِبُّ ٱلتَّوَّٰبِينَ وَيُحِبُّ ٱلْمُتَطَهِّرِينَ ۞ (القرآن ٢:٢٢٢)

Indeed, Allah loves those who are constantly repentant and loves those who purify themselves. (Quran 2:222)

يَوْمَ لَا يَنفَعُ مَالٌ وَلَا بَنُونَ ۞ إِلَّا مَنْ أَتَى ٱللَّهَ بِقَلْبٍ سَلِيمٍ ۞ (القرآن ٢٦: ٨٨-٨٩)

The day when neither wealth nor sons will help, except the one who brings to Allah a sound heart. (Quran 26:88-89)

كَلَّا ۖ بَلْ رَانَ عَلَىٰ قُلُوبِهِم مَّا كَانُوا۟ يَكْسِبُونَ ۞ (القرآن ٨٣:١٤)

Indeed upon their hearts is a stain for what they used to earn. (Quran 83:14)

إِنَّ ٱلنَّفْسَ لَأَمَّارَةٌۢ بِٱلسُّوٓءِ إِلَّا مَا رَحِمَ رَبِّىٓ ۚ إِنَّ رَبِّى غَفُورٌ رَّحِيمٌ ۞ (القرآن ١٢:٥٣)

Indeed, the soul is inclined to evil, except when My Lord bestows His Mercy. Indeed, My Lord is Oft-Forgiving, Most Merciful." (Quran 12:53)

وُجُوهٌ يَوْمَئِذٍ نَّاضِرَةٌ ۞ إِلَىٰ رَبِّهَا نَاظِرَةٌ ۞ (القرآن ٧٥: ٢٢-٢٣)

Some faces that Day shall be radiant, looking at their Lord. (Quran 75:22-23)

يَـٰٓأَيَّتُهَا ٱلنَّفْسُ ٱلْمُطْمَئِنَّةُ ۝ ٱرْجِعِىٓ إِلَىٰ رَبِّكِ رَاضِيَةً مَّرْضِيَّةً ۝ فَٱدْخُلِى فِى عِبَـٰدِى ۝ وَٱدْخُلِى جَنَّتِى ۝ (القرآن ٨٩: ٢٧-٣٠)

O satisfied soul! Return to your Lord, well-pleased & well-pleasing! Enter among My slaves and enter My Paradise! (Quran 89:27-30)

فَإِنَّهَا لَا تَعْمَى ٱلْأَبْصَـٰرُ وَلَـٰكِن تَعْمَى ٱلْقُلُوبُ ٱلَّتِى فِى ٱلصُّدُورِ ۝ (القرآن ٤٦:٢٢)

Indeed, it is not eyes that are blinded, but blinded are the hearts which are within the breasts. (Quran 22:46)

Reason (عَقْلانية)

Islam encourages us to think for ourselves. For us faith and reason are compatible. Religion and science are not in conflict. Any field of knowledge that seeks to understand any aspect of the creation of Allah the Exalted as a means of getting closer to Him is praiseworthy.

إِنَّ فِي خَلْقِ ٱلسَّمَـٰوَٰتِ وَٱلْأَرْضِ وَٱخْتِلَـٰفِ ٱلَّيْلِ وَٱلنَّهَارِ لَـَٔايَـٰتٍ لِّأُو۟لِي ٱلْأَلْبَـٰبِ ۝ (القرآن ٣:١٩٠)

Surely in the creation of the heavens and the earth, and the alteration of night and day, there are signs for intelligent people. (Quran 3:190)

وَكَأَيِّن مِّنْ ءَايَةٍ فِي ٱلسَّمَـٰوَٰتِ وَٱلْأَرْضِ يَمُرُّونَ عَلَيْهَا وَهُمْ عَنْهَا مُعْرِضُونَ ۝ (القرآن ١٢:١٠٥)

How many a sign in the heavens and the earth do they pass by while they are disregardful of it. (Quran 12:105)

ٱلَّذِى خَلَقَ سَبْعَ سَمَـٰوَٰتٍ طِبَاقًا ۖ مَّا تَرَىٰ فِي خَلْقِ ٱلرَّحْمَـٰنِ مِن تَفَـٰوُتٍ ۖ فَٱرْجِعِ ٱلْبَصَرَ هَلْ تَرَىٰ مِن فُطُورٍ ۝ ثُمَّ ٱرْجِعِ ٱلْبَصَرَ كَرَّتَيْنِ يَنقَلِبْ إِلَيْكَ ٱلْبَصَرُ خَاسِئًا وَهُوَ حَسِيرٌ ۝ (القرآن ٦٧: ٣-٤)

He created seven heavens in layers. You do not see in the creation of the Most Merciful any breaks. Return your vision; do you see any breaks? Then return your vision

again. Your vision will return to you humbled while it is fatigued. (Quran 67:3-4)

$$\text{أَفَلَا يَتَدَبَّرُونَ الْقُرْآنَ ۚ وَلَوْ كَانَ مِنْ عِندِ غَيْرِ اللَّهِ لَوَجَدُوا فِيهِ اخْتِلَافًا كَثِيرًا}$$ (القرآن ٤:٨٢)

Then do they not reflect upon the Quran? If it had been from other than Allah, they would have found within it much contradiction. (Quran 4:82)

$$\text{أَوَلَمْ يَتَفَكَّرُوا فِي أَنفُسِهِم ۗ مَّا خَلَقَ اللَّهُ السَّمَاوَاتِ وَالْأَرْضَ وَمَا بَيْنَهُمَا إِلَّا بِالْحَقِّ وَأَجَلٍ مُّسَمًّى}$$ (القرآن ٣٠:٨)

Do they not contemplate within themselves? Allah has not created the heavens and the earth and what is between them except in truth and for a specified term. (Quran 30:8)

$$\text{لَقَدْ أَنزَلْنَا إِلَيْكُمْ كِتَابًا فِيهِ ذِكْرُكُمْ ۖ أَفَلَا تَعْقِلُونَ}$$ (القرآن ٢١:١٠)

We have certainly sent down to you a Book in which is your mention. Then will you not reason? (Quran 21:10)

عَنْ أَبِي هُرَيْرَةَ ـ رضى الله عنه ـ عَنِ النَّبِيِّ صلى الله عليه وسلم أَنَّهُ قَالَ "لاَ يُلْدَغُ الْمُؤْمِنُ مِنْ جُحْرٍ وَاحِدٍ مَرَّتَيْنِ" (رواه البخاري، مسلم، أبو داوود، ابن ماجه – صحيح)

Abu Huraira reported: The Prophet (peace be upon him) said: "A believer will not be stung from the same hole twice". (Bukhari, Muslim, Abu Dawud, Ibn Majah - Sahih)

$$\text{فَٱنظُرْ إِلَىٰٓ ءَاثَٰرِ رَحْمَتِ ٱللَّهِ} \quad (\text{القرآن } 30:50)$$

So observe the effects of the mercy of Allah (Quran 30:50)

$$\text{وَمَا كَانَ لِنَفْسٍ أَن تُؤْمِنَ إِلَّا بِإِذْنِ ٱللَّهِ ۚ وَيَجْعَلُ ٱلرِّجْسَ عَلَى ٱلَّذِينَ لَا يَعْقِلُونَ} \quad (\text{القرآن } 10:100)$$

And it is not for a soul to believe except by permission of Allah, and He will disgrace those who will not use reason. (Quran 10:100)

$$\text{إِنَّ شَرَّ ٱلدَّوَآبِّ عِندَ ٱللَّهِ ٱلصُّمُّ ٱلْبُكْمُ ٱلَّذِينَ لَا يَعْقِلُونَ} \quad (\text{القرآن } 8:22)$$

Surely the worst of beasts in God's sight are those that are deaf and dumb and do not reason. (Quran 8:22)

Hope (أَمَل)

There is always hope for the Muslim. And why should we not remain perpetually hopeful? After all we Muslims place our reliance upon Allah the Exalted.

فَمَن كَانَ يَرْجُوا۟ لِقَآءَ رَبِّهِۦ فَلْيَعْمَلْ عَمَلًا صَٰلِحًا وَلَا يُشْرِكْ بِعِبَادَةِ رَبِّهِۦٓ أَحَدًۢا (القرآن ١٨:١١٠)

So whoever would hope for the meeting with his Lord, let him do righteous deeds and not associate anyone in the worship of his Lord. (Quran 18:110)

وَلَا تَا۟يْـَٔسُوا۟ مِن رَّوْحِ ٱللَّهِ إِنَّهُۥ لَا يَا۟يْـَٔسُ مِن رَّوْحِ ٱللَّهِ إِلَّا ٱلْقَوْمُ ٱلْكَٰفِرُونَ (القرآن ١٢:٨٧)

And despair not of relief from Allah. Indeed, no one despairs of relief from Allah except the disbelieving people. (Quran 12:87)

سَيَجْعَلُ ٱللَّهُ بَعْدَ عُسْرٍ يُسْرًا (القرآن ٦٥: ٧)

Allah will bring about, after hardship, ease. (Quran 65:7)

فَإِنَّ مَعَ ٱلْعُسْرِ يُسْرًا إِنَّ مَعَ ٱلْعُسْرِ يُسْرًا (القرآن ٩٤: ٥-٦)

For indeed, with every hardship there is relief. Indeed, with every hardship there is relief. (Quran 94:5-6)

فَلَا تَكُن مِّنَ ٱلْقَٰنِطِينَ ۝ (القرآن ١٥:٥٥)

So do not be among the despairing. (Quran 15:55)

عَنْ صُهَيْبٍ، قَالَ قَالَ رَسُولُ اللهِ صلى الله عليه وسلم "عَجَبًا لِأَمْرِ الْمُؤْمِنِ إِنَّ أَمْرَهُ كُلَّهُ خَيْرٌ وَلَيْسَ ذَاكَ لِأَحَدٍ إِلَّا لِلْمُؤْمِنِ إِنْ أَصَابَتْهُ سَرَّاءُ شَكَرَ فَكَانَ خَيْرًا لَهُ وَإِنْ أَصَابَتْهُ ضَرَّاءُ صَبَرَ فَكَانَ خَيْرًا لَهُ" (صحيح مسلم)

Narrated Suhaib: The Messenger of Allah (peace be upon him) said: "Wonderful is the affair of the believer. There is good in every affair of his and this is not the case with anyone else except the believer. He is thankful when joyful. That is good for him. And he is patient in adversity. That is good for him." (Muslim - Sahih)

وَلَا تَهِنُوا۟ وَلَا تَحْزَنُوا۟ وَأَنتُمُ ٱلْأَعْلَوْنَ إِن كُنتُم مُّؤْمِنِينَ ۝ (القرآن ٣:١٣٩)

So do not give up and do not be downhearted, and you will be uppermost if you are believers. (Quran 3:139)

عَنْ جَابِرِ بْنِ عَبْدِ اللهِ الْأَنْصَارِيِّ، قَالَ سَمِعْتُ رَسُولَ اللهِ صلى الله عليه وسلم قَبْلَ مَوْتِهِ بِثَلَاثَةِ أَيَّامٍ يَقُولُ "لَا يَمُوتَنَّ أَحَدُكُمْ إِلَّا وَهُوَ يُحْسِنُ الظَّنَّ بِاللهِ عَزَّ وَجَلَّ" (رواه مسلم، إبن ماجه، أبو داوود – صحيح)

Jabir bin Abdullah al-Ansari reported: I heard the Messenger of Allah (peace be upon him) say three days before his death: "None of you should die except hoping only good from Allah, the Exalted and Glorious." (Muslim, Ibn Majah, Abu Dawud - Sahih)

Integrity (إِسْتِقامة)

We are a people of honor and integrity. We strive our utmost to please our Lord, the Most Exalted. Our moral values come directly from the Quran and the Hadith.

يَٰٓأَيُّهَا ٱلَّذِينَ ءَامَنُوا۟ ٱتَّقُوا۟ ٱللَّهَ وَقُولُوا۟ قَوْلًا سَدِيدًا ۝ (القرآن ٣٣:٧٠)

O believers! Be mindful of Allah and speak straight, true words. (Quran 33:70)

يَٰٓأَيُّهَا ٱلَّذِينَ ءَامَنُوا۟ ٱتَّقُوا۟ ٱللَّهَ وَكُونُوا۟ مَعَ ٱلصَّٰدِقِينَ ۝ (القرآن ٩:١١٩)

O believers! Be mindful of Allah, and be with the truthful people. (Quran 9:119)

عَنْ عَائِشَةَ قَالَتْ، سَمِعْتُ رَسُولَ اللهِ صلى الله عليه وسلم يَقُولُ "مَنِ الْتَمَسَ رِضَاءَ اللهِ بِسَخَطِ النَّاسِ كَفَاهُ اللهُ مُؤْنَةَ النَّاسِ وَمَنِ الْتَمَسَ رِضَاءَ النَّاسِ بِسَخَطِ اللهِ وَكَّلَهُ اللهُ إِلَى النَّاسِ" (رواه الترمذي – حسن)

Narrated Aisha: The Messenger of Allah (peace be upon him) said: *"Whoever seeks Allah's pleasure by the people's wrath, Allah will suffice him from the people. And whoever seeks the people's pleasure by Allah's wrath, Allah will entrust him to the people."* (Tirmidhi – Hasan)

يَٰٓأَيُّهَا ٱلَّذِينَ ءَامَنُوا۟ كُونُوا۟ قَوَّٰمِينَ بِٱلْقِسْطِ شُهَدَآءَ لِلَّهِ وَلَوْ عَلَىٰٓ أَنفُسِكُمْ أَوِ ٱلْوَٰلِدَيْنِ وَٱلْأَقْرَبِينَ ۚ إِن يَكُنْ غَنِيًّا أَوْ فَقِيرًا فَٱللَّهُ أَوْلَىٰ بِهِمَا ۖ فَلَا تَتَّبِعُوا۟

ٱلْهَوَىٰٓ أَن تَعْدِلُوا۟ ۚ وَإِن تَلْوُۥٓا۟ أَوْ تُعْرِضُوا۟ فَإِنَّ ٱللَّهَ كَانَ بِمَا تَعْمَلُونَ خَبِيرًا ۝
(القرآن ٤: ١٣٥)

O believers! Be persistently standing firm in justice, witnesses for Allah, even against yourselves or parents and relatives. Whether one is rich or poor, Allah is more worthy of both. So follow not personal inclination, lest you not be just. And if you distort or refuse (your testimony), then indeed Allah is ever acquainted with what you do. (Quran 4:135)

Patience (صَبْر)

The secret ingredient of the success of the Islamic movement is patience. None of the Prophets (peace be upon them) were exempted from this requirement. A people who have not exercised patience cannot reasonably hope to receive divine assistance and victory.

There are four levels of patience.
- Patience (*Sabr*) means that we do not do anything forbidden (haram) as a result of any calamity or difficulty, big or small. Complaining about the calamity or difficulty to people does not nullify patience.
- Beautiful patience (*Sabr Jameel*) means that we do not complain about the calamity or difficulty except to to Allah alone.
- Satisfaction with the decree (*Rida bil Qada*) means that we accept the calamity or difficulty as the decree of Allah the Exalted and we thank Him that the calamity wasn't worse.
- Very few people reach the level of grateful servants (*Abd Shakur*). To achieve this level
    1. we realize that the decree of Allah the Exalted has a wisdom even if we cannot see the wisdom;
    2. we are sure that some benefit will eventually come out of this calamity; and
    3. we see the event not as a calamity, but as a favor from our Lord, the Most High.

يَـٰٓأَيُّهَا ٱلَّذِينَ ءَامَنُوا۟ ٱسْتَعِينُوا۟ بِٱلصَّبْرِ وَٱلصَّلَوٰةِ ۚ إِنَّ ٱللَّهَ مَعَ ٱلصَّـٰبِرِينَ ۝ (القرآن ٢:١٥٣)

O believers, seek help through patience and prayer. Indeed, Allah is with the patient. (Quran 2:153)

يَـٰٓأَيُّهَا ٱلَّذِينَ ءَامَنُوا۟ ٱصْبِرُوا۟ وَصَابِرُوا۟ وَرَابِطُوا۟ وَٱتَّقُوا۟ ٱللَّهَ لَعَلَّكُمْ تُفْلِحُونَ ۝ (القرآن ٣:٢٠٠)

O believers, persevere and endure and remain stationed and be mindful of Allah that you may be successful. (Quran 3:200)

عَنْ أَبِي هُرَيْرَةَ أَنَّ النَّبِيَّ صلى الله عليه وسلم قَالَ "لاَ تَمَنَّوْا لِقَاءَ الْعَدُوِّ فَإِذَا لَقِيتُمُوهُمْ فَاصْبِرُوا" (متفق عليه)

Narrated Abu Huraira: The Messenger of Allah (peace be upon him) said: "Do not desire an encounter with the enemy; but when you encounter them, be firm." (Muslim, Bukhari - Sahih)

وَبَشِّرِ ٱلصَّـٰبِرِينَ ۝ ٱلَّذِينَ إِذَآ أَصَـٰبَتْهُم مُّصِيبَةٌ قَالُوٓا۟ إِنَّا لِلَّهِ وَإِنَّآ إِلَيْهِ رَٰجِعُونَ ۝ (القرآن ٢: ١٥٥-١٥٦)

And give good news to the patient, who, when a misfortune befalls them, say: We belong to Allah and to Him we return." (Quran 2:155-156)

سَمِعْتُ أَنَسًا ـ رضى الله عنه ـ عَنِ النَّبِيِّ صلى الله عليه وسلم قَالَ "الصَّبْرُ عِنْدَ الصَّدْمَةِ الأُولَى" (رواه البخاري والترمذي وابن ماجه – صحيح)

Narrated Anas: The Prophet (peace be upon him) said, "The real patience is at the first stroke of a calamity." (Bukhari, Tirmidhi, Nasai, Ibn Majah - Sahih)

وَمَا لَنَا أَلَّا نَتَوَكَّلَ عَلَى اللَّهِ وَقَدْ هَدَىٰنَا سُبُلَنَا ۚ وَلَنَصْبِرَنَّ عَلَىٰ مَآ ءَاذَيْتُمُونَا ۚ وَعَلَى اللَّهِ فَلْيَتَوَكَّلِ الْمُتَوَكِّلُونَ ۝ (القرآن ١٤:١٢)

And why should we not rely upon Allah while He has guided us to our (good) ways. And we will surely be patient against whatever harm you should cause us. And upon Allah let those who would rely (indeed) rely. (Quran 14:12)

عَنِ ابْنِ عُمَرَ، قَالَ قَالَ رَسُولُ اللَّهِ ـ صلى الله عليه وسلم ـ "الْمُؤْمِنُ الَّذِي يُخَالِطُ النَّاسَ وَيَصْبِرُ عَلَى أَذَاهُمْ أَعْظَمُ أَجْرًا مِنَ الْمُؤْمِنِ الَّذِي لاَ يُخَالِطُ النَّاسَ وَلاَ يَصْبِرُ عَلَى أَذَاهُمْ" (رواه إبن ماجه – صحيح)

Narrated Ibn Umar: The Messenger of Allah (peace be upon him) said: "The believer who mixes with people and bears their annoyance with patience will have a greater reward than the believer who does not mix with people and does not put up with their annoyance." (Ibn Majah - Sahih)

فَاصْبِرْ صَبْرًا جَمِيلًا ۝ (القرآن ٧٠:٥)

So be patient with gracious patience. (Quran 70:5)

فَصَبْرٌ جَمِيلٌ ۖ وَاللَّهُ الْمُسْتَعَانُ عَلَىٰ مَا تَصِفُونَ ۝ (القرآن ١٢:١٨)

So (I shall maintain a) beautiful patience. And Allah is the one sought for help against that which you describe. (Quran 12:18)

Reliance (تَوَكُّل)

We place our reliance and ultimate dependence upon Allah the Exalted. This is because we are deeply aware of the reality that all matters in this world and in the next are in His hands. Nothing happens except by His permission. Reliance upon Allah the Exalted does not excuse laziness or passivity. Reliance upon Allah the Exalted requires us to exert full effort towards our goals while trusting in His judgement. As Muslims, we are not allowed to place our reliance on omens, charms, horoscopes, talismans or psychics. These are all forms of polytheism.

وَتَوَكَّلْ عَلَى ٱلْحَيِّ ٱلَّذِى لَا يَمُوتُ (القرآن ٢٥: ٥٨)

And rely upon the Ever-Living who does not die. (Quran 25:58)

وَمَن يَتَوَكَّلْ عَلَى ٱللَّهِ فَهُوَ حَسْبُهُۥ (القرآن ٦٥: ٣)

And whoever relies upon Allah - then He is sufficient for him. (Quran 65:3)

عَنْ أَنَسَ بْنَ مَالِكٍ، يَقُولُ قَالَ رَجُلٌ يَا رَسُولَ اللهِ أَعْقِلُهَا وَأَتَوَكَّلُ أَوْ أُطْلِقُهَا وَأَتَوَكَّلُ قَالَ "اعْقِلْهَا وَتَوَكَّلْ" (رواه الترمذي — حسن)

Anas bin Malik narrated that a man said: "O Messenger of Allah! Shall I tie it and rely (upon Allah), or leave it loose and rely (upon Allah)?" He said: "Tie it and rely (upon Allah)." (Tirmidhi - Hasan)

قُلْ هُوَ ٱلرَّحْمَٰنُ ءَامَنَّا بِهِۦ وَعَلَيْهِ تَوَكَّلْنَا (القرآن ٢٩:٦٧)

Say, "He is the Most Merciful; we have believed in Him, and upon Him we have relied. (Quran 67:29)

عَنْ عُمَرَ بْنِ الْخَطَّابِ، قَالَ قَالَ رَسُولُ اللَّهِ صلى الله عليه وسلم "لَوْ أَنَّكُمْ كُنْتُمْ تَوَكَّلُونَ عَلَى اللَّهِ حَقَّ تَوَكُّلِهِ لَرُزِقْتُمْ كَمَا تُرْزَقُ الطَّيْرُ تَغْدُو خِمَاصًا وَتَرُوحُ بِطَانًا" (رواه الترمذي — حسن)

Umar bin Al-Khattab narrated: The Messenger of Allah (peace be upon him) said: "If you were to rely upon Allah with the proper reliance, then He would provide for you just as a bird is provided for, it goes out in the morning empty, and returns full." (Tirmidhi - Hasan)

عَنْ أَبِي هُرَيْرَةَ، عَنِ النَّبِيِّ صلى الله عليه وسلم قَالَ "يَدْخُلُ الْجَنَّةَ أَقْوَامٌ أَفْئِدَتُهُمْ مِثْلُ أَفْئِدَةِ الطَّيْرِ" (صحيح مسلم)

Abu Huraira reported: The Messenger of Allah (peace be upon him) saying: "There would enter Paradise people whose hearts would be like those of the hearts of birds." (Muslim - Sahih)

إِنَّمَا ٱلْمُؤْمِنُونَ ٱلَّذِينَ إِذَا ذُكِرَ ٱللَّهُ وَجِلَتْ قُلُوبُهُمْ وَإِذَا تُلِيَتْ عَلَيْهِمْ ءَايَٰتُهُۥ زَادَتْهُمْ إِيمَٰنًا وَعَلَىٰ رَبِّهِمْ يَتَوَكَّلُونَ (القرآن ٨:٢)

The believers are only those who, when Allah is mentioned, their hearts become fearful, and when His verses are recited to them, it increases them in faith; and upon their Lord they rely. (Quran 8:2)

إِنْ يَنْصُرْكُمُ ٱللَّهُ فَلَا غَالِبَ لَكُمْ ۖ وَإِنْ يَخْذُلْكُمْ فَمَنْ ذَا ٱلَّذِى يَنْصُرُكُمْ مِنْ بَعْدِهِۦ ۗ وَعَلَى ٱللَّهِ فَلْيَتَوَكَّلِ ٱلْمُؤْمِنُونَ ۞ (القرآن ٣: ١٦٠)

If Allah should aid you, no one can overcome you; but if He should forsake you, who is there that can aid you after Him? And upon Allah let the believers rely. (Quran 3:160)

عَنْ عَبْدِ اللَّهِ بْنِ مَسْعُودٍ، عَنْ رَسُولِ اللَّهِ صلى الله عليه وسلم قَالَ "الطِّيَرَةُ شِرْكٌ الطِّيَرَةُ شِرْكٌ" . ثَلاَثًا " وَمَا مِنَّا إِلاَّ وَلَكِنَّ اللَّهَ يُذْهِبُهُ بِالتَّوَكُّلِ." (رواه أبو داود – صحيح)

Narrated Abdullah bin Masud: The Messenger of Allah (peace be upon him) said: "Omens are polytheism; omens are polytheism. Three times. Every one of us tends to have some, but Allah removes it through trust (in Him)." (Abu Dawud - Sahih)

Forgiveness (مَغْفِرَة)

Indeed Allah is the Ever Forgiving, Al Ghaffar. He promises to forgive us if we repent and He commands us to forgive those who wrong us. By forgiving others we simplify our own lives and acquire His pleasure.

وَلْيَعْفُوا۟ وَلْيَصْفَحُوٓا۟ ۗ أَلَا تُحِبُّونَ أَن يَغْفِرَ ٱللَّهُ لَكُمْ ۗ وَٱللَّهُ غَفُورٌ رَّحِيمٌ
(القرآن ٢٤:٢٢)

Pardon and overlook. Don't you love that Allah should forgive you. (Quran 24:22)

وَٱلْكَـٰظِمِينَ ٱلْغَيْظَ وَٱلْعَافِينَ عَنِ ٱلنَّاسِ ۗ وَٱللَّهُ يُحِبُّ ٱلْمُحْسِنِينَ
(القرآن ٣:١٣٤)

Those who restrain their anger and pardon people. Allah loves those who do good to others. (Quran 3:134)

وَٱلَّذِينَ يَجْتَنِبُونَ كَبَـٰٓئِرَ ٱلْإِثْمِ وَٱلْفَوَٰحِشَ وَإِذَا مَا غَضِبُوا۟ هُمْ يَغْفِرُونَ
(القرآن ٤٢:٣٧)

And those who avoid the major sins and immoralities, and when they are angry, they forgive. (Quran 42:37)

عَنْ أَبِي هُرَيْرَةَ، أَنَّ رَسُولَ اللهِ صلى الله عليه وسلم قَالَ "مَا نَقَصَتْ صَدَقَةٌ مِنْ مَالٍ وَمَا زَادَ اللهُ رَجُلًا بِعَفْوٍ إِلَّا عِزًّا وَمَا تَوَاضَعَ أَحَدٌ لِلَّهِ إِلَّا رَفَعَهُ اللهُ"
(رواه الترمذي ومسلم – صحيح)

Abu Hurairah narrated: The Messenger of Allah (peace be upon him) said: "Charity does not diminish wealth, Allah does not increase a man in anything for his pardoning others except in honor, and none humbles himself for Allah except Allah elevates him." (Tirmidhi, Muslim - Sahih)

خُذِ ٱلْعَفْوَ وَأْمُرْ بِٱلْعُرْفِ وَأَعْرِضْ عَنِ ٱلْجَٰهِلِينَ (القرآن ٧:١٩٩)

Increase forgiveness, promote the good, and turn away from the ignorant. (Quran 7:199)

عَنْ عَبْدِ اللهِ بْنِ الزُّبَيْرِ، قَالَ أَمَرَ اللهُ نَبِيَّهُ صلى الله عليه وسلم أَنْ يَأْخُذَ الْعَفْوَ مِنْ أَخْلَاقِ النَّاسِ. أَوْ كَمَا قَالَ. (صحيح البخاري)

Abdullah bin Az-Zubair said: "Allah ordered His Prophet to forgive the people their misbehavior." (Bukhari - Sahih)

عَنْ أَبِي هُرَيْرَةَ، أَنَّ رَسُولَ اللهِ صلى الله عليه وسلم قَالَ "كَانَ الرَّجُلُ يُدَايِنُ النَّاسَ، فَكَانَ يَقُولُ لِفَتَاهُ إِذَا أَتَيْتَ مُعْسِرًا فَتَجَاوَزْ عَنْهُ، لَعَلَّ اللهَ أَنْ يَتَجَاوَزَ عَنَّا. قَالَ فَلَقِيَ اللهَ فَتَجَاوَزَ عَنْهُ" (صحيح البخاري)

Narrated Abu Huraira: The Messenger of Allah (peace be upon him) said, "A man used to give loans to the people and used to say to his servant, 'If the debtor is poor, forgive him, so that Allah may forgive us.' So when he met Allah (after his death), Allah forgave him." (Bukhari - Sahih)

وَلَمَن صَبَرَ وَغَفَرَ إِنَّ ذَٰلِكَ لَمِنْ عَزْمِ ٱلْأُمُورِ (القرآن ٤٢:٤٣)

Whoever is patient and forgives, that is a matter of great resolution. (Quran 42:43)

وَٱخْفِضْ جَنَاحَكَ لِلْمُؤْمِنِينَ (القرآن ١٥:٨٨)

And lower your wing (of mercy) to the believers. (Quran 15:88)

قَالَ لَا تَثْرِيبَ عَلَيْكُمُ ٱلْيَوْمَ ۖ يَغْفِرُ ٱللَّهُ لَكُمْ ۖ وَهُوَ أَرْحَمُ ٱلرَّاحِمِينَ ۞

(القرآن ١٢:٩٢)

He said, "No blame will there be upon you today. Allah will forgive you; and He is the most Merciful of the merciful." (Quran 12:92)

قَالَ عَبْدُ اللهِ كَأَنِّي أَنْظُرُ إِلَى النَّبِيِّ صلى الله عليه وسلم يَحْكِي نَبِيًّا مِنَ الْأَنْبِيَاءِ ضَرَبَهُ قَوْمُهُ فَأَدْمَوْهُ، فَهُوَ يَمْسَحُ الدَّمَ عَنْ وَجْهِهِ وَيَقُولُ رَبِّ اغْفِرْ لِقَوْمِي، فَإِنَّهُمْ لاَ يَعْلَمُونَ. (صحيح البخاري)

Narrated Abdullah: I still recall the Prophet (peace be upon him) while he was speaking about one of the prophets whose people have beaten and wounded him, and he was wiping the blood off his face and saying, "O Lord! Forgive my people as they do not know." (Bukhari - Sahih)

Repentance (تَوْبَة)

By our very nature, we sin by night and by day. Our Lord, the Exalted and Glorified, loves to forgive and accept the repentance of His servants.

إِنَّ ٱللَّهَ يُحِبُّ ٱلتَّوَّٰبِينَ وَيُحِبُّ ٱلْمُتَطَهِّرِينَ ۝ (القرآن ٢:٢٢٢)

Indeed, Allah loves those who are constantly repentant and loves those who purify themselves. (Quran 2:222)

عَنْ أَنَسٍ، قَالَ قَالَ رَسُولُ اللهِ ـ صلى الله عليه وسلم ـ "كُلُّ بَنِي آدَمَ خَطَّاءٌ وَخَيْرُ الْخَطَّائِينَ التَّوَّابُونَ" (رواه ابن ماجه — حسن)

Narrated Anas: The Messenger of Allah (peace be upon him) said: "Every son of Adam sins, and the best of the sinners are those who repent." (Ibn Majah - Hasan)

إِنَّمَا ٱلتَّوْبَةُ عَلَى ٱللَّهِ لِلَّذِينَ يَعْمَلُونَ ٱلسُّوٓءَ بِجَهَٰلَةٍ ثُمَّ يَتُوبُونَ مِن قَرِيبٍ فَأُو۟لَٰٓئِكَ يَتُوبُ ٱللَّهُ عَلَيْهِمْ ۗ وَكَانَ ٱللَّهُ عَلِيمًا حَكِيمًا ۝ وَلَيْسَتِ ٱلتَّوْبَةُ لِلَّذِينَ يَعْمَلُونَ ٱلسَّيِّئَاتِ حَتَّىٰٓ إِذَا حَضَرَ أَحَدَهُمُ ٱلْمَوْتُ قَالَ إِنِّى تُبْتُ ٱلْـَٰٔنَ وَلَا ٱلَّذِينَ يَمُوتُونَ وَهُمْ كُفَّارٌ ۚ أُو۟لَٰٓئِكَ أَعْتَدْنَا لَهُمْ عَذَابًا أَلِيمًا ۝ (القرآن ٤: ١٧-١٨)

Indeed repentance is accepted by Allah for those who do wrong in ignorance and then repent soon after. It is those to whom Allah will turn in forgiveness, and Allah is ever Knowing and Wise. But repentance is not [accepted] from those who [continue to] do evil deeds until, when death

comes to one of them, he says, "Indeed, I have repented now," or of those who die while they are disbelievers. For them We have prepared a painful punishment. (Quran 4:17-18)

عَنْ أَبِي هُرَيْرَةَ، عَنِ النَّبِيِّ ـ صلى الله عليه وسلم ـ قَالَ : "لَوْ أَخْطَأْتُمْ حَتَّى تَبْلُغَ خَطَايَاكُمُ السَّمَاءَ ثُمَّ تُبْتُمْ لَتَابَ عَلَيْكُمْ" (رواه ابن ماجه – حسن)

Abu Hurairah reported: The Prophet (peace be upon him) said: "If you were to commit sin until your sins reach the heaven, then you were to repent, your repentance would be accepted." (Ibn Majah - Hasan)

إِلَّا ٱلَّذِينَ تَابُوا۟ وَأَصْلَحُوا۟ وَبَيَّنُوا۟ فَأُو۟لَٰٓئِكَ أَتُوبُ عَلَيْهِمْ ۚ وَأَنَا ٱلتَّوَّابُ ٱلرَّحِيمُ ۝ (القرآن ٢:١٦٠)

Except those who repent and amend and make manifest (the truth). For them I will accept their repentance, and I am the Accepting of repentance, the Merciful. (Quran 2:160)

عن أبي موسى، رضي الله عنه، عن النبي صلى الله عليه وسلم قال "إِنَّ الله تعالى يبسط يده بالليل ليتوب مسئ النهار، ويبسط يده بالنهار ليتوب مسئ الليل حتى تطلع الشمس من مغربها" (صحيح مسلم)

Abu Musa reported: The Prophet (peace be upon him) said: "Allah, the Exalted, stretches His Hand during the night so that those who commit sins by day may repent, and He stretches His Hand in the day so that those who commit sins by night may repent. He keeps doing so until the sun rises from the West." (Muslim - Sahih)

وَلَوْ أَنَّهُمْ إِذ ظَّلَمُوٓاْ أَنفُسَهُمْ جَآءُوكَ فَٱسْتَغْفَرُواْ ٱللَّهَ وَٱسْتَغْفَرَ لَهُمُ ٱلرَّسُولُ لَوَجَدُواْ ٱللَّهَ تَوَّابًا رَّحِيمًا ۩ (القرآن ٤:٦٤)

And if, when they wronged themselves, they had come to you, and asked forgiveness of Allah and the Messenger had asked forgiveness for them, they would have found Allah Accepting of repentance and Merciful. (Quran 4:64)

عن الأغر بن يسار المزني رضي الله عنه قال: قال رسول الله صلى الله عليه وسلم: "يَاأَيُّها النَّاسِ توبوا إلى الله واستغفروه فإنِّي أتوب في اليوم مائة مرَّة" (صحيح مسلم)

Al-Agharr bin Yasar Al-Muzani narrated: The Messenger of Allah (peace be upon him) said: "Turn you people in repentance to Allah and beg pardon of Him. I turn to Him in repentance a hundred times a day". (Muslim - Sahih)

أَفَلَا يَتُوبُونَ إِلَى ٱللَّهِ وَيَسْتَغْفِرُونَهُۥ ۚ وَٱللَّهُ غَفُورٌ رَّحِيمٌ ۩ (القرآن ٥:٧٤)

So will they not repent to Allah and seek His forgiveness? And Allah is Forgiving and Merciful. (Quran 5:74)

عَنْ عَائِشَةَ، أَنَّهَا قَالَتْ يَا رَسُولَ اللهِ أَرَأَيْتَ إِنْ وَافَقْتُ لَيْلَةَ الْقَدْرِ مَا أَدْعُو قَالَ "تَقُولِينَ اللَّهُمَّ إِنَّكَ عَفُوٌّ تُحِبُّ الْعَفْوَ فَاعْفُ عَنِّي" (رواه ابن ماجه والترمذي – صحيح)

Narrated Aisha that she said: O Messenger of Allah, what do you think I should say in my supplication, if I come upon Laylatul-Qadr? He said: "Say: "O Allah, You are Forgiving and love forgiveness, so forgive me." (Ibn Majah, Tirmidhi - Sahih)

أَلَمْ يَعْلَمُوٓاْ أَنَّ ٱللَّهَ هُوَ يَقْبَلُ ٱلتَّوْبَةَ عَنْ عِبَادِهِۦ وَيَأْخُذُ ٱلصَّدَقَٰتِ وَأَنَّ ٱللَّهَ هُوَ ٱلتَّوَّابُ ٱلرَّحِيمُ ۝ (القرآن ٩:١٠٤)

Do they not know that it is Allah who accepts repentance from His servants and receives charities and that it is Allah who is the Accepting of repentance, the Merciful? (Quran 9:104)

وَٱللَّهُ يُرِيدُ أَن يَتُوبَ عَلَيْكُمْ وَيُرِيدُ ٱلَّذِينَ يَتَّبِعُونَ ٱلشَّهَوَٰتِ أَن تَمِيلُواْ مَيْلًا عَظِيمًا ۝ (القرآن ٤:٢٧)

Allah wants to accept your repentance, but those who follow their passions want you to digress into a great deviation. (Quran 4:27)

Etiquette of Disagreement (أَدَبُ الخِلاف)

Unity does not mean uniformity. People are different and disagreements are natural. We are not required to agree on everything. We are required to disagree in a manner befitting our noble status as Muslims.

The noble companions disagreed among themselves in many significant matters. Scholars teach us that they handled their differnces in the following manner.

1. Their brotherhood in Islam transcended differences of opinion.
2. They treated corrections of their opinions as a favor from their brother. They did not perceive it as fault finding.
3. They were never bitter or embarrassed to admit their errors.
4. They tried to avoid differences whenever possible.
5. They expressed differences of opinion within the bounds of what is allowed.
6. They never disparaged the competence or rights of their Muslim brother.
7. They sincerely searched for the truth, and they willingly accepted it from wherever it came.
8. They disagreed about the branches, not the roots of Islam. The disagreed on fiqhi matters, not on akidah.

(وَلَا تَنَازَعُوا فَتَفْشَلُوا وَتَذْهَبَ رِيحُكُمْ (القرآن ٨:٤٦)

And do not dispute with one another lest you fail and your moral strength desert you (Quran 8:46)

وَلَوْ شَاءَ رَبُّكَ لَجَعَلَ ٱلنَّاسَ أُمَّةً وَٰحِدَةً ۖ وَلَا يَزَالُونَ مُخْتَلِفِينَ (القرآن ١١:١١٨)

If your Lord had willed, He would have made all humanity one community, but they will not cease to differ. (Quran 11:118)

عَنِ ابْنِ أَبِي مُلَيْكَةَ، قَالَ كَادَ الْخَيِّرَانِ أَنْ يَهْلِكَا ـ أَبَا بَكْرٍ وَعُمَرَ ـ رضى الله عنهما ـ رَفَعَا أَصْوَاتَهُمَا عِنْدَ النَّبِيِّ صلى الله عليه وسلم حِينَ قَدِمَ عَلَيْهِ رَكْبُ بَنِي تَمِيمٍ، فَأَشَارَ أَحَدُهُمَا بِالأَقْرَعِ بْنِ حَابِسٍ أَخِي بَنِي مُجَاشِعٍ، وَأَشَارَ الآخَرُ بِرَجُلٍ آخَرَ ـ قَالَ نَافِعٌ لاَ أَحْفَظُ اسْمَهُ ـ فَقَالَ أَبُو بَكْرٍ لِعُمَرَ مَا أَرَدْتَ إِلاَّ خِلاَفِي. قَالَ مَا أَرَدْتُ خِلاَفَكَ. فَارْتَفَعَتْ أَصْوَاتُهُمَا فِي ذَلِكَ، فَأَنْزَلَ اللَّهُ {يَا أَيُّهَا الَّذِينَ آمَنُوا لاَ تَرْفَعُوا أَصْوَاتَكُمْ} الآيَةَ. قَالَ ابْنُ الزُّبَيْرِ فَمَا كَانَ عُمَرُ يُسْمِعُ رَسُولَ اللَّهِ صلى الله عليه وسلم بَعْدَ هَذِهِ الآيَةِ حَتَّى يَسْتَفْهِمَهُ (صحيح البخاري)

Narrated Ibn Abi Mulaika, "The two righteous persons were about to be ruined. They were Abu Bakr and Umar who raised their voices in the presence of the Prophet (peace be upon him) when a mission from Bani Tamim came to him. One of the two recommended Al-Aqra' bin Habeas, the brother of Bani Mujashi to be their governor while the other recommended somebody else. Abu Bakr said to Umar, "You wanted nothing but to oppose me!" Umar said, "I did not intend to oppose you." Their voices grew loud in that argument, so Allah revealed: 'O you who believe! Raise not your voices above the voice of the Prophet.' (49:2) Ibn Az-Zubair said, "Since the revelation of this Verse, Umar used to speak in such a low tone that the Messenger of Allah (peace be upon him) had to ask him to repeat his statements." (Bukhari – Sahih)

عَنِ ابْنِ عُمَرَ ـ رضى الله عنهما ـ قَالَ قَالَ النَّبِيُّ صلى الله عليه وسلم يَوْمَ الأَحْزَابِ "لاَ يُصَلِّيَنَّ أَحَدٌ الْعَصْرَ إِلاَّ فِي بَنِي قُرَيْظَةَ". فَأَدْرَكَ بَعْضَهُمُ الْعَصْرُ فِي الطَّرِيقِ، فَقَالَ بَعْضُهُمْ لاَ نُصَلِّي حَتَّى نَأْتِيَهَا. وَقَالَ بَعْضُهُمْ بَلْ

نُصَلِّي، لَمْ يُرِدْ مِنَّا ذَلِكَ، فَذُكِرَ ذَلِكَ لِلنَّبِيِّ صلى الله عليه وسلم فَلَمْ يُعَنِّفْ وَاحِدًا مِنْهُمْ. (صحيح البخاري)

Narrated Ibn Umar: "On the day of Al-Ahzab, the Prophet (peace be upon him) said, 'None of you should offer the Asr prayer except at Banu Quraida's place.' The Asr prayer became due for some of them on the way. Some of those said, 'We will not offer it till we reach it, the place of Banu Quraida,' while some others said, 'No, we will pray at this spot, for he did not mean that for us.' Later on it was mentioned to the Prophet (peace be upon him) and he did not rebuke any of the two groups." (Bukhari – Sahih)

فَإِن تَنَازَعْتُمْ فِي شَيْءٍ فَرُدُّوهُ إِلَى ٱللَّهِ وَٱلرَّسُولِ إِن كُنتُمْ تُؤْمِنُونَ بِٱللَّهِ وَٱلْيَوْمِ ٱلْآخِرِ (القرآن ٤:٥٩)

If you differ in anything among yourselves, refer it to Allah and His Messenger, if you do believe in Allah and the Last Day: (Quran 4:59)

وَمَا ٱخْتَلَفَ ٱلَّذِينَ أُوتُوا۟ ٱلْكِتَـٰبَ إِلَّا مِنۢ بَعْدِ مَا جَآءَهُمُ ٱلْعِلْمُ بَغْيًۢا بَيْنَهُمْ (القرآن ٣:١٩)

The people of the scripture differed among themselves only after knowledge had come to them, out of mutual jealousy (Quran 3:19)

عَنْ الْبَرَاءِ بْنِ عَازِبٍ، يَقُولُ كَتَبَ عَلِيُّ بْنُ أَبِي طَالِبٍ الصُّلْحَ بَيْنَ النَّبِيِّ صلى الله عليه وسلم وَبَيْنَ الْمُشْرِكِينَ يَوْمَ الْحُدَيْبِيَةِ فَكَتَبَ "هَذَا مَا كَاتَبَ عَلَيْهِ مُحَمَّدٌ رَسُولُ اللَّهِ". فَقَالُوا لاَ تَكْتُبْ رَسُولُ اللَّهِ فَلَوْ نَعْلَمُ أَنَّكَ رَسُولُ اللَّهِ لَمْ نُقَاتِلْكَ. فَقَالَ النَّبِيُّ صلى الله عليه وسلم "لَعَلِيٌّ امْحُهُ". فَقَالَ مَا أَنَا بِالَّذِي أَمْحَاهُ. فَمَحَاهُ النَّبِيُّ صلى الله عليه وسلم بِيَدِهِ قَالَ وَكَانَ فِيمَا اشْتَرَطُوا أَنْ يَدْخُلُوا

مَكَّةَ فَتُقِيمُوا بِهَا ثَلَاثًا وَلاَ يَدْخُلُهَا بِسِلَاحٍ إِلاَّ جُلُبَّانَ السِّلَاحِ. قُلْتُ لِأَبِي إِسْحَاقَ وَمَا جُلُبَّانُ السِّلَاحِ قَالَ الْقِرَابُ وَمَا فِيهِ. (صحيح مسلم)

Al-Bara bin Azib said: Ali bin Abu Talib penned the treaty between the Prophet (peace be upon him) and the polytheists on the Day of Hudaibiya. He wrote: This is what Muhammad, the Messenger of Allah, has settled. They (the polytheists) said: Do not write words "the Messenger of Allah". If we knew that you were the Messenger of Allah, we would not fight against you. The Prophet (peace be upon him) said to Ali: Strike out these words. He (Ali) said: I am not going to strike them out. So the Prophet (peace be upon him) struck them out with his own hand. The narrator said that the conditions upon which the two sides had agreed included that the Muslims would enter Mecca (next year) and would stay there for three days, and that they would not enter bearing arms except in their sheaths. (Muslim - Sahih)

A Word Portrait Of The Messenger of Allah (*peace be upon him*)

Love and admiration is what a Muslim naturally feels towards *sayyiduna rasulullah* our master the Messenger of Allah (peace be upon him). Naturally generations of Muslims have sought to catch a glimpse of his beloved face and his personality.

Over the centuries, much has been written about this topic. Perhaps the most authoritative work is Ash Shamail al Muhammadiya written by Imam Tirmidhi. A selected passage from this masterpiece is produced below.

Whenever Ali bin Abi Talib, may Allah be pleased with him, described the noble features of Messenger of Allah (peace be upon him), he used to say:

> The Messenger of Allah (peace be upon him) was neither very tall nor short, but of a medium stature among people.
>
> His hair was not short and curly, nor was it long and straight, rather it would hang down in waves.
>
> His face was not overly plump, nor was it fleshy, yet it was somewhat circular.
>
> The complexion of the Messenger of Allah (peace be upon him) was white with redness in it.

The blessed eyes of the Messenger of Allah (peace be upon him) were extremely black. His eyelashes were long.

He was large-boned and broad shouldered.

His torso was hairless except for a thin line that stretched down his chest to his belly.

The hands and feet of the Messenger of Allah (peace be upon him) were fully fleshed.

When he walked, he lifted his legs with vigor, as if he were going down a slope.

When he looked at someone he turned his whole body towards that person.

The seal of prophet hood was located between his shoulders. He was a last of all prophets.

He was the most generous and the most truthful.

He was the most kind-hearted and was the most noble.

Any person who saw him suddenly would become overwhelmed with awe.

Anyone who came in close contact with him, and knew his excellent character was smitten with love due to his excellent attributes.

Anyone who described his noble features can only say: "I have not seen anyone like the Messenger of Allah (peace be upon him) neither before nor after him."

Source: *Shamail Muhammadiya* (Nobility of The Praiseworthy)

Characteristics Of The Complete Muslim

We are not Muslims by virtue of our lineage, ethnicity, tribe or country of birth. Rather we are Muslim due to the faith (Iman) that beats in our hearts and compels us to action. Faith is transformative. It has transformed entire nations and tribes. It has literally changed the world.

However, the first field of transformation is the life and character of the Muslim in whose heart the faith resides. Many scholars have written extensively about the characteristics a Muslim should possess.

Many contemporary scholars have identified eight characteristics that one should hold to be a complete Muslim. We list these characteristics in the following pages and identify verses and Hadith about them.

وَلَـٰكِنَّ ٱللَّهَ حَبَّبَ إِلَيْكُمُ ٱلْإِيمَـٰنَ وَزَيَّنَهُۥ فِى قُلُوبِكُمْ وَكَرَّهَ إِلَيْكُمُ ٱلْكُفْرَ وَٱلْفُسُوقَ وَٱلْعِصْيَانَ (القرآن ٤٩:٧)

But Allah has made beloved to you faith and has made it pleasing in your hearts and has made hateful to you disbelief, defiance and disobedience. (Quran 49:7)

عَنْ أَنَسٍ، عَنِ النَّبِيِّ صلى الله عليه وسلم قَالَ "ثَلاَثٌ مَنْ كُنَّ فِيهِ وَجَدَ بِهِنَّ حَلاَوَةَ الإِيمَانِ مَنْ كَانَ اللَّهُ وَرَسُولُهُ أَحَبَّ إِلَيْهِ مِمَّا سِوَاهُمَا وَأَنْ يُحِبَّ الْمَرْءَ لاَ يُحِبُّهُ إِلاَّ لِلَّهِ وَأَنْ يَكْرَهَ أَنْ يَعُودَ فِي الْكُفْرِ بَعْدَ أَنْ أَنْقَذَهُ اللَّهُ مِنْهُ كَمَا يَكْرَهُ أَنْ يُقْذَفَ فِي النَّارِ" (صحيح مسلم)

Reported Anas: The Prophet (peace be upon him) said: "There are the three qualities, whoever has them will taste the sweetness of faith: he to whom Allah and His Messenger are dearer than all else; he who loves someone for Allah's sake alone; and he who has as great an abhorrence of returning to unbelief after Allah has rescued him from it as he has of being cast into the fire." (Muslim - Sahih)

Pure Belief (سَلامَةُ العَقيدَة)

Iman (Faith) is our most precious asset. We thank Allah the Exalted for this enormous blessing and we seek His guidance every day to maintain this gift. In His mercy, He has taught us what we must believe in.

لَقَدْ جَاءَكَ ٱلْحَقُّ مِن رَّبِّكَ فَلَا تَكُونَنَّ مِنَ ٱلْمُمْتَرِينَ ۝ (القرآن ١٠:٩٤)

The truth has certainly come to you from your Lord, so do not be among the doubters. (Quran 10:94)

وَلَقَدْ أُوحِىَ إِلَيْكَ وَإِلَى ٱلَّذِينَ مِن قَبْلِكَ لَئِنْ أَشْرَكْتَ لَيَحْبَطَنَّ عَمَلُكَ وَلَتَكُونَنَّ مِنَ ٱلْخَٰسِرِينَ ۝ (القرآن ٣٩:٦٥)

And indeed it has been revealed to you, as it was to those before you: "If you join others in worship with Allah, surely your deeds will be in vain, and you will certainly be among the losers." (Quran 39:65)

ٱعْبُدُوا۟ ٱللَّهَ رَبِّى وَرَبَّكُمْ ۚ إِنَّهُۥ مَن يُشْرِكْ بِٱللَّهِ فَقَدْ حَرَّمَ ٱللَّهُ عَلَيْهِ ٱلْجَنَّةَ وَمَأْوَىٰهُ ٱلنَّارُ (القرآن ٧٢:٥)

Worship Allah, my Lord and your Lord. Verily, whoever sets up partners in worship with Allah, then Allah has forbidden Paradise for him, and the Fire will be his abode. (Quran 5:72)

عَنْ أَبِي هُرَيْرَةَ، قَالَ قَالَ رَسُولُ اللَّهِ صلى الله عليه وسلم "أَنْ تُؤْمِنَ بِاللَّهِ وَمَلَائِكَتِهِ وَكِتَابِهِ وَلِقَائِهِ وَرُسُلِهِ وَتُؤْمِنَ بِالْبَعْثِ وَتُؤْمِنَ بِالْقَدَرِ كُلِّهِ" (صحيح مسلم)

Abu Huraira narrated: The Messenger of Allah (peace be upon him) said: "(Faith is) that you affirm your faith in Allah, His angels, His books, His meeting, His messengers, that you believe in the resurrection and that you believe in the Divine decree) in all its entirety." (Muslim - Sahih)

ءَامَنَ ٱلرَّسُولُ بِمَآ أُنزِلَ إِلَيْهِ مِن رَّبِّهِۦ وَٱلْمُؤْمِنُونَ ۚ كُلٌّ ءَامَنَ بِٱللَّهِ وَمَلَـٰٓئِكَتِهِۦ وَكُتُبِهِۦ وَرُسُلِهِۦ لَا نُفَرِّقُ بَيْنَ أَحَدٍ مِّن رُّسُلِهِۦ ۚ وَقَالُوا۟ سَمِعْنَا وَأَطَعْنَا ۖ غُفْرَانَكَ رَبَّنَا وَإِلَيْكَ ٱلْمَصِيرُ (القرآن ٢:٢٨٥)

The Messenger has believed in what was revealed to him from his Lord, and [so have] the believers. All of them have believed in Allah and His angels and His books and His messengers, [saying], "We make no distinction between any of His messengers." And they say, "We hear and we obey. [We seek] Your forgiveness, our Lord, and to You is the return." (Quran 2:285)

وَٱللَّهُ خَلَقَكُمْ وَمَا تَعْمَلُونَ (القرآن ٣٧:٩٦)

And Allah created you and that which you do. (Quran 37:96)

عَنْ أَبِي هُرَيْرَةَ، قَالَ قَالَ رَسُولُ اللَّهِ صلى الله عليه وسلم "الإِيمَانُ بِضْعٌ وَسَبْعُونَ شُعْبَةً أَفْضَلُهَا لاَ إِلَهَ إِلاَّ اللَّهُ وَأَوْضَعُهَا إِمَاطَةُ الأَذَى عَنِ الطَّرِيقِ وَالْحَيَاءُ شُعْبَةٌ مِنَ الإِيمَانِ" (رواه النَّسائي – صحيح)

Narrated Abu Hurairah: The Messenger of Allah (peace be upon him) said: "Faith has seventy-odd branches, the most virtuous of which is there is none worthy of worship except Allah and the least of which is removing something harmful from the road. And modesty is a branch of faith." (Nasai - Sahih)

Correct Worship (صِحَّةُ العِبَادَةِ)

Our souls have a deep longing, an intense hunger to connect to our Lord. This can only be satisfied by worshipping Allah the Exalted. For our worship to be accepted, it must be done in the manner taught by our beloved Messenger (peace be upon him).

وَمَا خَلَقْتُ ٱلْجِنَّ وَٱلْإِنسَ إِلَّا لِيَعْبُدُونِ ۝ (القرآن ٥١:٥٦)

And I did not create the jinn and mankind except to worship Me. (Quran 51:56)

فَلْيَعْبُدُوا۟ رَبَّ هَٰذَا ٱلْبَيْتِ ۝ (القرآن ١٠٦:٣)

Let them worship the Lord of this House. (Quran 106:3)

عَنْ مُعَاذِ بْنِ جَبَلٍ، قَالَ قَالَ النَّبِيُّ صلى الله عليه وسلم "يَا مُعَاذُ أَتَدْرِي مَا حَقُّ اللَّهِ عَلَى الْعِبَادِ". قَالَ اللَّهُ وَرَسُولُهُ أَعْلَمُ. قَالَ " أَنْ يَعْبُدُوهُ وَلاَ يُشْرِكُوا بِهِ شَيْئًا، أَتَدْرِي مَا حَقُّهُمْ عَلَيْهِ". قَالَ اللَّهُ وَرَسُولُهُ أَعْلَمُ. قَالَ "أَنْ لاَ يُعَذِّبَهُمْ" (رواه البخاري ومسلم والترمذي – صحيح)

Narrated Muadh bin Jabal: The Prophet (peace be upon him) said: "O Muadh! Do you know what Allah's right upon His slaves is?" I said, "Allah and His Messenger know best." The Prophet (peace be upon him) said, "To worship Him alone and to join none in worship with Him. Do you know what their right upon Him is?" I replied, "Allah and His Messenger know best." The Prophet (peace be upon him) said, "Not to punish them (if they do so)." (Bukhari, Muslim, Tirmidhi - Sahih)

وَلَقَدْ بَعَثْنَا فِى كُلِّ أُمَّةٍ رَّسُولاً أَنِ ٱعْبُدُوا۟ ٱللَّهَ وَٱجْتَنِبُوا۟ ٱلطَّٰغُوتَ (القرآن ٣٦:١٦)

Certainly We raised a messenger in every nation (to preach) 'Worship Allah, and reject false gods'. (Quran 16:36)

إِنَّنِىٓ أَنَا ٱللَّهُ لَآ إِلَٰهَ إِلَّآ أَنَا۠ فَٱعْبُدْنِى وَأَقِمِ ٱلصَّلَوٰةَ لِذِكْرِىٓ (القرآن ٢٠:١٤)

Indeed, I am Allah. There is no deity except Me, so worship Me and establish prayer for My remembrance. (Quran 20:14)

وَأَنِ ٱعْبُدُونِى ۚ هَٰذَا صِرَٰطٌ مُّسْتَقِيمٌ (القرآن ٣٦:٦١)

Worship Me. This is a straight path. (Quran 36:61)

وَٱسْتَعِينُوا۟ بِٱلصَّبْرِ وَٱلصَّلَوٰةِ (القرآن ٢:٤٥)

And seek help in patience and prayer. (Quran 2:45)

يَٰٓأَيُّهَا ٱلَّذِينَ ءَامَنُوا۟ لَا تَقْرَبُوا۟ ٱلصَّلَوٰةَ وَأَنتُمْ سُكَٰرَىٰ حَتَّىٰ تَعْلَمُوا۟ مَا تَقُولُونَ (القرآن ٤:٤٣)

O believers! Do not approach prayer when you are intoxicated, until you know what you are saying. (Quran 4:43)

فَمَن كَانَ يَرْجُواْ لِقَآءَ رَبِّهِۦ فَلْيَعْمَلْ عَمَلًا صَٰلِحًا وَلَا يُشْرِكْ بِعِبَادَةِ رَبِّهِۦٓ أَحَدًۢا (القرآن ١٨: ١١٠)

So whoever hopes for the meeting with his Lord; let him do good deeds and not associate in the worship of his Lord anyone. (Quran 18:110)

وَٱتَّخَذُواْ مِن دُونِ ٱللَّهِ ءَالِهَةً لِّيَكُونُواْ لَهُمْ عِزًّا ۝ كَلَّا ۚ سَيَكْفُرُونَ بِعِبَادَتِهِمْ وَيَكُونُونَ عَلَيْهِمْ ضِدًّا (القرآن ١٩: ٨١-٨٢)

And they have taken besides Allah false deities as a source of honor. No indeed! Soon they will disown their worship, and they will become their enemies. (Quran 19:81-82)

وَيَعْبُدُونَ مِن دُونِ ٱللَّهِ مَا لَمْ يُنَزِّلْ بِهِۦ سُلْطَٰنًا وَمَا لَيْسَ لَهُم بِهِۦ عِلْمٌ ۗ وَمَا لِلظَّٰلِمِينَ مِن نَّصِيرٍ (القرآن ٢٢: ٧١)

And they worship besides Allah that for which He has not sent down authority and that of which they have no knowledge. And there will not be for the wrongdoers any helper. (Quran 22:71)

وَأَرِنَا مَنَاسِكَنَا (القرآن ٢: ١٢٨)

And show us our rituals (of worship). (Quran 2:128)

عَنْ أَبِي سُلَيْمَانَ و مَالِكِ بْنِ الْحُوَيْرِثِ قَالَ أَتَيْنَا النَّبِيَّ صلى الله عليه وسلم وَنَحْنُ شَبَبَةٌ مُتَقَارِبُونَ، فَأَقَمْنَا عِنْدَهُ عِشْرِينَ لَيْلَةً، فَظَنَّ أَنَّا اشْتَقْنَا أَهْلَنَا، وَسَأَلَنَا عَمَّنْ تَرَكْنَا فِي أَهْلِنَا، فَأَخْبَرْنَاهُ، وَكَانَ رَفِيقًا رَحِيمًا فَقَالَ "ارْجِعُوا إِلَى أَهْلِيكُمْ فَعَلِّمُوهُمْ وَمُرُوهُمْ، وَصَلُّوا كَمَا رَأَيْتُمُونِي أُصَلِّي، وَإِذَا حَضَرَتِ الصَّلَاةُ فَلْيُؤَذِّنْ لَكُمْ أَحَدُكُمْ، ثُمَّ لِيَؤُمَّكُمْ أَكْبَرُكُمْ" (صحيح البخاري)

Narrated Abu Sulaiman and Malik bin Huwairith: We came to the Prophet (peace be upon him) and we were young men of approximately equal age and stayed with him for twenty nights. Then he thought that we were anxious for our families, and he asked us whom we had left behind to look after our families, and we told him. He was kindhearted and merciful, so he said, "Return to your families and teach them (Islam) and command them (to do good deeds) and pray as you saw me praying, and when the stated time for the prayer becomes due, then one of you should pronounce its call (Adhan), and the eldest of you should lead you in prayer. (Bukhari - Sahih)

وَمَا آتَاكُمُ الرَّسُولُ فَخُذُوهُ وَمَا نَهَاكُمْ عَنْهُ فَانْتَهُوا (القرآن ٧:٥٩)

And take whatever the Messenger has given you and refrain from what he has forbidden you. (Quran 59:7)

لَقَدْ كَانَ لَكُمْ فِي رَسُولِ اللَّهِ أُسْوَةٌ حَسَنَةٌ لِّمَن كَانَ يَرْجُو اللَّهَ وَالْيَوْمَ الْآخِرَ وَذَكَرَ اللَّهَ كَثِيرًا (القرآن ٢١:٣٣)

Indeed in the Messenger of Allah you have a good example to follow for anyone whose hope is in Allah and the Last Day and remembers Allah often. (Quran 33:21)

عَنْ عَائِشَةَ، قَالَتْ قَالَ رَسُولُ اللَّهِ صلى الله عليه وسلم "مَنْ أَحْدَثَ فِي أَمْرِنَا هَذَا مَا لَيْسَ مِنْهُ فَهُوَ رَدٌّ" (رواه مسلم والبخاري وأبو دود وابن ماجه – صحيح)

Aisha reported: The Messenger of Allah (peace be upon him) as saying: "Anyone who brings something new to this matter of ours (Islam) will have it rejected". (Muslim, Bukhari, Abu Dawud, Ibn Majah - Sahih)

إِنَّمَا يَتَقَبَّلُ اللَّهُ مِنَ الْمُتَّقِينَ (القرآن ٢٧:٥)

Allah accepts only from those who are God conscious. (Quran 5:27)

وَمَن يَكْفُرْ بِالْإِيمَانِ فَقَدْ حَبِطَ عَمَلُهُ (القرآن ٥:٥)

Should anyone renounce his faith, his work shall fail. (Quran 5:5)

Good Character & Conduct (حُسْنُ الخُلُق)

The ideal Muslim seeks to emulate our beloved Messenger (peace be upon him). He was kind, gentle, courteous, forgiving, easy to deal with, a person of utmost integrity. He was not harsh, or lewd or obscene.

وَإِنَّكَ لَعَلَىٰ خُلُقٍ عَظِيمٍ ﴿٤﴾ (القرآن ٦٨:٤)

And indeed, you are of a great moral character. (Quran 68:4)

عَنْ أَبِي هُرَيْرَةَ، أَنَّ رَسُولَ اللهِ صلى الله عليه وسلم قَالَ: "إِنَّمَا بُعِثْتُ لِأُتَمِّمَ صَالِحَ الْأَخْلَاقِ" (آداب المفرد، موطأ الإمام مالك – صحيح)

Abu Hurayra reported: The Messenger of Allah (peace be upon him) said: "I was sent to perfect good character." (Adab al Mufrad, Muwatta Imam Malik – Sahih)

عَنْ عَائِشَةَ، عَنِ النَّبِيِّ ـ صلى الله عليه وسلم ـ قَالَ "إِنَّ اللَّهَ رَفِيقٌ يُحِبُّ الرِّفْقَ فِي الأَمْرِ كُلِّهِ" (رواه ابن ماجه – صحيح)

Aisha reported: The Prophet (peace be upon him) said: "Allah is Gentle and loves gentleness in all things." (Ibn Majah – Sahih)

وَعِبَادُ ٱلرَّحْمَٰنِ ٱلَّذِينَ يَمْشُونَ عَلَى ٱلْأَرْضِ هَوْنًا وَإِذَا خَاطَبَهُمُ ٱلْجَٰهِلُونَ قَالُوا۟ سَلَٰمًا ﴿٦٣﴾ (القرآن ٢٥:٦٣)

And the servants of the Most Merciful are those who walk upon the earth with humility, and when the ignorant argue with them, they say (words of) peace. (Quran 25:63)

عَنْ أَبِي الدَّرْدَاءِ، أَنَّ النَّبِيَّ صلى الله عليه وسلم قَالَ "مَا شَيْءٌ أَثْقَلُ فِي مِيزَانِ الْمُؤْمِنِ يَوْمَ الْقِيَامَةِ مِنْ خُلُقٍ حَسَنٍ وَإِنَّ اللَّهَ لَيُبْغِضُ الْفَاحِشَ الْبَذِيءَ" (رواه الترمذي – صحيح)

Abu Dardah narrated: The Messenger of Allah (peace be upon him) said: "Nothing is heavier on the believer's scale on the Day of Judgment than good character. For indeed Allah is angered by the shameless obscene person." (Tirmidhi – Sahih)

عَنْ أَبِي الدَّرْدَاءِ، قَالَ سَمِعْتُ النَّبِيَّ صلى الله عليه وسلم يَقُولُ "مَا مِنْ شَيْءٍ يُوضَعُ فِي الْمِيزَانِ أَثْقَلُ مِنْ حُسْنِ الْخُلُقِ وَإِنَّ صَاحِبَ حُسْنِ الْخُلُقِ لَيَبْلُغُ بِهِ دَرَجَةَ صَاحِبِ الصَّوْمِ وَالصَّلَاةِ" (رواه الترمذي – حسن)

Abu Dardah narrated: The Messenger of Allah (peace be upon him) said: "Nothing is heavier on the believer's Scale on the Day of Judgment than good character. Indeed the person with good character will have attained the rank of the person of fasting and prayer." (Tirmidhi – Hassan)

عَنْ عَبْدِ اللَّهِ بْنِ مَسْعُودٍ، قَالَ قَالَ رَسُولُ اللَّهِ صلى الله عليه وسلم "أَلاَ أُخْبِرُكُمْ بِمَنْ يَحْرُمُ عَلَى النَّارِ أَوْ بِمَنْ تَحْرُمُ عَلَيْهِ النَّارُ عَلَى كُلِّ قَرِيبٍ هَيِّنٍ لَيِّنٍ سَهْلٍ" رواه الترمذي – حسن)

Abdullah bin Masud narrated: The Messenger of Allah (peace be upon him) said: "Shall I not inform you for whom the hellfire is unlawful and he is unlawful for the hellfire? Every person who is tolerant, amicable, and easy to deal with." (Tirmidhi – Hassan)

أَبُو عَبْدِ اللَّهِ الْجَدَلِيِّ يَقُولُ، سَأَلْتُ عَائِشَةَ عَنْ خُلُقِ رَسُولِ اللَّهِ صلى الله عليه وسلم فَقَالَتْ لَمْ يَكُنْ فَاحِشًا وَلاَ مُتَفَحِّشًا وَلاَ صَخَّابًا فِي الأَسْوَاقِ وَلاَ يَجْزِي بِالسَّيِّئَةِ السَّيِّئَةَ وَلَكِنْ يَعْفُو وَيَصْفَحُ (رواه الترمذي والبخاري – صحيح)

Abu Abdullah Al-Jadali narrated: I asked Aisha about the character of the Messenger of Allah (peace be upon him). She said: "He was not obscene, nor uttering obscenities, nor shouting in the markets, he would not return a harm with a harm, but rather he was pardoning and forgiving." (Tirmidhi, Bukhari – Sahih)

عَنْ أَبِي هُرَيْرَةَ، قَالَ: سُئِلَ النَّبِيُّ صلى الله عليه وسلم: مَا أَكْثَرُ مَا يُدْخِلُ الْجَنَّةَ قَالَ: "التَّقْوَى وَحُسْنُ الْخُلُقِ". وَسُئِلَ: مَا أَكْثَرُ مَا يُدْخِلُ النَّارَ قَالَ: "الأَجْوَفَانِ: الْفَمُ وَالْفَرْجُ" (رواه ابن ماجه – صحيح)

Narrated Abu Hurairah: The Prophet (peace be upon him) was asked: "What most admits people to Paradise?" He said: "Piety and good manners." And he was asked: "What most leads people to Hell?" He said: "The mouth and the private part." (Ibn Majah – Sahih)

يَٰٓأَيُّهَا ٱلَّذِينَ ءَامَنُوا۟ لَا تَدْخُلُوا۟ بُيُوتًا غَيْرَ بُيُوتِكُمْ حَتَّىٰ تَسْتَأْنِسُوا۟ وَتُسَلِّمُوا۟ عَلَىٰٓ أَهْلِهَا ۚ ذَٰلِكُمْ خَيْرٌ لَّكُمْ لَعَلَّكُمْ تَذَكَّرُونَ ۝ فَإِن لَّمْ تَجِدُوا۟ فِيهَآ أَحَدًا فَلَا تَدْخُلُوهَا حَتَّىٰ يُؤْذَنَ لَكُمْ ۖ وَإِن قِيلَ لَكُمُ ٱرْجِعُوا۟ فَٱرْجِعُوا۟ ۖ هُوَ أَزْكَىٰ لَكُمْ ۚ وَٱللَّهُ بِمَا تَعْمَلُونَ عَلِيمٌ ۝ (القرآن ٢٤: ٢٧-٢٨)

O believers, do not enter houses other than your own houses until you receive permission and greet their inhabitants. That is best for you; perhaps you will be reminded. And if you do not find anyone therein, do not enter them until permission has been given you. And if it is said to you, "Go back," then go back; it is purer for you. And Allah is knowing of what you do. (Quran 24:27-28)

وَإِذَا حُيِّيتُم بِتَحِيَّةٍ فَحَيُّوا۟ بِأَحْسَنَ مِنْهَآ أَوْ رُدُّوهَآ ۗ إِنَّ ٱللَّهَ كَانَ عَلَىٰ كُلِّ شَىْءٍ حَسِيبًا ۝ (القرآن ٤: ٨٦)

And when you are greeted with a greeting, return a better greeting or a similar greeting. Indeed, Allah is ever, over all things, an Accountant. (Quran 4:86)

يَـٰٓأَيُّهَا ٱلَّذِينَ ءَامَنُوا۟ ٱجْتَنِبُوا۟ كَثِيرًا مِّنَ ٱلظَّنِّ إِنَّ بَعْضَ ٱلظَّنِّ إِثْمٌ ۖ وَلَا تَجَسَّسُوا۟ وَلَا يَغْتَب بَّعْضُكُم بَعْضًا (القرآن ٤٩:١٢)

O believers, avoid much suspicion. Indeed, some suspicion is sin. And do not spy or backbite each other. (Quran 49:12)

عَنْ أَبِي هُرَيْرَةَ، عَنِ النَّبِيِّ صلى الله عليه وسلم قَالَ" إِيَّاكُمْ وَالظَّنَّ، فَإِنَّ الظَّنَّ أَكْذَبُ الْحَدِيثِ، وَلاَ تَحَسَّسُوا، وَلاَ تَجَسَّسُوا، وَلاَ تَحَاسَدُوا، وَلاَ تَدَابَرُوا، وَلاَ تَبَاغَضُوا، وَكُونُوا عِبَادَ اللهِ إِخْوَانًا" (صحيح البخاري)

Abu Huraira reported: The Prophet (peace be upon him) said, "Beware of suspicion, for suspicion is the worst of false tales; and do not look for the others' faults and do not spy, and do not be jealous of one another, and do not cut off relations with one another, and do not hate one another; and O Allah's worshipers! Be brothers!" (Bukhari - Sahih)

وَأَنفِقُوا۟ فِى سَبِيلِ ٱللَّهِ وَلَا تُلْقُوا۟ بِأَيْدِيكُمْ إِلَى ٱلتَّهْلُكَةِ ۛ وَأَحْسِنُوٓا۟ ۛ إِنَّ ٱللَّهَ يُحِبُّ ٱلْمُحْسِنِينَ ۝ (القرآن ٢:١٩٥)

And spend in the way of Allah and do not destroy yourselves with your own hands, and do good. Indeed, Allah loves the doers of good. (Quran 2:195)

وَإِذَا سَمِعُوا۟ ٱللَّغْوَ أَعْرَضُوا۟ عَنْهُ وَقَالُوا۟ لَنَآ أَعْمَـٰلُنَا وَلَكُمْ أَعْمَـٰلُكُمْ سَلَـٰمٌ عَلَيْكُمْ لَا نَبْتَغِى ٱلْجَـٰهِلِينَ ۝ (القرآن ٢٨:٥٥)

And when they hear ill speech, they turn away from it and say, "For us are our deeds, and for you are your deeds. Peace to you; we seek not the ignorant." (Quran 28:55)

وَٱلَّذِينَ هُمْ عَنِ ٱللَّغْوِ مُعْرِضُونَ ۝ (القرآن ٢٣:٣)

And they who turn away from ill speech. (Quran 23:3)

وَلَا تَمْشِ فِي ٱلْأَرْضِ مَرَحًا ۖ إِنَّكَ لَن تَخْرِقَ ٱلْأَرْضَ وَلَن تَبْلُغَ ٱلْجِبَالَ طُولًا ۝ (القرآن ١٧:٣٧)

And do not walk upon the earth proudly. Indeed, you cannot tear the earth nor reach the mountains in height. (Quran 17:37)

إِنَّ ٱللَّهَ لَا يُحِبُّ كُلَّ مُخْتَالٍ فَخُورٍ ۝ (القرآن ٣١:١٨)

Indeed, Allah does not like everyone self-deluded and boastful. (Quran 31:18)

عَنْ أَبِي أُمَامَةَ، قَالَ قَالَ رَسُولُ اللهِ صلى الله عليه وسلم "أَنَا زَعِيمٌ بِبَيْتٍ فِي رَبَضِ الْجَنَّةِ لِمَنْ تَرَكَ الْمِرَاءَ وَإِنْ كَانَ مُحِقًّا وَبِبَيْتٍ فِي وَسَطِ الْجَنَّةِ لِمَنْ تَرَكَ الْكَذِبَ وَإِنْ كَانَ مَازِحًا وَبِبَيْتٍ فِي أَعْلَى الْجَنَّةِ لِمَنْ حَسَّنَ خُلُقَهُ" (رواه أبو داود – حسن)

Narrated Abu Umamah: The Prophet (peace be upon him) said: "I guarantee a house in the outskirts of Paradise for anyone who avoids quarrelling even if he were in the right, a house in the middle of Paradise for anyone who avoids lying even if he were joking, and a house in the upper part of Paradise for anyone who made his character good." (Abu Dawud - Hasan)

عَنْ جَابِرٍ، أَنَّ رَسُولَ اللهِ صلى الله عليه وسلم قَالَ "إِنَّ مِنْ أَحَبِّكُمْ إِلَيَّ وَأَقْرَبِكُمْ مِنِّي مَجْلِسًا يَوْمَ الْقِيَامَةِ أَحَاسِنَكُمْ أَخْلَاقًا وَإِنَّ أَبْغَضَكُمْ إِلَيَّ وَأَبْعَدَكُمْ

مِنِّي مَجْلِسًا يَوْمَ الْقِيَامَةِ الثَّرْثَارُونَ وَالْمُتَشَدِّقُونَ وَالْمُتَفَيْهِقُونَ". قَالُوا يَا رَسُولَ اللهِ قَدْ عَلِمْنَا الثَّرْثَارُونَ وَالْمُتَشَدِّقُونَ فَمَا الْمُتَفَيْهِقُونَ قَالَ "الْمُتَكَبِّرُونَ"
(رواه الترمذي — حسن)

Jabir narrated: The Messenger of Allah (peace be upon him) said: "Indeed the most beloved among you to me, and the nearest to sit with me on the Day of Judgment is the best of you in character. And indeed, the most disliked among you to me, and the one sitting furthest from me on the Day of Judgement are those who brag loudly, and those who rant and the Muthafaihiqun." They said: O Messenger of Allah! We know about those who brag, and those who rant, but what about the Muthafaihiqun? He said: "The arrogant."
(Tirmidhi - Hasan)

Enlightened Intellect (ثَقافَةُ الفِكْرِ)

Intellect and enlightenment are hallmarks of the Muslim. We have an obligation to develop and grow our minds. Our entire civilization is based on knowledge.

اَقْرَأْ بِٱسْمِ رَبِّكَ ٱلَّذِى خَلَقَ ۝ (القرآن ٩٦:١)

Read in the name of your Lord who created. (Quran 96:1)

عن أبي هريرة رضي الله عنه أن رسول الله صلى الله عليه وسلم قال: "ومن سلك طريقًا يلتمس فيه علما سهل الله له به طريقًا إلى الجنة"

Abu Hurairah reported: The Messenger of Allah (peace be upon him) said, "Allah makes the way to Jannah easy for him who treads the path in search of knowledge." (Muslim - Sahih)

ٱلرَّحْمَٰنُ ۝ عَلَّمَ ٱلْقُرْءَانَ ۝ خَلَقَ ٱلْإِنسَٰنَ ۝ عَلَّمَهُ ٱلْبَيَانَ ۝ (القرآن ٥٥ :١-٤)

The Most Merciful, taught the Quran, created humanity, and taught them to communicate. (Quran 55:1-4)

اَقْرَأْ وَرَبُّكَ ٱلْأَكْرَمُ ۝ ٱلَّذِى عَلَّمَ بِٱلْقَلَمِ ۝ عَلَّمَ ٱلْإِنسَٰنَ مَا لَمْ يَعْلَمْ ۝ (القرآن ٩٦ :٣-٤)

Read, and your Lord is the most Generous, Who taught by the pen, taught humanity what they did not know. (Quran 96:3-5)

قُلْ هَلْ يَسْتَوِى ٱلَّذِينَ يَعْلَمُونَ وَٱلَّذِينَ لَا يَعْلَمُونَ ۗ إِنَّمَا يَتَذَكَّرُ أُوْلُوا ٱلْأَلْبَٰبِ (القرآن ٣٩:٩)

Say, "Are those who know equal to those who do not know?" Only people of understanding will take heed. (Quran 39:9)

إِنَّمَا يَخْشَى ٱللَّهَ مِنْ عِبَادِهِ ٱلْعُلَمَٰٓؤُا۟ (القرآن ٣٥:٢٨)

It is only those who have knowledge among His servants that truly fear Allah. (Quran 35:28)

يَرْفَعِ ٱللَّهُ ٱلَّذِينَ ءَامَنُوا۟ مِنكُمْ وَٱلَّذِينَ أُوتُوا۟ ٱلْعِلْمَ دَرَجَٰتٍ (القرآن ٥٨:١١)

Allah will raise those who have believed among you and those who were given knowledge, by degrees. (Quran 58:11)

وَقُل رَّبِّ زِدْنِى عِلْمًا (القرآن ٢٠:١١٤)

And say, "My Lord, increase me in knowledge." (Quran 20:114)

وَلَقَدْ ءَاتَيْنَا دَاوُۥدَ وَسُلَيْمَٰنَ عِلْمًا ۖ وَقَالَا ٱلْحَمْدُ لِلَّهِ ٱلَّذِى فَضَّلَنَا عَلَىٰ كَثِيرٍ مِّنْ عِبَادِهِ ٱلْمُؤْمِنِينَ (القرآن ٢٧:١٥)

And We had certainly given to Dawud and Suleiman knowledge, and they said, "Praise to Allah, who has favored us over many of His believing servants." (Quran 27:15)

عَنْ أَبِي مُوسَى، عَنِ النَّبِيِّ صلى الله عليه وسلم قَالَ "مَثَلُ مَا بَعَثَنِي اللهُ بِهِ مِنَ الْهُدَى وَالْعِلْمِ كَمَثَلِ الْغَيْثِ الْكَثِيرِ أَصَابَ أَرْضًا، فَكَانَ مِنْهَا نَقِيَّةٌ قَبِلَتِ الْمَاءَ، فَأَنْبَتَتِ الْكَلَأَ وَالْعُشْبَ الْكَثِيرَ، وَكَانَتْ مِنْهَا أَجَادِبُ أَمْسَكَتِ الْمَاءَ، فَنَفَعَ اللهُ بِهَا النَّاسَ، فَشَرِبُوا وَسَقَوْا وَزَرَعُوا، وَأَصَابَتْ مِنْهَا طَائِفَةً أُخْرَى، إِنَّمَا هِيَ قِيعَانٌ لاَ تُمْسِكُ مَاءً، وَلاَ تُنْبِتُ كَلَأً، فَذَلِكَ مَثَلُ مَنْ فَقِهَ فِي دِينِ اللهِ وَنَفَعَهُ مَا بَعَثَنِي اللهُ بِهِ، فَعَلِمَ وَعَلَّمَ، وَمَثَلُ مَنْ لَمْ يَرْفَعْ بِذَلِكَ رَأْسًا، وَلَمْ يَقْبَلْ هُدَى اللهِ الَّذِي أُرْسِلْتُ بِهِ" (صحيح البخاري)

Narrated Abu Musa: The Prophet (peace be upon him) said, "The example of guidance and knowledge with which Allah has sent me is like abundant rain falling on the land, some of which was fertile soil that absorbed rain water and brought forth vegetation and grass in abundance. Another portion of it was hard and held the rain water and Allah benefited the people with it and they utilized it for drinking, making their animals drink from it and for irrigation of the land for cultivation. Another portion of it was barren which could neither hold the water nor bring forth vegetation. The first is the example of the person who comprehends Allah's religion and benefits from the knowledge which Allah has revealed through me and learns and then teaches others. The last example is that of a person who does not care for it and does not take Allah's guidance revealed through me." (Bukhari - Sahih)

Healthy Body (قُوَّةُ الجِسْمِ)

Every Muslim should take care to maintain a healthy body. Our bodies are a trust given to us by Allah the Exalted. Thus we have a duty to take care of our physical and emotional health.

عَنْ أَبِي هُرَيْرَةَ، قَالَ قَالَ رَسُولُ اللَّهِ صلى الله عليه وسلم "الْمُؤْمِنُ الْقَوِيُّ خَيْرٌ وَأَحَبُّ إِلَى اللَّهِ مِنَ الْمُؤْمِنِ الضَّعِيفِ وَفِي كُلٍّ خَيْرٌ" (صحيح مسلم)

Abu Huraira reported: The Messenger of Allah (peace be upon him) said: "A strong believer is better and beloved to Allah than a weak believer, and there is good in everyone." (Muslim - Sahih)

عَنْ عُقْبَةَ بْنَ عَامِرٍ، يَقُولُ سَمِعْتُ رَسُولَ اللَّهِ صلى الله عليه وسلم وَهُوَ عَلَى الْمِنْبَرِ يَقُولُ "وَأَعِدُّوا لَهُمْ مَا اسْتَطَعْتُمْ مِنْ قُوَّةٍ أَلاَ إِنَّ الْقُوَّةَ الرَّمْىُ أَلاَ إِنَّ الْقُوَّةَ الرَّمْىُ أَلاَ إِنَّ الْقُوَّةَ الرَّمْىُ" (صحيح مسلم)

Narrated Uqbah bin Amir: I heard the Messenger of Allah (peace be upon him) say-as he was delivering a sermon from the pulpit: "Prepare to meet them with as much strength as you can afford. (Quran 8:60) Indeed, throwing (archery/shooting) is strength. Indeed, throwing (archery/shooting) is strength. Indeed, throwing (archery/shooting) is strength." (Muslim - Sahih)

يَٰٓأَيُّهَا ٱلنَّاسُ كُلُواْ مِمَّا فِي ٱلْأَرْضِ حَلَٰلًا طَيِّبًا (القرآن ٢:١٦٨)

O humanity, eat from what is on earth that is lawful and healthy. (Quran 2:168)

كُلُوا۟ مِن طَيِّبَـٰتِ مَا رَزَقْنَـٰكُمْ وَلَا تَطْغَوْا۟ فِيهِ (القرآن ٢٠:٨١)

Eat from the good things We have provided you and do not transgress therein. (Quran 20:81)

فَٱبْعَثُوٓا۟ أَحَدَكُم بِوَرِقِكُمْ هَـٰذِهِۦٓ إِلَى ٱلْمَدِينَةِ فَلْيَنظُرْ أَيُّهَآ أَزْكَىٰ طَعَامًا فَلْيَأْتِكُم بِرِزْقٍ مِّنْهُ (القرآن ١٨:١٩)

So send one of you with money to the city and let him find pure food and as sustenance. (Quran 18:19)

عَنْ عَبْدِ اللهِ بْنِ عَمْرٍو، قَالَ دَخَلَ عَلَيَّ رَسُولُ اللهِ صلى الله عليه وسلم فَقَالَ "أَلَمْ أُخْبَرْ أَنَّكَ تَقُومُ اللَّيْلَ وَتَصُومُ النَّهَارَ". قُلْتُ بَلَى. قَالَ "فَلَا تَفْعَلْ، قُمْ وَنَمْ، وَصُمْ وَأَفْطِرْ، فَإِنَّ لِجَسَدِكَ عَلَيْكَ حَقًّا، وَإِنَّ لِعَيْنِكَ عَلَيْكَ حَقًّا، وَإِنَّ لِزَوْرِكَ عَلَيْكَ حَقًّا، وَإِنَّ لِزَوْجِكَ عَلَيْكَ حَقًّا" (صحيح البخاري)

Narrated Abdullah bin Amr: The Messenger of Allah (peace be upon him) entered upon me and said, "Have I not been informed that you offer prayer all the night and fast the whole day?" I said, "Yes." He said, "Do not do so; Offer prayer at night and also sleep; Fast for a few days and give up fasting for a few days because your body has a right on you, and your eye has a right on you, and your guest has a right on you, and your wife has a right on you." (Bukhari - Sahih)

عَنْ عَبْدِ اللهِ، عَنِ النَّبِيِّ صلى الله عليه وسلم قَالَ "مَا أَنْزَلَ اللهُ دَاءً إِلَّا أَنْزَلَ لَهُ دَوَاءً" (رواه ابن ماجه – صحيح)

Narrated Abdullah that the Prophet (peace be upon him) said: "Allah does not send down any disease, but He also sends down the cure for it." (Ibn Majah - Sahih)

عَنْ مُعَاذِ بْنِ عَبْدِ اللهِ بْنِ خُبَيْبٍ، عَنْ أَبِيهِ، عَنْ عَمِّهِ، قَالَ كُنَّا فِي مَجْلِسٍ فَجَاءَ النَّبِيُّ صلى الله عليه وسلم وَعَلَى رَأْسِهِ أَثَرُ مَاءٍ فَقَالَ لَهُ بَعْضُنَا نَرَاكَ الْيَوْمَ

طَيِّبَ النَّفْسِ . فَقَالَ "أَجَلْ وَالْحَمْدُ لِلَّهِ" . ثُمَّ أَفَاضَ الْقَوْمُ فِي ذِكْرِ الْغِنَى فَقَالَ "لاَ بَأْسَ بِالْغِنَى لِمَنِ اتَّقَى وَالصِّحَّةُ لِمَنِ اتَّقَى خَيْرٌ مِنَ الْغِنَى وَطِيبُ النَّفْسِ مِنَ النِّعَمِ" (رواه ابن ماجه – صحيح)

Narrated from Muadh bin Abdullah bin Khubaib, from his father, that his paternal uncle said: We were sitting in a gathering, and the Prophet (peace be upon him) came with traces of water on his head. One of us said to him, "We see that you are of good cheer today." He said, "Yes, praise is to Allah." Then he spoke to the people about being rich. He said, "There is nothing wrong with being rich for one who has piety, but good health for one who has piety is better than riches, and being of good cheer is a blessing." (Ibn Majah - Sahih)

Capable Of Earning A Living (القُدْرَةُ عَلَى الكَسْبِ)

Dignified even in adversity, begging is not easy for a Muslim. We have been taught the value of work. Our daily struggle to earn lawful wealth to feed our families is an act of worship we perform to please Allah the Exalted.

هُوَ ٱلَّذِى جَعَلَ لَكُمُ ٱلْأَرْضَ ذَلُولاً فَٱمْشُواْ فِى مَنَاكِبِهَا وَكُلُواْ مِن رِّزْقِهِۦ وَإِلَيْهِ ٱلنُّشُورُ ۝ (القرآن ٦٧:١٥)

It is He who subjected the earth for you, so walk among its paths and eat of His provision, and to Him is the resurrection. (Quran 67:15)

فَٱنتَشِرُواْ فِى ٱلْأَرْضِ وَٱبْتَغُواْ مِن فَضْلِ ٱللَّهِ (القرآن ٦٢:١٠)

Disperse within the land and seek from the bounty of Allah. (Quran 62:10)

عَنْ الزُّبَيْرِ بْنِ الْعَوَّامِ رضى الله عنه عَنْ النَّبِيِّ صلى الله عليه وسلم قَالَ "لَأَنْ يَأْخُذَ أَحَدُكُمْ حَبْلَهُ فَيَأْتِيَ بِحُزْمَةِ الْحَطَبِ عَلَى ظَهْرِهِ فَيَبِيعَهَا فَيَكُفَّ اللَّهُ بِهَا وَجْهَهُ، خَيْرٌ لَهُ مِنْ أَنْ يَسْأَلَ النَّاسَ أَعْطَوْهُ أَوْ مَنَعُوهُ" (صحيح البخاري)

Narrated Az-Zubair bin Al-Awwam: The Prophet (peace be upon him) said, "It is better for anyone of you to take a rope and bring a bundle of wood over his back and sell it and Allah will save his face (from the Hell-Fire) because of that, rather than to ask the people who may give him or not." (Bukhari - Sahih)

وَجَعَلْنَا ٱلنَّهَارَ مَعَاشًا ۝ (القرآن ١١:٧٨)

And He appointed the day for livelihood. (Quran 78:11)

عَنْ مُعَاوِيَةَ، قَالَ قَالَ رَسُولُ اللهِ صلى الله عليه وسلم "لَا تُلْحِفُوا فِي الْمَسْأَلَةِ" (رواه مسلم والنّسائي – صحيح)

Muawiya reported: The Messenger of Allah (peace be upon him) said: "Do not be insistent in begging or asking." (Muslim, Nasai - Sahih)

لِلْفُقَرَآءِ ٱلَّذِينَ أُحْصِرُوا۟ فِى سَبِيلِ ٱللَّهِ لَا يَسْتَطِيعُونَ ضَرْبًا فِى ٱلْأَرْضِ يَحْسَبُهُمُ ٱلْجَاهِلُ أَغْنِيَآءَ مِنَ ٱلتَّعَفُّفِ تَعْرِفُهُم بِسِيمَٰهُمْ لَا يَسْـَٔلُونَ ٱلنَّاسَ إِلْحَافًا (القرآن ٢:٢٧٣)

[Charity is] for the poor who have been restricted for the cause of Allah, unable to move about in the land. They appear to an unfamiliar person to be self-sufficient because of their restraint, but you can recognize them from their characteristic sign, they do not beg of people at all. (Quran 2:273)

عَنْ أَنَسِ بْنِ مَالِكٍ، قَالَ كُنَّا مَعَ رَسُولِ اللهِ صلى الله عليه وسلم فِي السَّفَرِ فَمِنَّا الصَّائِمُ وَمِنَّا الْمُفْطِرُ فَنَزَلْنَا فِي يَوْمٍ حَارٍّ وَاتَّخَذْنَا ظِلَالًا فَسَقَطَ الصَّوَّامُ وَقَامَ الْمُفْطِرُونَ فَسَقَوُا الرِّكَابَ فَقَالَ رَسُولُ اللهِ صلى الله عليه وسلم "ذَهَبَ الْمُفْطِرُونَ الْيَوْمَ بِالْأَجْرِ" (رواه النّسائي ومسلم – صحيح)

Narrated Anas bin Malik: We were with the Messenger of Allah (peace be upon him) on a journey, and some of us were fasting and some of us were not. We made a stop on a hot day and looked for shade. Those who were fasting fell to the ground, but those who were not fasting got up and watered the animals. The Messenger of

Allah said: "Those who were not fasting today have taken the reward." (Nasai, Muslim - Sahih)

عَنْ أَبِي هُرَيْرَةَ ـ رضى الله عنه ـ يَقُولُ قَالَ النَّبِيُّ صلى الله عليه وسلم "لَيْسَ الْمِسْكِينُ الَّذِي تَرُدُّهُ التَّمْرَةُ وَالتَّمْرَتَانِ وَلاَ اللُّقْمَةُ وَلاَ اللُّقْمَتَانِ. إِنَّمَا الْمِسْكِينُ الَّذِي يَتَعَفَّفُ وَاقْرَءُوا إِنْ شِئْتُمْ يَعْنِي قَوْلَهُ {لاَ يَسْأَلُونَ النَّاسَ إِلْحَافًا}" (صحيح البخاري)

Narrated Abu Huraira: The Prophet (peace be upon him) said, "The poor person is not the one who needs a date or two or a morsel or two. Rather the poor person is he who does not (beg or) ask the people or show his poverty at all. Recite if you wish: 'They do not beg of people at all.'" (2:273) (Bukhari - Sahih)

عَنْ أَبِي سَعِيدٍ، أَخْبَرَهُ أَنَّ أُنَاسًا مِنَ الأَنْصَارِ سَأَلُوا رَسُولَ اللَّهِ صلى الله عليه وسلم فَلَمْ يَسْأَلْهُ أَحَدٌ مِنْهُمْ إِلاَّ أَعْطَاهُ حَتَّى نَفِدَ مَا عِنْدَهُ فَقَالَ لَهُمْ حِينَ نَفِدَ كُلُّ شَىْءٍ أَنْفَقَ بِيَدَيْهِ "مَا يَكُنْ عِنْدِي مِنْ خَيْرٍ لاَ أَدَّخِرْهُ عَنْكُمْ، وَإِنَّهُ مَنْ يَسْتَعْفِفْ يُعِفُّهُ اللَّهُ، وَمَنْ يَتَصَبَّرْ يُصَبِّرْهُ اللَّهُ، وَمَنْ يَسْتَغْنِ يُغْنِهِ اللَّهُ، وَلَنْ تُعْطَوْا عَطَاءً خَيْرًا وَأَوْسَعَ مِنَ الصَّبْرِ" (صحيح البخاري)

Narrated Abu Said: Some people from the Ansar asked the Messenger of Allah (peace be upon him) (to give them something) and he gave to everyone of them who asked him, until all that he had was finished. When everything was finished and he had spent all that was in his hand, he said to them, "If I have any wealth, I will not withhold it from you. The one who refrains from begging, Allah will make contented and not in need of others; and the one who remains patient, Allah will grant patience upon him, and the one who is satisfied with what he has, Allah will make him self-sufficient. And there is no gift better and more vast (you may be given) than patience." (Bukhari - Sahih)

عَنْ أَبِي هُرَيْرَةَ، قَالَ قَالَ رَسُولُ اللَّهِ صلى الله عليه وسلم "إِنَّ اللَّهَ يَرْضَى لَكُمْ ثَلاَثًا وَيَكْرَهُ لَكُمْ ثَلاَثًا فَيَرْضَى لَكُمْ أَنْ تَعْبُدُوهُ وَلاَ تُشْرِكُوا بِهِ شَيْئًا وَأَنْ تَعْتَصِمُوا بِحَبْلِ اللَّهِ جَمِيعًا وَلاَ تَفَرَّقُوا وَيَكْرَهُ لَكُمْ قِيلَ وَقَالَ وَكَثْرَةَ السُّؤَالِ وَإِضَاعَةَ الْمَالِ" (صحيح مسلم)

Abu Huraira narrated: The Messenger of Allah (peace be upon him) said: "Verily Allah likes three things for you and He disapproves three things for you. He is pleased with you that you worship Him and associate nor anything with Him, that you hold fast the rope of Allah, and be not scattered; and He disapproves for you irrelevant talk, persistent questioning and the wasting of wealth." (Muslim - Sahih)

Organized (تَنْظِيمُ الشُؤُون)

It is indeed a mercy from Allah the Exalted that He has taught us the importance of being organized and prepared. Islam teaches us that it is better to take provisions for a journey instead of hoping for the kindness of strangers along the way and the need to take precautions for potential problems.

We have been commanded to be organized with a cohesive leadership structure at all times, even in something as simple as a journey for personal or business reasons.

The Messenger of Allah (peace be upon him) taught us how to be organized in everyday life when he modeled for us how to pray in congregation behind an Imam and to stand in straight lines.

وَتَزَوَّدُواْ فَإِنَّ خَيْرَ ٱلزَّادِ ٱلتَّقْوَىٰ (القرآن ١٩٧:٢)

And take provisions (for your journey), indeed, the best provision is rememberance of Allah. (Quran 2:197)

عَنْ أَبِي سَعِيدٍ الْخُدْرِيِّ، أَنَّ رَسُولَ اللهِ صلى الله عليه وسلم قَالَ "إِذَا خَرَجَ ثَلَاثَةٌ فِي سَفَرٍ فَلْيُؤَمِّرُوا أَحَدَهُمْ" (رواه أبو داود – حسن)

Narrated Abu Said al-Khudri: The Prophet (peace be upon him) said, "When three are on a journey, they should appoint one of them as their leader." (Abu Dawud - Hasan)

$$\text{يَٰٓأَيُّهَا ٱلَّذِينَ ءَامَنُواْ خُذُواْ حِذْرَكُمْ فَٱنفِرُواْ ثُبَاتٍ أَوِ ٱنفِرُواْ جَمِيعًا}$$

(القرآن ٤:٧١)

O believers, take your precautions and proceed in groups or proceed all together. (Quran 4:71)

$$\text{وَأَعِدُّواْ لَهُم مَّا ٱسْتَطَعْتُم مِّن قُوَّةٍ وَمِن رِّبَاطِ ٱلْخَيْلِ}$$ (القرآن ٨:٦٠)

And prepare against them whatever you are able of power and of groups of horses. (Quran 8:60)

عَنْ أَبِي سَعِيدٍ الْخُدْرِيِّ، قَالَ قَالَ رَسُولُ اللهِ صلى الله عليه وسلم "إِذَا كَانُوا ثَلَاثَةً فَلْيَؤُمَّهُمْ أَحَدُهُمْ وَأَحَقُّهُمْ بِالْإِمَامَةِ أَقْرَؤُهُمْ" (صحيح مسلم)

Abu Said al-Khudri reported: The Messenger of Allah (peace be upon him) said: "When there are three persons, one of them should lead them. The one among them most worthy to act as Imam is one who is best versed in the Quran." (Muslim - Sahih)

عَنْ أَنَسٍ، عَنِ النَّبِيِّ صلى الله عليه وسلم قَالَ "سَوُّوا صُفُوفَكُمْ فَإِنَّ تَسْوِيَةَ الصُّفُوفِ مِنْ إِقَامَةِ الصَّلَاةِ" (صحيح البخاري)

Narrated Anas: The Prophet (peace be upon him) said, "Straighten your rows as the straightening of rows is part of establishing prayer." (Bukhari - Sahih)

عَنْ النُّعْمَانَ بْنَ بَشِيرٍ، قَالَ سَمِعْتُ رَسُولَ اللهِ صلى الله عليه وسلم يَقُولُ "لَتُسَوُّنَّ صُفُوفَكُمْ أَوْ لَيُخَالِفَنَّ اللهُ بَيْنَ وُجُوهِكُمْ" (صحيح مسلم)

Numan bin Bashir reported: I heard the Messenger of Allah (peace be upon him) say: "Straighten your rows, or Allah would create dissension amongst you." (Muslim - Sahih)

Mindful Of The Importance Of Time (الحِرْصُ عَلى الوَقْتِ)

Contrary to popular belief, time is not money. Time is much more important than money. Our entire lives are actually nothing more than a series of moments in time. Thus we don't allow time to be wasted.

Allah the Exalted has taken repeated oaths by various sections of time to emphasize this matter to us. He, the Most High also commanded us to perform specific acts of worship at specified times. One of the many benefits of worship is that we get used to being timely.

أَوَلَمْ نُعَمِّرْكُم مَّا يَتَذَكَّرُ فِيهِ مَن تَذَكَّرَ (القرآن ٣٥:٣٧)

Did We not give you lives long enough, so that whoever wanted could receive a reminder? (Quran 35:37)

وَلِكُلِّ أُمَّةٍ أَجَلٌ فَإِذَا جَاءَ أَجَلُهُمْ لَا يَسْتَأْخِرُونَ سَاعَةً وَلَا يَسْتَقْدِمُونَ (القرآن ٧:٣٤)

And for every nation is a term. So when their time has come, they will not remain behind an hour, nor will they precede it. (Quran 7:34)

وَٱلْفَجْرِ وَلَيَالٍ عَشْرٍ (القرآن ٨٩: ١-٢)

By the dawn, and by the ten nights. (Quran 89:1-2)

وَٱلْعَصْرِ ۝ (القرآن ١٠٣:١)

By the declining day. (Quran 103:1)

وَٱلَّيْلِ إِذَا يَغْشَىٰ ۝ وَٱلنَّهَارِ إِذَا تَجَلَّىٰ ۝ (القرآن ٩٢: ١-٢)

By the night when it covers, and the day when it appears. (Quran 92:1-2)

وَٱلضُّحَىٰ ۝ وَٱلَّيْلِ إِذَا سَجَىٰ ۝ (القرآن ٩٣: ١-٢)

By the morning brightness, and the night when it covers with darkness. (Quran 93:1-2)

إِنَّ ٱلصَّلَوٰةَ كَانَتْ عَلَى ٱلْمُؤْمِنِينَ كِتَٰبًا مَّوْقُوتًا ۝ (القرآن ٤:١٠٣)

Indeed, prayer has been decreed upon the believers at specified times. (Quran 4:103)

ٱلْحَجُّ أَشْهُرٌ مَّعْلُومَٰتٌ (القرآن ٢:١٩٧)

Hajj is [to be performed during] well-known months. (Quran 2:197)

جَعَلَ ٱللَّهُ ٱلْكَعْبَةَ ٱلْبَيْتَ ٱلْحَرَامَ قِيَٰمًا لِّلنَّاسِ وَٱلشَّهْرَ ٱلْحَرَامَ (القرآن ٥:٩٧)

Allah has made the Kabah, the Sacred House for the people to stand, and [has sanctified] the sacred months. (Quran 5:97)

$$\text{كَأَنَّهُمْ يَوْمَ يَرَوْنَهَا لَمْ يَلْبَثُوٓا۟ إِلَّا عَشِيَّةً أَوْ ضُحَىٰهَا} \quad (\text{القرآن } 79:46)$$

On the Day they will perceive they had not remained in the world except for an afternoon or a morning thereof. (Quran 79:46)

$$\text{وَيَوْمَ يَحْشُرُهُمْ كَأَن لَّمْ يَلْبَثُوٓا۟ إِلَّا سَاعَةً مِّنَ ٱلنَّهَارِ} \quad (\text{القرآن } 10:45)$$

And on the Day when He will gather them, it will be as if they had not remained in the world but an hour of the day. (Quran 10:45)

عَنِ ابْنِ عَبَّاسٍ ـ رضى الله عنهما ـ قَالَ قَالَ النَّبِيُّ صلى الله عليه وسلم "نِعْمَتَانِ مَغْبُونٌ فِيهِمَا كَثِيرٌ مِنَ النَّاسِ، الصِّحَّةُ وَالْفَرَاغُ" (رواه البخاري والترمذي – صحيح)

Narrated Ibn Abbas: The Prophet (peace be upon him) said, "There are two blessings which many people waste: Health and free time for doing good." (Bukhari, Tirmidhi - Sahih)

عن أبي برزة رضي الله عنه، قال: قال رسول الله صلى الله عليه وسلم: "لا تزول قدما عبد يوم القيامة حتى يسأل عن عمره فيما أفناه ، وعن علمه فيما فعل فيه، وعن ماله من أين اكتسبه، وفيما أنفقه، وعن جسمه فيم أبلاه" (رواه الترمذي – حسن)

Abu Burzah reported. The Messenger of Allah (peace be upon him) said, "Man's feet will not move on the Day of Resurrection before he is asked about his life, how did he consume it, his knowledge, what did he do with it, his wealth, how did he earn it and how did he dispose of it, and about his body, how did he wear it out." (Tirmidhi - Hasan)

Self-Restrained (مُجَاهَدَةُ النَّفْسِ)

Ideally, we should minimize our ego, and restrain ourselves from the tyranny of their passions, whims and desires. Thus we can protect ourselves from the whispers of Shaytan.

Part of self-restraint is to avoid sins. Classical Islamic scholars have described one aspect of Taqwa (piety) as restraining oneself from sinning and Waraa (scrupulousness) as leaving the doubtful for fear of falling into the sin.

يَـٰٓأَيُّهَا ٱلَّذِينَ ءَامَنُوا۟ ٱتَّقُوا۟ ٱللَّهَ حَقَّ تُقَاتِهِۦ وَلَا تَمُوتُنَّ إِلَّا وَأَنتُم مُّسْلِمُونَ ۝
(القرآن ٣:١٠٢)

O believers, be careful of your duty to Allah with the care which is due to Him and do not die except as Muslims [in a state of submission]. (Quran 3:102)

وَأَمَّا مَنْ خَافَ مَقَامَ رَبِّهِۦ وَنَهَى ٱلنَّفْسَ عَنِ ٱلْهَوَىٰ ۝ فَإِنَّ ٱلْجَنَّةَ هِىَ ٱلْمَأْوَىٰ ۝ (القرآن ٧٩: ٤٠-٤١)

But as for he who feared the position of his Lord and restrained his soul from its desires, indeed, Paradise will be his refuge. (Quran 79:40-41)

عَنْ أَبِي شُرَيْحٍ، أَنَّ النَّبِيَّ صلى الله عليه وسلم قَالَ "وَاللَّهِ لاَ يُؤْمِنُ، وَاللَّهِ لاَ يُؤْمِنُ، وَاللَّهِ لاَ يُؤْمِنُ". قِيلَ وَمَنْ يَا رَسُولَ اللَّهِ قَالَ "الَّذِي لاَ يَأْمَنُ جَارُهُ بَوَايِقَهُ" (صحيح البخاري)

Narrated Abu Shuraih: The Prophet (peace be upon him) said, "By Allah, he does not believe! By Allah, he does not believe! By Allah, he does not believe!" It was said, "Who is that, O Messenger of Allah?" He said, "That person whose neighbor does not feel safe from his evil." (Bukhari - Sahih)

$$\text{أَنَّمَا يَتَّبِعُونَ أَهْوَاءَهُمْ ۚ وَمَنْ أَضَلُّ مِمَّنِ اتَّبَعَ هَوَاهُ بِغَيْرِ هُدًى مِنَ اللَّهِ}$$
(القرآن ٢٨:٥٠)

They only follow their desires. And who is more astray than one who follows his desire without guidance from Allah? (Quran 28:50)

$$\text{أَفَمَنْ أَسَّسَ بُنْيَانَهُ عَلَىٰ تَقْوَىٰ مِنَ اللَّهِ وَرِضْوَانٍ خَيْرٌ أَم مَّنْ أَسَّسَ بُنْيَانَهُ عَلَىٰ شَفَا جُرُفٍ هَارٍ فَانْهَارَ بِهِ فِي نَارِ جَهَنَّمَ ۗ وَاللَّهُ لَا يَهْدِي الْقَوْمَ الظَّالِمِينَ}$$
(القرآن ٩:١٠٩)

Is the one who laid the foundation of his building on mindfulness of Allah and His approval better or one who laid the foundation of his building on the edge of a bank about to collapse, so it collapsed with him into the fire of Hell? And Allah does not guide the wrongdoing people. (Quran 9:109)

عَنْ النُّعْمَانِ بْنِ بَشِيرٍ، قَالَ سَمِعْتُ رَسُولَ اللَّهِ صلى الله عليه وسلم يَقُولُ "الْحَلاَلُ بَيِّنٌ وَالْحَرَامُ بَيِّنٌ وَبَيْنَ ذَلِكَ أُمُورٌ مُشْتَبِهَاتٌ لاَ يَدْرِي كَثِيرٌ مِنَ النَّاسِ أَمِنَ الْحَلاَلِ هِيَ أَمْ مِنَ الْحَرَامِ فَمَنْ تَرَكَهَا اسْتِبْرَاءً لِدِينِهِ وَعِرْضِهِ فَقَدْ سَلِمَ وَمَنْ وَاقَعَ شَيْئًا مِنْهَا يُوشِكُ أَنْ يُوَاقِعَ الْحَرَامَ كَمَا أَنَّهُ مَنْ يَرْعَى حَوْلَ الْحِمَى يُوشِكُ أَنْ يُوَاقِعَهُ أَلاَ وَإِنَّ لِكُلِّ مَلِكٍ حِمًى أَلاَ وَإِنَّ حِمَى اللَّهِ مَحَارِمُهُ" (رواه الترمذي والنسائي وابن ماجه – صحيح)

An-Numan bin Bashir narrated: The Messenger of Allah (peace be upon him) said: "The lawful is clear and the unlawful is clear, and between them are matters that are not clear; many people do not know if they are lawful or unlawful. So whoever leaves them to protect his religion and his honor, then he will be safe, and whoever falls into something from them, then he soon will have fallen into the unlawful. Just like if someone grazes (his animals) around a sanctuary, he is likely to trespass into it. Indeed for every king is a sanctuary (pasture), and indeed Allah's sanctuary is what He made unlawful." (Tirmidhi, Nasai, Ibn Majah - Sahih)

عَنْ أَبِي هُرَيْرَةَ ـ رضى الله عنه ـ أَنَّ رَسُولَ اللَّهِ صلى الله عليه وسلم قَالَ "لَيْسَ الشَّدِيدُ بِالصُّرَعَةِ، إِنَّمَا الشَّدِيدُ الَّذِي يَمْلِكُ نَفْسَهُ عِنْدَ الْغَضَبِ" (صحيح البخاري)

Narrated Abu Huraira: The Messenger of Allah (peace be upon him) said, "The strong is not the one who overcomes the people by his strength, but the strong is the one who controls himself while in anger." (Bukhari - Sahih)

Beneficial To Others (النَّفْعُ لِلْغَيْر)

How can people love Islam if Muslims have not benefited them? Allah the Exalted, in His infinite wisdom, has made our beloved Prophet (peace be upon him) a "mercy to all the worlds". And He has further commanded us to take our beloved Prophet (peace be upon him) as our example.

وَمَآ أَرْسَلْنَٰكَ إِلَّا رَحْمَةً لِّلْعَٰلَمِينَ ۝ (القرآن ٢١:١٠٧)

And We have not sent you, [O Muhammad], except as a mercy to the worlds. (Quran 21:107)

عَنِ ابْنِ عُمَرَ أَنَّ النَّبِيَّ صَلَّى اللهُ عَلَيْهِ وَسَلَّمَ قَالَ "أَحَبُّ النَّاسِ إِلَى اللهِ أَنْفَعُهُمْ لِلنَّاسِ وَأَحَبُّ الْأَعْمَالِ إِلَى اللهِ سُرُورٌ تُدْخِلُهُ عَلَى مُسْلِمٍ أَوْ تَكْشِفُ عَنْهُ كُرْبَةً أَوْ تَقْضِي عَنْهُ دَيْنًا أَوْ تَطْرُدُ عَنْهُ جُوعًا وَلَأَنْ أَمْشِيَ مَعَ أَخِي فِي حَاجَةٍ أَحَبُّ إِلَيَّ مِنْ أَنْ أَعْتَكِفَ فِي هَذَا الْمَسْجِدِ يَعْنِي مَسْجِدَ الْمَدِينَةِ شَهْرًا وَمَنْ كَفَّ غَضَبَهُ سَتَرَ اللهُ عَوْرَتَهُ وَمَنْ كَظَمَ غَيْظَهُ وَلَوْ شَاءَ أَنْ يُمْضِيَهُ أَمْضَاهُ مَلَأَ اللهُ عَزَّ وَجَلَّ قَلْبَهُ أَمْنًا يَوْمَ الْقِيَامَةِ وَمَنْ مَشَى مَعَ أَخِيهِ فِي حَاجَةٍ حَتَّى أَثْبَتَهَا لَهُ أَثْبَتَ اللهُ عَزَّ وَجَلَّ قَدَمَهُ عَلَى الصِّرَاطِ يَوْمَ تَزِلُّ فِيهِ الْأَقْدَامُ" (الطبراني – صحيح)

Ibn Umar reported: The Prophet (peace be upon him) said, "The most beloved people to Allah are those who are most beneficial to the people. The most beloved deed to Allah is to make a Muslim happy, or to remove one of his troubles, or to forgive his debt, or to feed his hunger. That I walk with a brother regarding a need is more beloved to me than that I seclude myself in this mosque in Medina for a month. Whoever swallows his anger, then Allah will conceal his faults. Whoever suppresses his rage, even though he could fulfill his anger if he wished, then Allah will secure his heart on the Day of Resurrection. Whoever walks with his brother regarding a need until he secures it for him, then Allah the Exalted will make his footing firm across the bridge on the day when the footings are shaken." (Tabarani - Sahih)

وَٱعْبُدُواْ ٱللَّهَ وَلَا تُشْرِكُواْ بِهِۦ شَيْـًٔا ۖ وَبِٱلْوَٰلِدَيْنِ إِحْسَٰنًا وَبِذِى ٱلْقُرْبَىٰ وَٱلْيَتَٰمَىٰ وَٱلْمَسَٰكِينِ وَٱلْجَارِ ذِى ٱلْقُرْبَىٰ وَٱلْجَارِ ٱلْجُنُبِ وَٱلصَّاحِبِ بِٱلْجَنۢبِ وَٱبْنِ ٱلسَّبِيلِ وَمَا مَلَكَتْ أَيْمَٰنُكُمْ ۗ إِنَّ ٱللَّهَ لَا يُحِبُّ مَن كَانَ مُخْتَالًا فَخُورًا

(القرآن ٤:٣٦)

Worship Allah and associate nothing with Him, and to parents do good, and to relatives, orphans, the needy, the near neighbor, the neighbor farther away, the companion at your side, the traveler, and your slaves. Indeed, Allah does not like those who are self-deluding and boastful. (Quran 4:36)

عَنْ أَبِي هُرَيْرَةَ، قَالَ قَالَ رَسُولُ اللَّهِ صلى الله عليه وسلم "مَنْ نَفَّسَ عَنْ مُؤْمِنٍ كُرْبَةً مِنْ كُرَبِ الدُّنْيَا نَفَّسَ اللَّهُ عَنْهُ كُرْبَةً مِنْ كُرَبِ الآخِرَةِ وَمَنْ سَتَرَ عَلَى مُسْلِمٍ سَتَرَهُ اللَّهُ فِي الدُّنْيَا وَالآخِرَةِ وَاللَّهُ فِي عَوْنِ الْعَبْدِ مَا كَانَ الْعَبْدُ فِي عَوْنِ أَخِيهِ" (متفق عليه)

Narrated Abu Hurairah: The Messenger of Allah (peace be upon him) said: "Whoever relieves a Muslim of a burden from the burdens of the world, Allah will relieve him of a burden from the burdens of the Hereafter. And whoever covers (the faults of) a Muslim, Allah will cover (his faults) for him in the world and the Hereafter. And Allah is engaged in helping the worshipper as long as the worshipper is engaged in helping his brother." (Muslim, Bukhari - Sahih)

لَقَدْ جَاءَكُمْ رَسُولٌ مِنْ أَنفُسِكُمْ عَزِيزٌ عَلَيْهِ مَا عَنِتُّمْ حَرِيصٌ عَلَيْكُم بِٱلْمُؤْمِنِينَ رَءُوفٌ رَّحِيمٌ ﴿١٢٨﴾ (القرآن ٩:١٢٨)

There has certainly come to you a Messenger from among yourselves. It grieves him that you should receive any injury or difficulty. He is anxious over you, for the believers he is full of pity, kind, and merciful. (Quran 9:128)

Examples Of Complete Muslims

Once a slave of Abu Dharr (may Allah be pleased with him) brought to him a sheep with a broken leg. On asking him who had broken its leg, the slave answered, "I have done this deliberately to enrage you so you may hit me and commit a sin". Abu Dharr (may Allah be pleased with him) replied, "I shall enrage the one who drove you to do so (Shaytan)" and then set the slave free.

One night, Umar ibn Abdul Aziz entered a masjid when it was so dark that he stumbled upon a sleeping man. The man raised his head and exclaimed, "Are you crazy?", "No" replied Umar. The soldiers of Umar wanted to punish the man for his insolence when Umar prevented them, saying, "He just asked me 'Are you crazy?' and I said, 'No'."

A man said evil words about Ali ibn Al-Hussein ibn Ali (may Allah be pleased with them all) so his servants were enraged, but he told them to calm down and said to the man, "What you do not know about us is much more than what you have said. Do you have any need that we can fulfill for you?" The man felt ashamed and said nothing, so Ali gave him the garment he was just wearing and instructed his servants to give him a thousand Dirhams. After that the man used to say, "I testify that you are a descendant of the Messenger (peace be upon him)."

A man told Wahb ibn Munabbih that someone had insulted him and Wahb said, "And are you the only postman that Shaytan found to deliver this message to me?"

Source: *Mukhtasar Minhaj Alqasidin* (Path of the Seekers - Abridged)

Leadership Qualities & Concepts

The Messenger of Allah (peace be upon him) was the ideal servant leader. He modeled the best characteristics that the leader should posess. We take lessons from his noble character in attempting to improve ourselves.

Muslims are taught to prepare for leadership but not compete for it. The Quran describes how believers aspire to possess leadership skills.

لَقَدْ كَانَ لَكُمْ فِي رَسُولِ ٱللَّهِ أُسْوَةٌ حَسَنَةٌ لِمَن كَانَ يَرْجُوا۟ ٱللَّهَ وَٱلْيَوْمَ ٱلْأَخِرَ وَذَكَرَ ٱللَّهَ كَثِيرًا (القرآن ٣٣:٢١)

Indeed in the Messenger of Allah you have a good example to follow for anyone whose hope is in Allah and the Last Day and remembers Allah often. (Quran 33:21)

عَنْ أَنَسِ بْنِ مَالِكٍ، قَالَ: قَالَ رَسُولُ اللهِ صَلَّى اللهُ عَلَيْهِ وَعَلَى آلِهِ وَسَلَّمَ: "سَيِّدُ الْقَوْمِ خَادِمُهُمْ" (رواه العجلوني – حسن لغيره)

Narrated Anas bin Malik: The Messenger of Allah (peace be upon him) said: *"The leader of a people is their servant."* (Ajluni - Hasan Lighairihi)

وَٱلَّذِينَ يَقُولُونَ رَبَّنَا هَبْ لَنَا مِنْ أَزْوَاجِنَا وَذُرِّيَّتِنَا قُرَّةَ أَعْيُنٍ وَٱجْعَلْنَا لِلْمُتَّقِينَ إِمَامًا (القرآن ٢٥:٧٤)

And those who say, "Our Lord, grant us comfort to our eyes from our spouses and offspring and make us leaders (or examples) among the righteous." (Quran 25:74)

Trust (أَمَانَة)

Our beloved Messenger (peace be upon him) was known as Al-Ameen, the trustworthy. As Muslims, we strive to be trustworthy, for this is a characteristic dear to Allah the Exalted.

وَٱلَّذِينَ هُمْ لِأَمَٰنَٰتِهِمْ وَعَهْدِهِمْ رَٰعُونَ ۝ وَٱلَّذِينَ هُمْ عَلَىٰ صَلَوَٰتِهِمْ يُحَافِظُونَ ۝ أُوْلَٰٓئِكَ هُمُ ٱلْوَٰرِثُونَ ۝ ٱلَّذِينَ يَرِثُونَ ٱلْفِرْدَوْسَ هُمْ فِيهَا خَٰلِدُونَ ۝
(القرآن ٢٣: ٨-١١)

Those who are attentive to their trusts and their promises and carefully guard their prayers. They shall inherit the paradise and live therein forever. (Quran 23:8-11)

عَنْ أَبِي هُرَيْرَةَ ـ رضى الله عنه ـ عَنِ النَّبِيِّ صلى الله عليه وسلم قَالَ "قَالَ اللَّهُ تَعَالَى ثَلاَثَةٌ أَنَا خَصْمُهُمْ يَوْمَ الْقِيَامَةِ رَجُلٌ أَعْطَى بِي ثُمَّ غَدَرَ، وَرَجُلٌ بَاعَ حُرًّا فَأَكَلَ ثَمَنَهُ، وَرَجُلٌ اسْتَأْجَرَ أَجِيرًا فَاسْتَوْفَى مِنْهُ وَلَمْ يُعْطِهِ أَجْرَهُ"
(صحيح البخاري)

Narrated Abu Huraira: The Prophet (peace be upon him) said: "God says, 'There are three people whom I shall be their opponent on the Day of Judgment: A man who was given something in My name and then betrays; A man who sells-off a free man as a slave and consumes the price; and a man who hires a laborer, makes use of his service then does not give him his wages.'" (Bukhari - Sahih)

يَٰٓأَيُّهَا ٱلَّذِينَ ءَامَنُوٓاْ أَوْفُواْ بِٱلْعُقُودِ (القرآن ٥:١)

O believers, fulfill your agreements. (Quran 5:1)

يَٰٓأَيُّهَا ٱلَّذِينَ ءَامَنُوا۟ لَا تَخُونُوا۟ ٱللَّهَ وَٱلرَّسُولَ وَتَخُونُوٓا۟ أَمَٰنَٰتِكُمْ وَأَنتُمْ تَعْلَمُونَ ۝ (القرآن ٨:٢٧)

O believers, do not betray Allah and the Messenger or betray your trusts knowingly. (Quran 8:27)

وَيَٰقَوْمِ أَوْفُوا۟ ٱلْمِكْيَالَ وَٱلْمِيزَانَ بِٱلْقِسْطِ ۖ وَلَا تَبْخَسُوا۟ ٱلنَّاسَ أَشْيَآءَهُمْ وَلَا تَعْثَوْا۟ فِى ٱلْأَرْضِ مُفْسِدِينَ ۝ (القرآن ٨٥:١١)

And O my people, give full measure and weight in justice and do not deprive the people of their due and do not commit abuse on the earth, spreading corruption. (Quran 11:85)

إِنَّ ٱللَّهَ يَأْمُرُكُمْ أَن تُؤَدُّوا۟ ٱلْأَمَٰنَٰتِ إِلَىٰٓ أَهْلِهَا وَإِذَا حَكَمْتُم بَيْنَ ٱلنَّاسِ أَن تَحْكُمُوا۟ بِٱلْعَدْلِ ۚ إِنَّ ٱللَّهَ نِعِمَّا يَعِظُكُم بِهِۦٓ ۗ إِنَّ ٱللَّهَ كَانَ سَمِيعًۢا بَصِيرًا ۝ (القرآن ٥٨:٤)

Indeed, Allah commands you to render trusts to whom they are due and when you judge between people to judge with justice. Excellent is that which Allah instructs you. Indeed, Allah is ever Hearing and Seeing. (Quran 4:58)

عَنْ أَبِي هُرَيْرَةَ، أَنَّ رَسُولَ اللهِ صلى الله عليه وسلم قَالَ "آيَةُ الْمُنَافِقِ ثَلَاثٌ إِذَا حَدَّثَ كَذَبَ، وَإِذَا وَعَدَ أَخْلَفَ، وَإِذَا اؤْتُمِنَ خَانَ" (متفق عليه)

Narrated Abu Huraira: The Messenger of Allah (peace be upon him) said: "A hypocrite is known by three traits: When he speaks, he lies; when he promises, he reneges; when he is entrusted, he cheats." (Bukhari, Muslim)

عَنْ أَبِي هُرَيْرَةَ، وَ حُذَيْفَةَ، قَالَا قَالَ رَسُولُ اللهِ صلى الله عليه وسلم "... فَيَأْتُونَ مُحَمَّدًا صلى الله عليه وسلم فَيَقُومُ فَيُؤْذَنُ لَهُ وَتُرْسَلُ الْأَمَانَةُ وَالرَّحِمُ فَتَقُومَانِ جَنَبَتَىِ الصِّرَاطِ يَمِينًا وَشِمَالًا فَيَمُرُّ أَوَّلُكُمْ كَالْبَرْقِ" (صحيح مسلم)

Abu Huraira and Hudhaifa reported: The Messenger of Allah (peace be upon him) said: "... (on the day of judgement) Muhammad (peace be upon him) would be permitted (to open the door of Paradise). Trustworthiness and kinship would be dispatched, and they would stand on the right and left of the Sirat (bridge over hell) and the first of you would pass like lightning." (Muslim - Sahih)

وَمَا كَانَ لِنَبِيٍّ أَن يَغُلَّ ۚ وَمَن يَغْلُلْ يَأْتِ بِمَا غَلَّ يَوْمَ ٱلْقِيَٰمَةِ ۚ ثُمَّ تُوَفَّىٰ كُلُّ نَفْسٍ مَّا كَسَبَتْ وَهُمْ لَا يُظْلَمُونَ ۝ (القرآن ٣: ١٦١)

It is not befitting for the prophet to cheat. And whoever betrays, will come with what he took on the Day of Resurrection. Then will every soul be compensated for what it earned, and they will not be wronged. (Quran 3:161)

وَيْلٌ لِّلْمُطَفِّفِينَ ۝ ٱلَّذِينَ إِذَا ٱكْتَالُوا۟ عَلَى ٱلنَّاسِ يَسْتَوْفُونَ ۝ وَإِذَا كَالُوهُمْ أَو وَّزَنُوهُمْ يُخْسِرُونَ ۝ أَلَا يَظُنُّ أُو۟لَٰٓئِكَ أَنَّهُم مَّبْعُوثُونَ ۝ لِيَوْمٍ عَظِيمٍ ۝ يَوْمَ يَقُومُ ٱلنَّاسُ لِرَبِّ ٱلْعَٰلَمِينَ ۝ (القرآن ٨٣: ١-٦)

Woe unto those who give short measure, who demand full measure for themselves, but give less than what is due to others. Do they not know that they will be resurrected on a tremendous Day, the Day when all people shall stand before the Lord of the worlds? (Quran 83:1-6)

عَنْ أَبِي سَعِيدٍ الْخُدْرِيِّ، يَقُولُ قَالَ رَسُولُ اللَّهِ صلى الله عليه وسلم "إِنَّ مِنْ أَشَرِّ النَّاسِ عِنْدَ اللَّهِ مَنْزِلَةً يَوْمَ الْقِيَامَةِ الرَّجُلَ يُفْضِي إِلَى امْرَأَتِهِ وَتُفْضِي إِلَيْهِ ثُمَّ يَنْشُرُ سِرَّهَا" (صحيح مسلم)

Abu Said al-Khudri reported: The Messenger of Allah (peace be upon him) said: "The most wicked among the people to Allah on the Day of judgment is the men who goes to his wife and she comes to him, and then he divulges her secret." (Muslim - Sahih)

فَٱسْتَخَفَّ قَوْمَهُۥ فَأَطَاعُوهُ ۚ إِنَّهُمْ كَانُوا۟ قَوْمًا فَٰسِقِينَ ۝ فَلَمَّآ ءَاسَفُونَا ٱنتَقَمْنَا مِنْهُمْ فَأَغْرَقْنَٰهُمْ أَجْمَعِينَ ۝ فَجَعَلْنَٰهُمْ سَلَفًا وَمَثَلًا لِّلْءَاخِرِينَ ۝ (القرآن ٤٣: ٥٤-٥٦)

So Pharaoh deceived his people, and they followed him. Indeed, they became wrongdoers. And when they angered Us, We punished them and drowned them all. And We made them a precedent for the future. (Quran 43:54-56)

Stewardship (خِلَافَة)

We have been appointed stewards of this Earth. We possess agency. We are responsible. Either individually or collectively. We are responsible for ourselves, our spiritual growth, our actions, our families, our communities, all of humanity and the entire earth.

We ask Allah the Exalted to help us on the day we are held accountable for our areas of responsibility.

وَإِذْ قَالَ رَبُّكَ لِلْمَلَٰٓئِكَةِ إِنِّى جَاعِلٌ فِى ٱلْأَرْضِ خَلِيفَةً (القرآن ٢:٣٠)

And when your Lord said to the angels, "Indeed, I will make upon the earth a steward." (Quran 2:30)

وَهُوَ ٱلَّذِى جَعَلَكُمْ خَلَٰٓئِفَ ٱلْأَرْضِ وَرَفَعَ بَعْضَكُمْ فَوْقَ بَعْضٍ دَرَجَٰتٍ لِّيَبْلُوَكُمْ فِى مَآ ءَاتَىٰكُمْ ۗ إِنَّ رَبَّكَ سَرِيعُ ٱلْعِقَابِ وَإِنَّهُۥ لَغَفُورٌ رَّحِيمٌ (٦:١٦٥)

And Allah made you stewards upon the earth and has raised some of you above others in degrees to test you through what He has given you. Indeed, your Lord is swift in penalty; but indeed, He is Forgiving and Merciful." (Quran 6:165).

وَلَقَدْ كَرَّمْنَا بَنِىٓ ءَادَمَ وَحَمَلْنَٰهُمْ فِى ٱلْبَرِّ وَٱلْبَحْرِ وَرَزَقْنَٰهُم مِّنَ ٱلطَّيِّبَٰتِ وَفَضَّلْنَٰهُمْ عَلَىٰ كَثِيرٍ مِّمَّنْ خَلَقْنَا تَفْضِيلًا (القرآن ١٧:٧٠)

And indeed We have honored the children of Adam, and We have carried them on land and sea, and have provided them with the good things, and have preferred them to many of Our creations with a marked preferment. (Quran 17:70)

إِنَّا عَرَضْنَا ٱلْأَمَانَةَ عَلَى ٱلسَّمَوَٰتِ وَٱلْأَرْضِ وَٱلْجِبَالِ فَأَبَيْنَ أَن يَحْمِلْنَهَا وَأَشْفَقْنَ مِنْهَا وَحَمَلَهَا ٱلْإِنسَٰنُ ۖ إِنَّهُۥ كَانَ ظَلُومًا جَهُولًا ۞ (القرآن ٧٢:٣٣)

We offered the trust to the heavens and the Earth and the mountains, but they declined to undertake it, and were afraid of it. And the human undertook it. Indeed he was unjust (to himself) and ignorant (of the consequences of his undertaking). (Quran 33:72).

يَٰدَاوُۥدُ إِنَّا جَعَلْنَٰكَ خَلِيفَةً فِى ٱلْأَرْضِ فَٱحْكُم بَيْنَ ٱلنَّاسِ بِٱلْحَقِّ وَلَا تَتَّبِعِ ٱلْهَوَىٰ فَيُضِلَّكَ عَن سَبِيلِ ٱللَّهِ ۚ إِنَّ ٱلَّذِينَ يَضِلُّونَ عَن سَبِيلِ ٱللَّهِ لَهُمْ عَذَابٌ شَدِيدٌۢ بِمَا نَسُوا۟ يَوْمَ ٱلْحِسَابِ ۞ (القرآن ٢٦:٣٨)

O Dawud, indeed We have made you a steward upon the earth, so judge between the people in truth and do not follow your own desire, as it will lead you astray from the way of Allah. Indeed, those who go astray from the way of Allah will have a severe punishment for having forgotten the Day of Account. (Quran 38:26)

ٱلَّذِينَ إِن مَّكَّنَّٰهُمْ فِى ٱلْأَرْضِ أَقَامُوا۟ ٱلصَّلَوٰةَ وَءَاتَوُا۟ ٱلزَّكَوٰةَ وَأَمَرُوا۟ بِٱلْمَعْرُوفِ وَنَهَوْا۟ عَنِ ٱلْمُنكَرِ ۗ وَلِلَّهِ عَٰقِبَةُ ٱلْأُمُورِ ۞ (القرآن ٤١:٢٢)

Those who, if We give them authority in the land, establish prayer and give charity and promote good and forbid evil. And to Allah belongs the outcome of matters. (Quran 22:41)

$$\text{وَكُلُّ إِنسَـٰنٍ أَلْزَمْنَـٰهُ طَـٰٓئِرَهُۥ فِى عُنُقِهِۦ} \quad (\text{القرآن ١٣:١٧})$$

And each man is held responsible for his own actions. (Quran 17: 13)

$$\text{قَالَ عَبْدُ اللهِ بْنِ عَمْرٍو قَالَ رَسُولُ اللهِ صلى الله عليه وسلم "كَفَى بِالْمَرْءِ إِثْمًا أَنْ يَحْبِسَ عَمَّنْ يَمْلِكُ قُوتَهُ" (صحيح مسلم)}$$

Abdullah bin Umar said: The Messenger of Allah (peace be upon him) has said: "This sin is enough for a man that he withholds the subsistence from one who he is responsible for." (Muslim - Sahih)

$$\text{وَكُلُّهُمْ ءَاتِيهِ يَوْمَ ٱلْقِيَـٰمَةِ فَرْدًا} \quad (\text{القرآن ١٩:٩٥})$$

And everyone shall come to Him on the Day of Resurrection alone. (Quran 19:95)

$$\text{وَهُوَ ٱلَّذِى جَعَلَكُمْ خَلَـٰٓئِفَ ٱلْأَرْضِ وَرَفَعَ بَعْضَكُمْ فَوْقَ بَعْضٍ دَرَجَـٰتٍ لِّيَبْلُوَكُمْ فِى مَآ ءَاتَىٰكُمْ ۗ إِنَّ رَبَّكَ سَرِيعُ ٱلْعِقَابِ وَإِنَّهُۥ لَغَفُورٌ رَّحِيمٌ}$$
$$(\text{القرآن ٦:١٦٥})$$

And Allah made you stewards upon the earth and has raised some of you above others in degrees to test you through what He has given you. Indeed, your Lord is swift in penalty; but indeed, He is Forgiving and Merciful." (Quran 6:165).

$$\text{عَنْ عَبْدِ اللهِ بْنِ عُمَرَ ـ رضى الله عنهما ـ أَنَّ رَسُولَ اللهِ صلى الله عليه وسلم قَالَ "أَلاَ كُلُّكُمْ رَاعٍ، وَكُلُّكُمْ مَسْئُولٌ عَنْ رَعِيَّتِهِ، فَالإِمَامُ الَّذِي عَلَى النَّاسِ رَاعٍ وَهُوَ مَسْئُولٌ عَنْ رَعِيَّتِهِ، وَالرَّجُلُ رَاعٍ عَلَى أَهْلِ بَيْتِهِ وَهُوَ مَسْئُولٌ عَنْ رَعِيَّتِهِ، وَالْمَرْأَةُ رَاعِيَةٌ عَلَى أَهْلِ بَيْتِ زَوْجِهَا وَوَلَدِهِ وَهِيَ مَسْئُولَةٌ عَنْهُمْ،}$$

وَعَبْدُ الرَّجُلِ رَاعٍ عَلَى مَالِ سَيِّدِهِ وَهُوَ مَسْئُولٌ عَنْهُ، أَلاَ فَكُلُّكُمْ رَاعٍ وَكُلُّكُمْ مَسْئُولٌ عَنْ رَعِيَّتِهِ" (متفق عليه)

Narrated Abdullah bin Umar: The Messenger of Allah (peace be upon him) said, "Every one of you is a shepherd and is responsible for his flock. The leader of people is a guardian and is responsible for his subjects. A man is the guardian of his family and he is responsible for them. A woman is the guardian of her husband's home and his children and she is responsible for them. The servant of a man is a guardian of the property of his master and he is responsible for it. Surely, every one of you is a shepherd and responsible for his flock." (Bukhari & Muslim - Sahih)

مَّنِ ٱهْتَدَىٰ فَإِنَّمَا يَهْتَدِى لِنَفْسِهِ ۖ وَمَن ضَلَّ فَإِنَّمَا يَضِلُّ عَلَيْهَا ۚ وَلَا تَزِرُ وَازِرَةٌ وِزْرَ أُخْرَىٰ ۗ وَمَا كُنَّا مُعَذِّبِينَ حَتَّىٰ نَبْعَثَ رَسُولًا ۝ (القرآن ١٧:١٥)

He who is guided will be guided for himself, and he who strays, will stray for himself, and no soul will carry the burden of another's soul, nor would We visit with Our Wrath until We had sent a messenger. (Quran 17:15)

كُلُّ نَفْسٍ بِمَا كَسَبَتْ رَهِينَةٌ ۝ (القرآن ٧٤:٣٨)

Every soul will be held in pledge for its deeds. (Quran 74:38)

لَا يُكَلِّفُ ٱللَّهُ نَفْسًا إِلَّا مَا ءَاتَىٰهَا ۚ سَيَجْعَلُ ٱللَّهُ بَعْدَ عُسْرٍ يُسْرًا ۝ (القرآن ٦٥:٧)

Allah does not hold a soul responsible for anything other than what He has provided it. Surely Allah will make ease after hardship. (Quran 65:7)

وَلَا نُكَلِّفُ نَفْسًا إِلَّا وُسْعَهَا ۖ وَلَدَيْنَا كِتَٰبٌ يَنطِقُ بِٱلْحَقِّ ۚ وَهُمْ لَا يُظْلَمُونَ ۝ (القرآن ٢٣:٦٢)

And We charge no soul except its capacity, and with Us is a record which speaks with truth; and they will not be wronged. (Quran 23:62)

فَلَنَسْـَٔلَنَّ ٱلَّذِينَ أُرْسِلَ إِلَيْهِمْ وَلَنَسْـَٔلَنَّ ٱلْمُرْسَلِينَ ۝ (القرآن ٧:٦)

Then We will surely question those to whom [a message] was sent, and We will surely question the messengers. (Quran 7:6)

ظَهَرَ ٱلْفَسَادُ فِى ٱلْبَرِّ وَٱلْبَحْرِ بِمَا كَسَبَتْ أَيْدِى ٱلنَّاسِ لِيُذِيقَهُم بَعْضَ ٱلَّذِى عَمِلُوا۟ لَعَلَّهُمْ يَرْجِعُونَ ۝ (القرآن ٣٠:٤١)

Corruption has appeared on land and sea because of what the hands of men have earned, that (Allah) may show them the consequences of some of their deeds: in order that they may turn back. (Quran 30:41)

Altruism (إِيثَار)

Beautiful indeed is the religion that teaches us to give preference to our brother over our selves. That is the highest level of altruism. The lowest level is to desire for our brother what we desire for ourselves. This is popularly called the golden rule.

عَنْ أَنَسٍ، عَنِ النَّبِيِّ صلى الله عليه وسلم قَالَ ''لاَ يُؤْمِنُ أَحَدُكُمْ حَتَّى يُحِبَّ لأَخِيهِ مَاَ يُحِبُّ لِنَفْسِهِ'' (رواه البخاري ومسلم والترمذي وابن ماجه – صحيح)

Narrated Anas: The Prophet (peace be upon him) said, "None of you will have faith till he wishes for his (Muslim) brother what he likes for himself." (Bukhari, Muslim, Tirmidhi, Ibn Majah - Sahih)

عَنْ أَبِي مُوسَى - رضى الله عنه - عَنِ النَّبِيِّ صلى الله عليه وسلم قَالَ ''الْمُؤْمِنُ لِلْمُؤْمِنِ كَالْبُنْيَانِ يَشُدُّ بَعْضُهُ بَعْضًا'' وشَبَّكَ بين أصابعه (متفق عليه)

Narrated Abu Musa: The Prophet (peace be upon him) said, "A believer to another believer is like a building whose different parts strengthen each other." The Prophet (peace be upon him) then clasped his hands with the fingers interlaced. (Bukhari, Muslim - Sahih)

لَن تَنَالُوا ٱلْبِرَّ حَتَّىٰ تُنفِقُوا مِمَّا تُحِبُّونَ ۚ وَمَا تُنفِقُوا مِن شَىْءٍ فَإِنَّ ٱللَّهَ بِهِۦ عَلِيمٌ ۝ (القرآن ٣:٩٢)

Never will you achieve righteousness until you spend (in charity) from that which you love. Indeed, Allah knows whatever you spend. (Quran 3:92)

وَيُطْعِمُونَ ٱلطَّعَامَ عَلَىٰ حُبِّهِۦ مِسْكِينًا وَيَتِيمًا وَأَسِيرًا ۝ إِنَّمَا نُطْعِمُكُمْ لِوَجْهِ ٱللَّهِ لَا نُرِيدُ مِنكُمْ جَزَآءً وَلَا شُكُورًا ۝ (القرآن ٧٦: ٨-٩)

They give food, despite their own love for it, to the poor, the orphan and the slave, saying: We feed you only for Allah's pleasure, we desire from you neither reward nor thanks. (Quran 76:8-9)

وَلَا تَمْنُن تَسْتَكْثِرُ ۝ (القرآن ٧٤:٦)

And do not confer a favor to acquire more. (Quran 74:6)

عَنْ عَائِشَةَ، أَنَّهَا قَالَتْ جَاءَتْنِي مِسْكِينَةٌ تَحْمِلُ ابْنَتَيْنِ لَهَا فَأَطْعَمْتُهَا ثَلَاثَ تَمَرَاتٍ فَأَعْطَتْ كُلَّ وَاحِدَةٍ مِنْهُمَا تَمْرَةً وَرَفَعَتْ إِلَى فِيهَا تَمْرَةً لِتَأْكُلَهَا فَاسْتَطْعَمَتْهَا ابْنَتَاهَا فَشَقَّتِ التَّمْرَةَ الَّتِي كَانَتْ تُرِيدُ أَنْ تَأْكُلَهَا بَيْنَهُمَا فَأَعْجَبَنِي شَأْنُهَا فَذَكَرْتُ الَّذِي صَنَعَتْ لِرَسُولِ اللهِ صلى الله عليه وسلم فَقَالَ "إِنَّ اللَّهَ قَدْ أَوْجَبَ لَهَا بِهَا الْجَنَّةَ أَوْ أَعْتَقَهَا بِهَا مِنَ النَّارِ" (صحيح مسلم)

Aisha reported: A poor woman came to me along with her daughters. I gave her three dates. She gave a date to each of them and then raised one date to her mouth to eat, but her daughters asked for it. She then divided the date that she intended to eat between them. Her kindness impressed me and I mentioned it to the Messenger of Allah (peace be upon him). Thereupon he said: "Verily Allah has assured paradise for her due to this, or He has rescued her from Hell-Fire." (Muslim - Sahih)

وَيُؤْثِرُونَ عَلَىٰ أَنفُسِهِمْ وَلَوْ كَانَ بِهِمْ خَصَاصَةٌ ۚ وَمَن يُوقَ شُحَّ نَفْسِهِ فَأُو۟لَـٰٓئِكَ هُمُ ٱلْمُفْلِحُونَ ۞ (القرآن ٥٩:٩)

They give preference over themselves, even though they are in need. And whoever is protected from the stinginess of his soul - it is those who will be the successful. (Quran 59:9)

عن النّعمان بن بشير رضي الله عنهما قال: قال رسول الله صلى الله عليه وسلّم "مثل المؤمنين في توادهم وتراحمهم وتعاطفهم، مثل الجسد إذا اشتكى منه عضو تداعى له سائر الجسد بالسهر والحمّى" (متفّق عليه)

Numan bin Bashir reported: The Messenger of Allah (peace be upon him) said, "The believers in their mutual kindness, compassion and sympathy are like one body. When one of the limbs suffers, the whole body responds to it with wakefulness and fever." (Muslim, Bukhari - Sahih)

عَنْ جَابِرِ بْنِ عَبْدِ اللهِ، قَالَ قَالَ رَسُولُ اللهِ صلى الله عليه وسلم "كُلُّ مَعْرُوفٍ صَدَقَةٌ وَإِنَّ مِنَ الْمَعْرُوفِ أَنْ تَلْقَى أَخَاكَ بِوَجْهٍ طَلْقٍ وَأَنْ تُفْرِغَ مِنْ دَلْوِكَ فِي إِنَاءِ أَخِيكَ" (رواه التّرمذي – صحيح)

Jabir bin Abdullah narrated: The Messenger of Allah (peace be upon him) said: "Every good is charity. Indeed among the good is to meet your brother with a smiling face, and to pour what is left in your bucket into the buket of your brother." (Tirmidhi - Sahih)

بَلْ تُؤْثِرُونَ ٱلْحَيَوٰةَ ٱلدُّنْيَا ۞ وَٱلْـَٔاخِرَةُ خَيْرٌ وَأَبْقَىٰ ۞ (القرآن ٨٧: ١٦-١٧)

But you prefer the worldly life, while the Hereafter is better and more enduring. (Quran 87:16-17)

عَنْ أَبِي هُرَيْرَةَ، رضى الله عنه أَنَّهُ كَانَ يَقُولُ: شَرُّ الطَّعَامِ طَعَامُ الْوَلِيمَةِ يُدْعَى لَهَا الْأَغْنِيَاءُ، وَيُتْرَكُ الْفُقَرَاءُ، وَمَنْ تَرَكَ الدَّعْوَةَ فَقَدْ عَصَى اللَّهَ وَرَسُولَهُ صلى الله عليه وسلم (رواه البخاري ومسلم وابن ماجه – صحيح)

Narrated Abu Huraira: *The worst food is that of a wedding banquet to which only the rich are invited while the poor are not invited. And he who refuses an invitation disobeys Allah and His Messenger (peace be upon him).* (Bukhari, Muslim, Ibn Majah - Sahih)

Courage (شَجَاعَة)

A Muslim fears only Allah, the Exalted. We don't seek to engage the enemies of Islam, but when confronted with the enemy, we hold our own. We cultivate courage.

ٱلَّذِينَ يُبَلِّغُونَ رِسَٰلَٰتِ ٱللَّهِ وَيَخْشَوْنَهُۥ وَلَا يَخْشَوْنَ أَحَدًا إِلَّا ٱللَّهَ ۗ وَكَفَىٰ بِٱللَّهِ حَسِيبًا ۝ (القرآن ٣٣:٣٩)

Those who convey the messages of Allah and fear Him and do not fear anyone but Allah. And sufficient is Allah as Accountant. (Quran 33:39)

إِنَّمَا ذَٰلِكُمُ ٱلشَّيْطَٰنُ يُخَوِّفُ أَوْلِيَآءَهُۥ فَلَا تَخَافُوهُمْ وَخَافُونِ إِن كُنتُم مُّؤْمِنِينَ ۝ (القرآن ٣:١٧٥)

That is only Shaytan who frightens [you] of his supporters. So fear them not, but fear Me, if you are [indeed] believers. (Quran 3:175)

أَمْ حَسِبْتُمْ أَن تَدْخُلُوا۟ ٱلْجَنَّةَ وَلَمَّا يَأْتِكُم مَّثَلُ ٱلَّذِينَ خَلَوْا۟ مِن قَبْلِكُم ۖ مَّسَّتْهُمُ ٱلْبَأْسَآءُ وَٱلضَّرَّآءُ وَزُلْزِلُوا۟ حَتَّىٰ يَقُولَ ٱلرَّسُولُ وَٱلَّذِينَ ءَامَنُوا۟ مَعَهُۥ مَتَىٰ نَصْرُ ٱللَّهِ ۗ أَلَآ إِنَّ نَصْرَ ٱللَّهِ قَرِيبٌ ۝ (القرآن ٢:٢١٤)

Or do you think that you will enter Paradise while such [trial] has not yet come to you as came to those who passed on before you? They were touched by poverty and hardship

and were shaken until [even their] messenger and those who believed with him said, "When is the help of Allah?" Unquestionably, the help of Allah is near. (Quran 2:214)

عَنْ أَبِي هُرَيْرَةَ ـ رضي الله عنه ـ عَنِ النَّبِيِّ صلى الله عليه وسلم قَالَ "لاَ تَمَنَّوْا لِقَاءَ الْعَدُوِّ، فَإِذَا لَقِيتُمُوهُمْ فَاصْبِرُوا" (صحيح البخاري)

Narrated Abu Huraira: The Prophet (peace be upon him) said: "Do not wish to meet the enemy, but when you meet (face) the enemy, be patient." (Bukhari - Sahih)

إِذْ هَمَّت طَّآئِفَتَانِ مِنكُمْ أَن تَفْشَلَا وَٱللَّهُ وَلِيُّهُمَا ۗ وَعَلَى ٱللَّهِ فَلْيَتَوَكَّلِ ٱلْمُؤْمِنُونَ ۝ (القرآن ٣:١٢٢)

When two parties among you were about to lose courage, but Allah was their ally; and upon Allah the believers should rely. (Quran 3:122)

عَنْ أَنَسٍ، قَالَ كَانَ النَّبِيُّ صلى الله عليه وسلم أَحْسَنَ النَّاسِ وَأَشْجَعَ النَّاسِ، وَلَقَدْ فَزِعَ أَهْلُ الْمَدِينَةِ لَيْلَةً فَخَرَجُوا نَحْوَ الصَّوْتِ فَاسْتَقْبَلَهُمُ النَّبِيُّ صلى الله عليه وسلم وَقَدِ اسْتَبْرَأَ الْخَبَرَ، وَهُوَ عَلَى فَرَسٍ لأَبِي طَلْحَةَ عُرْىٍ وَفِي عُنُقِهِ السَّيْفُ وَهْوَ يَقُولُ "لَمْ تُرَاعُوا لَمْ تُرَاعُوا" (رواه مسلم والترمذي وابن ماجه – صحيح)

Narrated Anas: The Prophet (peace be upon him) was the best and the bravest amongst the people. One night the people of Medina were terrified at night by a loud noise. They went in the direction of the noise. The Prophet (peace be upon him) met them on his way back after he had looked into the matter. He was riding an unsaddled horse belonging to Abu Talha and a sword was hanging by his neck, and he was saying, "Don't be afraid! Don't be afraid!" (Bukhari, Muslim, Tirmidhi, Ibn Majah - Sahih)

ٱلَّذِينَ قَالَ لَهُمُ ٱلنَّاسُ إِنَّ ٱلنَّاسَ قَدْ جَمَعُوا۟ لَكُمْ فَٱخْشَوْهُمْ فَزَادَهُمْ إِيمَٰنًا وَقَالُوا۟ حَسْبُنَا ٱللَّهُ وَنِعْمَ ٱلْوَكِيلُ ۞ (القرآن ٣:١٧٣)

Those to whom men said: people have gathered against you, so fear them; but this increased their faith, and they said: Allah is sufficient for us and He is an excellent Guardian. (Quran 3:173)

وَلَا يَحْزُنكَ ٱلَّذِينَ يُسَٰرِعُونَ فِى ٱلْكُفْرِ ۚ إِنَّهُمْ لَن يَضُرُّوا۟ ٱللَّهَ شَيْـًٔا ۗ يُرِيدُ ٱللَّهُ أَلَّا يَجْعَلَ لَهُمْ حَظًّا فِى ٱلْءَاخِرَةِ ۖ وَلَهُمْ عَذَابٌ عَظِيمٌ ۞ (القرآن ٣:١٧٦)

And do not be grieved, by those who hasten into disbelief. Indeed, they will never harm Allah at all. Allah intends that He should give them no share in the Hereafter, and for them is a great punishment. (Quran 3:176)

يَٰٓأَيُّهَا ٱلَّذِينَ ءَامَنُوٓا۟ إِن تَنصُرُوا۟ ٱللَّهَ يَنصُرْكُمْ (القرآن ٤٧:٧)

O believers! If you help Allah, He will help you (Quran 47:7)

مَّا كَانَ ٱللَّهُ لِيَذَرَ ٱلْمُؤْمِنِينَ عَلَىٰ مَآ أَنتُمْ عَلَيْهِ حَتَّىٰ يَمِيزَ ٱلْخَبِيثَ مِنَ ٱلطَّيِّبِ ۗ وَمَا كَانَ ٱللَّهُ لِيُطْلِعَكُمْ عَلَى ٱلْغَيْبِ وَلَٰكِنَّ ٱللَّهَ يَجْتَبِى مِن رُّسُلِهِۦ مَن يَشَآءُ ۖ فَـَٔامِنُوا۟ بِٱللَّهِ وَرُسُلِهِۦ ۚ وَإِن تُؤْمِنُوا۟ وَتَتَّقُوا۟ فَلَكُمْ أَجْرٌ عَظِيمٌ ۞ (القرآن ٣:١٧٩)

Allah would not leave the believers in that condition you are in until He separates the evil from the good. Nor would

Allah reveal to you the unseen. But Allah chooses of His messengers whom He wills, so believe in Allah and His messengers. And if you believe and fear Him, then for you is a great reward. (Quran 3:179)

عَنْ أَبِي هُرَيْرَةَ، قَالَ قَالَ رَسُولُ اللَّهِ صلى الله عليه وسلم "الْمُؤْمِنُ الْقَوِيُّ خَيْرٌ وَأَحَبُّ إِلَى اللَّهِ مِنَ الْمُؤْمِنِ الضَّعِيفِ وَفِي كُلٍّ خَيْرٌ" (رواه مسلم وابن ماجه – صحيح)

Abu Huraira reported: The Messenger of Allah (peace be upon him) said: "A strong believer is better and is more lovable to Allah than a weak believer, and there is good in both." (Muslim, Ibn Majah – Sahih)

Consultation (شُورَى)

Mandated by Allah the Exalted, one of the secrets of our success is consultation. Better ideas and an ability to avoid problems before they occur naturally flow from practicing consultation.

Furthermore, Allah the Exalted has blessed consultation. In general, any decision will be better through this process. Sometimes we delay a decision for a few days, just so we get an opportunity to take the advice of our brothers and sisters. We do this even when the advice leads us to the same decision we would have done without the consultation, just so that we can get the blessings of team work.

فَبِمَا رَحْمَةٍ مِّنَ ٱللَّهِ لِنتَ لَهُمْ ۖ وَلَوْ كُنتَ فَظًّا غَلِيظَ ٱلْقَلْبِ لَٱنفَضُّوا۟ مِنْ حَوْلِكَ ۖ فَٱعْفُ عَنْهُمْ وَٱسْتَغْفِرْ لَهُمْ وَشَاوِرْهُمْ فِى ٱلْأَمْرِ ۖ فَإِذَا عَزَمْتَ فَتَوَكَّلْ عَلَى ٱللَّهِ ۚ إِنَّ ٱللَّهَ يُحِبُّ ٱلْمُتَوَكِّلِينَ ۝ (القرآن ٣:١٥٩)

Indeed by mercy from Allah, (O Muhammad), you were lenient with them. If you had been rude and harsh in heart, they would have disbanded from about you. So pardon them and ask forgiveness for them and consult them in the matters. And when you have decided, then rely upon Allah. Indeed, Allah loves those who rely upon Him. (Quran 3:159)

وَٱلَّذِينَ ٱسْتَجَابُوا۟ لِرَبِّهِمْ وَأَقَامُوا۟ ٱلصَّلَوٰةَ وَأَمْرُهُمْ شُورَىٰ بَيْنَهُمْ وَمِمَّا رَزَقْنَـٰهُمْ يُنفِقُونَ ۝ (القرآن ٤٢:٣٨)

And those who have responded to their Lord and established prayer and whose affair is determined by consultation among themselves, and from what We have provided them, they spend. (Quran 42:38)

فَإِنْ أَرَادَا فِصَالاً عَن تَرَاضٍ مِّنْهُمَا وَتَشَاوُرٍ فَلَا جُنَاحَ عَلَيْهِمَا (القرآن ٢:٢٣٣)

But if both (parents) desire to wean (the child) by their mutual consent and consultation, then there is no blame on either of them. (Quran 2:233)

عَنْ ابْنِ عُمَرَ رضي الله عنهما أَنَّ رَسُولَ اللَّهِ صَلَّى اللهُ عَلَيْهِ وَسَلَّمَ قَالَ: "إِنَّ اللَّهَ لَا يَجْمَعُ أُمَّتِي عَلَى ضَلَالَةٍ، وَيَدُ اللَّهِ مَعَ الْجَمَاعَةِ" (رواه الترمذي وابن ماجه والترمذي وأبو داود والحاكم — حسن لغيره)

Ibn Umar narrated: The Messenger of Allah (peace be upon him) said: "Allah will not gather my nation upon an error, and Allah's hand is with the Congregation"(Tirmidhi, Ibn Majah, Abu Dawud, Hakim- Hasan li ghairihi)

Instances of Shura employed by the Messenger (peace be upon him):
- Instituting the Adhan (1 Hijri)
- Strategy for Battle of Badr (2 Hijri)
- Dealing with prisoners of war after Badr (2 Hijri)
- Strategy for Battle of Uhud (3 Hijri)
- Strategy for Battle of Ahzab (5 Hijri)
- How to handle the sacrifice after the treaty of Hudaibiyah (6 Hijri)
- Dealing with prisoners of war of Hawazin (8 Hijri)

Juristic Effort (إِجْتِهَاد)

Intellectual struggle in scholarship, ijtihad, helps determine the correct ruling, in Islamic jurisprudence, for any particular situation at hand. It is one of the main reasons for the vibrancy of Islam till today. It is an integral part of the role of reason in Islam.

$$\text{هُوَ ٱلَّذِىٓ أَنزَلَ عَلَيْكَ ٱلْكِتَٰبَ مِنْهُ ءَايَٰتٌ مُّحْكَمَٰتٌ هُنَّ أُمُّ ٱلْكِتَٰبِ وَأُخَرُ مُتَشَٰبِهَٰتٌ}$$ (القرآن ٣:٧)

It is He Who sent down upon you the Book, in it are decisive verses that are the essence of the book, and others are allegorical. (Quran 3:7)

$$\text{فَسْـَٔلُوٓاْ أَهْلَ ٱلذِّكْرِ إِن كُنتُمْ لَا تَعْلَمُونَ}$$ (القرآن ١٦:٤٣)

So ask the people of understanding if you do not know. (Quran 16:43)

عَنْ عَمْرِو بْنِ الْعَاصِ، أَنَّهُ سَمِعَ رَسُولَ اللهِ صلى الله عليه وسلم يَقُولُ "إِذَا حَكَمَ الْحَاكِمُ فَاجْتَهَدَ ثُمَّ أَصَابَ فَلَهُ أَجْرَانِ، وَإِذَا حَكَمَ فَاجْتَهَدَ ثُمَّ أَخْطَأَ فَلَهُ أَجْرٌ" (متفق عليه)

Narrated Amr bin Al-As that he heard the Messenger of Allah (peace be upon him) saying: "If a judge makes a ruling, striving to apply his reasoning and he is correct, then he will have two rewards. If a judge makes a ruling, striving to apply his reasoning and he is mistaken, then he will have one reward." (Bukhari, Muslim - Sahih)

فَلَوْلَا نَفَرَ مِن كُلِّ فِرْقَةٍ مِّنْهُمْ طَآئِفَةٌ لِّيَتَفَقَّهُوا۟ فِى ٱلدِّينِ وَلِيُنذِرُوا۟ قَوْمَهُمْ إِذَا رَجَعُوٓا۟ إِلَيْهِمْ لَعَلَّهُمْ يَحْذَرُونَ ۝ (القرآن ٩:١٢٢)

Of every group of them, a team only should go forth, that they may learn the religion, and warn their people when they return to them, so that they may teach them. (Quran 9:122)

ذَٰلِكُمْ وَصَّىٰكُم بِهِۦ لَعَلَّكُمْ تَعْقِلُونَ ۝ (القرآن ٦:١٥١)

This He has instructed you that you may use reason. (Quran 6:151)

قُلْ هَاتُوا۟ بُرْهَٰنَكُمْ إِن كُنتُمْ صَٰدِقِينَ ۝ (القرآن ٢:١١١)

Say: Bring your proof if you are truthful. (Quran 2:111)

وَٱتَّبِعْ سَبِيلَ مَنْ أَنَابَ إِلَىَّ ۚ ثُمَّ إِلَىَّ مَرْجِعُكُمْ فَأُنَبِّئُكُم بِمَا كُنتُمْ تَعْمَلُونَ ۝ (القرآن ٣١:١٥)

And follow the way of those who turn to Me. Then to Me will be your return, and I will inform you about what you used to do. (Quran 31:15)

وَلَا تَقْفُ مَا لَيْسَ لَكَ بِهِۦ عِلْمٌ ۚ إِنَّ ٱلسَّمْعَ وَٱلْبَصَرَ وَٱلْفُؤَادَ كُلُّ أُو۟لَٰٓئِكَ كَانَ عَنْهُ مَسْـُٔولًا ۝ (القرآن ١٧:٣٦)

And do not pursue that of which you have no knowledge. Indeed everyone shall be questioned about the hearing, the sight and the heart. (Quran 17:36)

عَنْ حُذَيْفَةَ، قَالَ قَالَ رَسُولُ اللهِ صلى الله عليه وسلم "لاَ تَكُونُوا إِمَّعَةً تَقُولُونَ إِنْ أَحْسَنَ النَّاسُ أَحْسَنَّا وَإِنْ ظَلَمُوا ظَلَمْنَا وَلَكِنْ وَطِّنُوا أَنْفُسَكُمْ إِنْ أَحْسَنَ النَّاسُ أَنْ تُحْسِنُوا وَإِنْ أَسَاءُوا فَلاَ تَظْلِمُوا" (رواه الترمذي — حسن)

Hudhaifah narrated: The Messenger of Allah (peace be upon him) said: "Do not let yourselves be 'yes-men', saying: 'If the people are good then we will be good, and if they are wrong then we will be wrong.' Rather, make up your own minds, if the people are good then you are good, and if they are evil, then do not behave unjustly." (Tirmidhi - Hasan)

وَمَا لَهُم بِهِۦ مِنْ عِلْمٍ ۖ إِن يَتَّبِعُونَ إِلَّا ٱلظَّنَّ ۖ وَإِنَّ ٱلظَّنَّ لَا يُغْنِى مِنَ ٱلْحَقِّ شَيْـًٔا (القرآن ٢٨:٥٣)

And they have no knowledge about it. They follow not except assumption, and indeed, assumption avails not against the truth at all. (Quran 53:28)

Asceticism (زُهْد)

Zuhd does not mean renouncing the world. Zuhd is to assign to this life and the next life their true values. It means not being in love with the world and focusing on what brings benefit in the hereafter.

The ascetic (Zahid) assigns the next life a much higher priority in comparison to this life and its frivolity. People mistakenly assume that a rich person cannot be a Zahid. Uthman bin Affan and Abudrahman bin Awf (may Allah be pleased with them) are wealthy people who lived ascetic lives because the increase of their wealth made them less happy than their worship and the loss of their wealth made them less sad than the displeasure of Allah.

Conversely, many poor people, being immersed in a materialistic frame of mind, cannot reach Zuhd without changing their mindset and entire outlook on life.

مَا عِندَكُمْ يَنفَدُ ۖ وَمَا عِندَ ٱللَّهِ بَاقٍ ۗ وَلَنَجْزِيَنَّ ٱلَّذِينَ صَبَرُوٓاْ أَجْرَهُم بِأَحْسَنِ مَا كَانُواْ يَعْمَلُونَ ۝ (القرآن ١٦:٩٦)

Whatever you have will end, but what Allah has is lasting. And We will surely give those who were patient their reward according to the best of what they used to do. (Quran 16:96)

عَنْ أَبِي هُرَيْرَةَ، قَالَ قَالَ رَسُولُ اللَّهِ ـ صلى الله عليه وسلم ـ "لَيْسَ الْغِنَى عَنْ كَثْرَةِ الْعَرَضِ وَلَكِنَّ الْغِنَى غِنَى النَّفْسِ" (رواه ابن ماجه – صحيح)

Narrated Abu Hurairah: The Messenger of Allah (peace be upon him) said: "Richness is not an abundance of worldly goods, rather richness is contentment with one's lot." (Ibn Majah - Sahih)

عَنْ الْمُسْتَوْرِدَ يَقُولُ سَمِعْتُ رَسُولَ اللَّهِ صلى الله عليه وسلم يَقُولُ "مَا مَثَلُ الدُّنْيَا فِي الْآخِرَةِ إِلَّا مَثَلُ مَا يَجْعَلُ أَحَدُكُمْ إِصْبَعَهُ فِي الْيَمِّ فَلْيَنْظُرْ بِمَ يَرْجِعُ" (رواه ابن ماجه – صحيح)

Al-Mustawrid said: I heard the Messenger of Allah (peace be upon him) say: "The likeness of this world in comparison to the Hereafter is that of anyone of you dipping his finger into the sea: let him see what he brings forth." (Ibn Majah - Sahih)

ٱعْلَمُوٓاْ أَنَّمَا ٱلْحَيَوٰةُ ٱلدُّنْيَا لَعِبٌ وَلَهْوٌ وَزِينَةٌ وَتَفَاخُرٌ بَيْنَكُمْ وَتَكَاثُرٌ فِى ٱلْأَمْوَٰلِ وَٱلْأَوْلَٰدِ ۖ كَمَثَلِ غَيْثٍ أَعْجَبَ ٱلْكُفَّارَ نَبَاتُهُۥ ثُمَّ يَهِيجُ فَتَرَىٰهُ مُصْفَرًّا ثُمَّ يَكُونُ حُطَٰمًا ۖ وَفِى ٱلْءَاخِرَةِ عَذَابٌ شَدِيدٌ وَمَغْفِرَةٌ مِّنَ ٱللَّهِ وَرِضْوَٰنٌ ۚ وَمَا ٱلْحَيَوٰةُ ٱلدُّنْيَآ إِلَّا مَتَٰعُ ٱلْغُرُورِ (القرآن ٥٧: ٢٠)

Know that the life of this world is but amusement and diversion and adornment and boasting to one another and competition in increase of wealth and children - like the example of a rain whose [resulting] plant growth pleases the tillers; then it dries and you see it turned yellow; then it becomes debris. And in the Hereafter is severe punishment and forgiveness from Allah and approval. And what is the worldly life except the enjoyment of delusion. (Quran 57:20)

عَنْ أَبِي هُرَيْرَةَ، قَالَ قَالَ رَسُولُ اللَّهِ صلى الله عليه وسلم "تَعِسَ عَبْدُ الدِّينَارِ وَعَبْدُ الدِّرْهَمِ وَعَبْدُ الْقَطِيفَةِ وَعَبْدُ الْخَمِيصَةِ إِنْ أُعْطِيَ رَضِيَ وَإِنْ لَمْ يُعْطَ لَمْ يَفِ" (رواه ابن ماجه – صحيح)

Narrated Abu Hurairah: The Messenger of Allah (peace be upon him) said: "Wretched is the slave of the Dinar and the slave of the Dirham, and the slave of velvet and the slave of the music. If he is given, he is pleased and if he is not given, he does not fulfill (his oath of allegiance)." (Ibn Majah - Sahih)

عَنْ سلمة بن عُبَيْدِ اللَّهِ بْنِ مِحْصَنٍ الأَنْصَارِيِّ، قَالَ قَالَ رَسُولُ اللَّهِ ـ صلى الله عليه وسلم ـ "مَنْ أَصْبَحَ مِنْكُمْ مُعَافًى فِي جَسَدِهِ آمِنًا فِي سِرْبِهِ عِنْدَهُ قُوتُ يَوْمِهِ فَكَأَنَّمَا حِيزَتْ لَهُ الدُّنْيَا" (رواه ابن ماجه – صحيح)

Narrated Ubaidullah bin Mihsan Al-Ansari: The Messenger of Allah (peace be upon him) said: "Whoever among you wakes up physically healthy, feeling safe and secure within himself, with food for the day, it is as if he acquired the whole world." (Ibn Majah - Hasan)

عَنْ أَبِي هُرَيْرَةَ، قَالَ قَالَ رَسُولُ اللَّهِ ـ صلى الله عليه وسلم ـ "انْظُرُوا إِلَى مَنْ هُوَ أَسْفَلَ مِنْكُمْ وَلاَ تَنْظُرُوا إِلَى مَنْ هُوَ فَوْقَكُمْ فَإِنَّهُ أَجْدَرُ أَنْ لاَ تَزْدَرُوا نِعْمَةَ اللَّهِ" . قَالَ أَبُو مُعَاوِيَةَ "عَلَيْكُمْ" (رواه ابن ماجه – صحيح)

Abu Hurairah narrated: The Messenger of Allah (peace be upon him) said: "Look at those who are beneath you and do not look at those who are above you, for it is more suitable that you should not consider as less the blessing of Allah." (Ibn Majah - Sahih)

عَنْ أَبِي أَيُّوبَ، قَالَ جَاءَ رَجُلٌ إِلَى النَّبِيِّ ـ صلى الله عليه وسلم ـ فَقَالَ يَا رَسُولَ اللَّهِ عَلِّمْنِي وَأَوْجِزْ. قَالَ "إِذَا قُمْتَ فِي صَلاَتِكَ فَصَلِّ صَلاَةَ مُوَدِّعٍ وَلاَ تَكَلَّمْ بِكَلاَمٍ تَعْتَذِرُ مِنْهُ وَأَجْمِعِ الْيَأْسَ عَمَّا فِي أَيْدِي النَّاسِ" (رواه ابن ماجه – صحيح)

Narrated Abu Ayyub: "A man came to the Prophet (peace be upon him) and said: O Messenger of Allah (peace be upon him), teach me but make it concise. He said: "When you stand to pray, pray like a man bidding farewell. Do not say anything for which you will have to apologize. And give up hope for what other people have." (Ibn Majah - Hasan)

Humor (خِفَّةُ الظِّلّ)

There exists a long tradition of humor in Islam. Muslims are serious people who also have the ability to laugh. As a comprehensive way of life, Islam teaches us the value of laughter and the limits of humor.

وَأَنَّهُ هُوَ أَضْحَكَ وَأَبْكَىٰ ۝ (القرآن ٥٣:٤٣)

And that it is He who makes one laugh and weep. (Quran 53:43)

عَنْ أَنَسٍ، أَنَّ رَجُلًا، أَتَى النَّبِيَّ صلى الله عليه وسلم فَقَالَ يَا رَسُولَ اللهِ احْمِلْنِي. قَالَ النَّبِيُّ صلى الله عليه وسلم "إِنَّا حَامِلُوكَ عَلَى وَلَدِ نَاقَةٍ". قَالَ وَمَا أَصْنَعُ بِوَلَدِ النَّاقَةِ فَقَالَ النَّبِيُّ صلى الله عليه وسلم "وَهَلْ تَلِدُ الإِبِلَ إِلَّا النُّوقُ" (رواه أبو داود والترمذي — صحيح)

Narrated Anas ibn Malik: A man came to the Prophet (peace be upon him) and said: O Messenger of Allah! Give me a mount. The Prophet (peace be upon him) said: "We shall give you a she-camel's child to ride on. He said: What shall I do with a she-camel's child? The Prophet (peace be upon him) replied: "Do any others than she-camels give birth to camels?" (Abu Dawud, Tirmidhi - Sahih)

عَنِ الْحَسَنِ، قَالَ: أَتَتْ عَجُوزٌ إِلَى النَّبِيِّ صلى الله عليه وسلم، فَقَالَتْ: يَا رَسُولَ اللهِ، ادْعُ اللهَ أَنْ يُدْخِلَنِي الْجَنَّةَ، فَقَالَ: "يَا أُمَّ فُلَانٍ، إِنَّ الْجَنَّةَ لَا تَدْخُلُهَا عَجُوزٌ"، قَالَ: فَوَلَّتْ تَبْكِي، فَقَالَ: "أَخْبِرُوهَا أَنَّهَا لَا تَدْخُلُهَا وَهِيَ عَجُوزٌ إِنَّ اللهَ تَعَالَى: يَقُولُ: إِنَّا أَنْشَأْنَاهُنَّ إِنْشَاءً، فَجَعَلْنَاهُنَّ أَبْكَارًا، عُرُبًا أَتْرَابًا"
(الشمائل المحمدية — حسن)

An old woman came to the Prophet (peace be upon him) and said: O Messenger of Allah, pray to Allah that I will enter Paradise. He said, "No old women will enter Paradise." The old woman went away crying, so he (peace be upon him) said, "Tell her that she will not enter Paradise as an old woman, for Allah says: '**We have created (their companions) of special creation, and made them young**'" *(Quran 56:35-36)."* (Shamail Muhammadiyah- Hasan)

عَنْ أَبِي هُرَيْرَةَ، قَالُوا: يَا رَسُولَ اللهِ، إِنَّكَ تُدَاعِبُنَا؟ قَالَ: "إِنِّي لَا أَقُولُ إِلا حَقًّا" (أدب المُفرد – صحيح، رواه الترمذي – حسن)

Abu Hurayra reported: The people said, "O Messenger of Allah, you joke with us!" He replied, "But I only speak the truth." (Adab al Mufrad – Sahih, Tirmidhi - Hasan)

عَنْ عَبْدِ اللَّهِ ـ رضى الله عنه ـ قَالَ النَّبِيُّ صلى الله عليه وسلم "إِنِّي لَأَعْلَمُ آخِرَ أَهْلِ النَّارِ خُرُوجًا مِنْهَا، وَآخِرَ أَهْلِ الْجَنَّةِ دُخُولًا رَجُلٌ يَخْرُجُ مِنَ النَّارِ كَبْوًا، فَيَقُولُ اللَّهُ اذْهَبْ فَادْخُلِ الْجَنَّةَ. فَيَأْتِيهَا فَيُخَيَّلُ إِلَيْهِ أَنَّهَا مَلْأَى، فَيَرْجِعُ فَيَقُولُ يَا رَبِّ وَجَدْتُهَا مَلْأَى، فَيَقُولُ اذْهَبْ فَادْخُلِ الْجَنَّةَ. فَيَأْتِيهَا فَيُخَيَّلُ إِلَيْهِ أَنَّهَا مَلْأَى. فَيَقُولُ يَا رَبِّ وَجَدْتُهَا مَلْأَى، فَيَقُولُ اذْهَبْ فَادْخُلِ الْجَنَّةَ، فَإِنَّ لَكَ مِثْلَ الدُّنْيَا وَعَشَرَةَ أَمْثَالِهَا. أَوْ إِنَّ لَكَ مِثْلَ عَشَرَةِ أَمْثَالِ الدُّنْيَا. فَيَقُولُ تَسْخَرُ مِنِّي، أَوْ تَضْحَكُ مِنِّي وَأَنْتَ الْمَلِكُ ". فَلَقَدْ رَأَيْتُ رَسُولَ اللَّهِ صلى الله عليه وسلم ضَحِكَ حَتَّى بَدَتْ نَوَاجِذُهُ، وَكَانَ يُقَالُ ذَلِكَ أَدْنَى أَهْلِ الْجَنَّةِ مَنْزِلَةً. (صحيح البخاري)

The Prophet (peace be upon him) said, "I know the person who will be the last to come out of the (Hell) Fire, and the last to enter Paradise. He will be a man who will come out of the (Hell) Fire crawling, and Allah will say to him, 'Go and enter Paradise.' He will go to it, but he will imagine that it had been filled, and then he will return and say, 'O Lord, I have found it full.' Allah will say, 'Go and enter Paradise, and you will have what equals the world and ten times as much.' The man will say, 'Do you mick me or do you laugh at me although You are the King?'" I saw the Messenger of Allah (peace be upon him) laughing so that his premolar teeth could be seen. It is said that will be the lowest in degree amongst the people of Paradise. (Bukhari - Sahih)

يَـٰٓأَيُّهَا ٱلَّذِينَ ءَامَنُوا۟ لَا يَسْخَرْ قَوْمٌ مِّن قَوْمٍ عَسَىٰٓ أَن يَكُونُوا۟ خَيْرًا مِّنْهُمْ وَلَا نِسَآءٌ مِّن نِّسَآءٍ عَسَىٰٓ أَن يَكُنَّ خَيْرًا مِّنْهُنَّ ۖ وَلَا تَلْمِزُوٓا۟ أَنفُسَكُمْ وَلَا تَنَابَزُوا۟ بِٱلْأَلْقَـٰبِ ۖ (القرآن ٤٩:١١)

Let not a people ridicule another people; perhaps they may be better than them; nor let some women ridicule other women; perhaps they may be better than them. And do not insult one another and do not call each other by offensive nicknames. (Quran 49:11)

وَلَئِن سَأَلْتَهُمْ لَيَقُولُنَّ إِنَّمَا كُنَّا نَخُوضُ وَنَلْعَبُ ۚ قُلْ أَبِٱللَّهِ وَءَايَـٰتِهِۦ وَرَسُولِهِۦ كُنتُمْ تَسْتَهْزِءُونَ ۝ لَا تَعْتَذِرُوا۟ قَدْ كَفَرْتُم بَعْدَ إِيمَـٰنِكُمْ ۚ (القرآن ٩: ٦٥-٦٦)

And if you ask them, they will surely say, "We were only conversing and playing." Say, "Is it Allah and His verses and His Messenger that you were mocking?" Make no excuse; you have disbelieved after your belief. (Quran 9:65-66)

حَدَّثَنَا بَهْزُ بْنُ حَكِيمٍ، حَدَّثَنِي أَبِي، عَنْ جَدِّي، قَالَ سَمِعْتُ النَّبِيَّ صلى الله عليه وسلم يَقُولُ "وَيْلٌ لِلَّذِي يُحَدِّثُ بِالْحَدِيثِ لِيُضْحِكَ بِهِ الْقَوْمَ فَيَكْذِبُ وَيْلٌ لَهُ وَيْلٌ لَهُ" (رواه الترمذي وأبو داود – حسن)

Bahz bin Hakim narrated from his father, from his grandfather that he heard the Prophet (peace be upon him) say: "Woe to the one who lies to make the people laugh. Woe to him. Then again, woe to him." (Tirmidhi, Abu Daud – Hassan)

An Exemplary Leadership

Abu Bakr, may Allah be pleased with him, was the best Muslim in our ummah. He was personally trained by the Messenger of Allah and he led the Muslims as the first Khalifah. Below is his inauguration speech, a model of conciseness, precision and comprehensiveness. In less than a hundred words he described his law and order policy, international relation policy, religious policy, and form of government.

أيُّها الناسُ فإني قد وُلِّيتُ عليكم ولست بخيرِكم فإنْ أَحْسَنْتُ فَأَعِينُونِي وإنْ أَسَأْتُ فَقَوِّمُونِي. الصِدْقُ أمانةٌ والكَذِبُ خِيَانَةٌ . والضعيفُ فيكم قويٌّ عندِي حتى أرجعَ إليه حقَّه إن شاء اللَّه، والقويّ فيكم ضعيفٌ عندِي حتى آخذ الحقَّ منه إن شاء اللَّه. لا يَدَعُ قومٌ الجِهادَ في سبيلِ اللَّه إلا خَذَلَهم اللَّهُ بالذُلِّ ولا تَشِيعُ الفاحشةُ في قومٍ إلا عَمَّهم اللَّهُ بالبلاءِ. أَطِيعُونِي ما أَطَعْتُ اللَّهَ ورسولَه فإذا عَصَيْتُ اللَّهَ ورسولَه فلا طاعةَ لي عليكم. قُومُوا إلى صلاتكم يَرْحَمْكُمُ اللَّه

"O people, I have been appointed over you, although I am not the best among you. If I do well, then help me; and if I act wrongly, then correct me. Truthfulness is fulfilling the trust, and lying is treachery. The weak among you is deemed strong by me, until I return to them that which is rightfully theirs, if Allah wills. And the strong among you is deemed weak by me, until I take from them what is rightfully someone else's, if Allah wills. No group of people abandons the struggle in the path of Allah, except that Allah makes them suffer humiliation. And evil does not become widespread among a people, except that Allah inflicts them with widespread calamity. Obey me so long as I obey Allah and His Messenger. And if I disobey Allah and His Messenger, then I have no right to your obedience. Arise for prayer, may Allah have mercy on you."

Source: *Al-Bidaayah wan-Nihaayah* (The Beginning and The Ending)

Characteristics of the Islamic Movement

Throughout the history of this ummah, Allah the Exalted has tasked us with the duty to promote Islam and work towards improving society through the message of Islam.

The revivalist movement in Islam is not new. It traces its roots to the life and teachings of our beloved Prophet (peace be upon him).

Many contemporary scholars have identified eight characteristics that every Islamic movement must possess. We list these characteristics in the following pages and identify verses and Hadith about them.

ادْعُ إِلَىٰ سَبِيلِ رَبِّكَ بِٱلْحِكْمَةِ وَٱلْمَوْعِظَةِ ٱلْحَسَنَةِ (القرآن ١٦:١٢٥)

Invite to the way of your Lord with wisdom and good instruction. (Quran 16:125)

كُنتُمْ خَيْرَ أُمَّةٍ أُخْرِجَتْ لِلنَّاسِ تَأْمُرُونَ بِٱلْمَعْرُوفِ وَتَنْهَوْنَ عَنِ ٱلْمُنكَرِ وَتُؤْمِنُونَ بِٱللَّهِ (القرآن ٣:١١٠)

You are the best of the nations raised up for (the benefit of) humanity; you enjoin what is right and forbid the wrong and believe in Allah. (Quran 3:110)

عَنْ أَبِي هُرَيْرَةَ، فِيمَا أَعْلَمُ عَنْ رَسُولِ اللهِ صلى الله عليه وسلم قَالَ "إِنَّ اللهَ يَبْعَثُ لِهَذِهِ الأُمَّةِ عَلَى رَأْسِ كُلِّ مِائَةِ سَنَةٍ مَنْ يُجَدِّدُ لَهَا دِينَهَا" (رواه أبو داود – صحيح)

Narrated Abu Hurayrah: The Prophet (peace be upon him) said: "Allah will raise for this ummah at the head of every hundred years one who will renovate its religion for it." (Abu Dawud - Sahih)

Godliness (رَبَّانِية)

Ours is a purely Islamic movement, in every sense of the word. We strive to understand Islam according to the Quran and the teachings of the Messenger of Allah (peace be upon him).

We strive to practice the teachings of Islam with integrity and sincerity in our private lives and in our collective work. We advocate the values and principles of Islam for the benefit of all people. For us, these activities are the path to getting closer to our Lord the Exalted and upon Him we place all our hopes.

كُونُوا۟ رَبَّٰنِيِّـۧنَ   (القرآن ٣:٧٩)

Be you Godly persons. (Quran 3:79)

إِنَّ ٱلَّذِينَ ءَامَنُوا۟ وَعَمِلُوا۟ ٱلصَّٰلِحَٰتِ سَيَجْعَلُ لَهُمُ ٱلرَّحْمَٰنُ وُدًّا ۝
(القرآن ١٩:٩٦)

Indeed! Those who believe and do good deeds, the Most Merciful will bestow upon them love. (Quran 19:96)

عَنْ أَبِي هُرَيْرَةَ، عَنِ النَّبِيِّ صلى الله عليه وسلم قَالَ "إِذَا أَحَبَّ اللَّهُ عَبْدًا نَادَى جِبْرِيلَ إِنَّ اللَّهَ يُحِبُّ فُلاَنًا، فَأَحِبَّهُ. فَيُحِبُّهُ جِبْرِيلُ، فَيُنَادِي جِبْرِيلُ فِي أَهْلِ السَّمَاءِ إِنَّ اللَّهَ يُحِبُّ فُلاَنًا، فَأَحِبُّوهُ. فَيُحِبُّهُ أَهْلُ السَّمَاءِ، ثُمَّ يُوضَعُ لَهُ الْقَبُولُ فِي أَهْلِ الأَرْضِ" (صحيح البخاري)

Narrated Abu Huraira: The Prophet (peace be upon him) said, "If Allah loves a person, He calls Gabriel saying: 'Allah loves so and so; O Gabriel, love him.' Gabriel would love him, and then Gabriel would make an announcement among the residents of the Heaven,

'Allah loves so-and-so, therefore, you should love him also.' So, all the residents of the Heavens would love him and then he is granted the pleasure of the people of the earth." (Bukhari - Sahih)

قُلْ إِنَّ صَلَاتِي وَنُسُكِي وَمَحْيَايَ وَمَمَاتِي لِلَّهِ رَبِّ ٱلْعَالَمِينَ ۝ (القرآن ٦:١٦٢)

Say: "Surely my prayers and my sacrifices and my life and my death are all for Allah, the Lord of the worlds." (Quran 6:162)

وَإِنَّ ٱللَّهَ بِكُمْ لَرَءُوفٌ رَّحِيمٌ ۝ (القرآن ٩:٥٧)

And indeed, Allah is to you Kind and Merciful. (Quran 57:9)

قُلْ إِن كُنتُمْ تُحِبُّونَ ٱللَّهَ فَٱتَّبِعُونِى يُحْبِبْكُمُ ٱللَّهُ وَيَغْفِرْ لَكُمْ ذُنُوبَكُمْ ۗ وَٱللَّهُ غَفُورٌ رَّحِيمٌ ۝ (القرآن ٣:٣١)

Say, (O Muhammad), "If you love Allah, then follow me, Allah will love you and forgive you your sins. And Allah is Forgiving and Merciful." (Quran 3:31)

عَنْ أَبِي هُرَيْرَةَ، قَالَ قَالَ رَسُولُ اللَّهِ صلى الله عليه وسلم "إِنَّ اللَّهَ قَالَ مَنْ عَادَى لِي وَلِيًّا فَقَدْ آذَنْتُهُ بِالْحَرْبِ، وَمَا تَقَرَّبَ إِلَىَّ عَبْدِي بِشَىْءٍ أَحَبَّ إِلَىَّ مِمَّا افْتَرَضْتُ عَلَيْهِ، وَمَا يَزَالُ عَبْدِي يَتَقَرَّبُ إِلَىَّ بِالنَّوَافِلِ حَتَّى أُحِبَّهُ، فَإِذَا أَحْبَبْتُهُ كُنْتُ سَمْعَهُ الَّذِي يَسْمَعُ بِهِ، وَبَصَرَهُ الَّذِي يُبْصِرُ بِهِ، وَيَدَهُ الَّتِي يَبْطِشُ بِهَا وَرِجْلَهُ الَّتِي يَمْشِي بِهَا، وَإِنْ سَأَلَنِي لأُعْطِيَنَّهُ، وَلَئِنِ اسْتَعَاذَنِي لأُعِيذَنَّهُ، وَمَا تَرَدَّدْتُ عَنْ شَىْءٍ أَنَا فَاعِلُهُ تَرَدُّدِي عَنْ نَفْسِ الْمُؤْمِنِ، يَكْرَهُ الْمَوْتَ وَأَنَا أَكْرَهُ مَسَاءَتَهُ" (صحيح البخاري)

Narrated Abu Huraira: The Messenger of Allah (peace be upon him) said: "Allah the Exalted has said: 'I will declare war against him who shows hostility to a pious worshipper of Mine. And the most beloved thing with which My slave comes nearer to Me is what I have commanded upon him; and My servant keeps on coming closer to Me through performing the optional deeds (Nawafil) till I love him. When I love him I become his hearing with which he hears, his seeing with which he sees, his hand with which he strikes, and his leg with which he walks; and if he asks from Me, I give him, and if he seeks My Protection, I protect him". (Bukhari - Sahih)

وَمَا خَلَقْتُ ٱلْجِنَّ وَٱلْإِنسَ إِلَّا لِيَعْبُدُونِ ۝ (القرآن ٥١:٥٦)

And I did not create the jinn and humanity except to worship Me. (Quran 51:56)

يَٰٓأَيُّهَا ٱلَّذِينَ ءَامَنُوا۟ ٱتَّقُوا۟ ٱللَّهَ وَٱبْتَغُوٓا۟ إِلَيْهِ ٱلْوَسِيلَةَ وَجَٰهِدُوا۟ فِى سَبِيلِهِۦ لَعَلَّكُمْ تُفْلِحُونَ ۝ (القرآن ٥:٣٥)

O believers, do your duty toward Allah, seek means of approach unto Him and strive in His cause, that you may be successful. (Quran 5:35)

فَـَٔاتَىٰهُمُ ٱللَّهُ ثَوَابَ ٱلدُّنْيَا وَحُسْنَ ثَوَابِ ٱلْءَاخِرَةِ ۗ وَٱللَّهُ يُحِبُّ ٱلْمُحْسِنِينَ ۝ (القرآن ٣:١٤٨)

So, Allah gave them the return in this world and also the better rewards in the Hereafter. Allah loves those who do good. (Quran 3:148)

فَٱسْتَجَابَ لَهُمْ رَبُّهُمْ أَنِّى لَآ أُضِيعُ عَمَلَ عَـٰمِلٍ مِّنكُم مِّن ذَكَرٍ أَوْ أُنثَىٰ ۖ بَعْضُكُم مِّنْ بَعْضٍ ۖ فَٱلَّذِينَ هَاجَرُوا۟ وَأُخْرِجُوا۟ مِن دِيَـٰرِهِمْ وَأُوذُوا۟ فِى سَبِيلِى وَقَـٰتَلُوا۟ وَقُتِلُوا۟ لَأُكَفِّرَنَّ عَنْهُمْ سَيِّـَٔاتِهِمْ وَلَأُدْخِلَنَّهُمْ جَنَّـٰتٍ تَجْرِى مِن تَحْتِهَا ٱلْأَنْهَـٰرُ ثَوَابًا مِّنْ عِندِ ٱللَّهِ ۗ وَٱللَّهُ عِندَهُۥ حُسْنُ ٱلثَّوَابِ ۝ (القرآن ٣:١٩٥)

So their Lord responded to them, "Never will I allow to be lost the work of any worker among you, male or female; you are of one another. Those who emigrated or were evicted from their homes or were harmed in My cause or fought or were killed - I will surely remove from them their misdeeds, and I will surely admit them to gardens beneath which rivers flow as reward from Allah , and Allah has with Him the best reward." (Quran 3:195)

Cooperation & Teamwork (جَمَاعَة)

We value brotherhood, unity, cooperation and partnership. We cooperate with others in matters on which we agree, and excuse each other in the matters on which we disagree. Organized dedicated collective work is necessary to attain great goals.

وَٱعْتَصِمُواْ بِحَبْلِ ٱللَّهِ جَمِيعًا وَلَا تَفَرَّقُواْ (القرآن ٣:١٠٣)

And hold firmly to the rope of Allah all of you together and do not become divided. (Quran 3:103)

عَنِ النُّعْمَانِ بْنِ بَشِيرٍ، قَالَ قَالَ رَسُولُ اللَّهِ صلى الله عليه وسلم "مَثَلُ الْمُؤْمِنِينَ فِي تَوَادِّهِمْ وَتَرَاحُمِهِمْ وَتَعَاطُفِهِمْ مَثَلُ الْجَسَدِ إِذَا اشْتَكَى مِنْهُ عُضْوٌ تَدَاعَى لَهُ سَائِرُ الْجَسَدِ بِالسَّهَرِ وَالْحُمَّى" (صحيح مسلم)

Numan bin Bashir reported: The Messenger of Allah (peace be upon him) said: "The believers in their mutual love, mercy and sympathy are just like one body. When one of the limbs suffers, the whole body responds to it with sleeplessness and fever." (Muslim - Sahih)

وَٱلْمُؤْمِنُونَ وَٱلْمُؤْمِنَٰتُ بَعْضُهُمْ أَوْلِيَآءُ بَعْضٍ ۚ يَأْمُرُونَ بِٱلْمَعْرُوفِ وَيَنْهَوْنَ عَنِ ٱلْمُنكَرِ وَيُقِيمُونَ ٱلصَّلَوٰةَ وَيُؤْتُونَ ٱلزَّكَوٰةَ وَيُطِيعُونَ ٱللَّهَ وَرَسُولَهُۥٓ (القرآن ٩:٧١)

The believers, men and women, are helpers of one another; they command good and forbid evil and establish the prayer and pay the charity and obey Allah and the Messenger. (Quran 9:71)

وَتَعَاوَنُوا۟ عَلَى ٱلْبِرِّ وَٱلتَّقْوَىٰ ۖ وَلَا تَعَاوَنُوا۟ عَلَى ٱلْإِثْمِ وَٱلْعُدْوَٰنِ ۚ (القرآن ٥: ٢)

Cooperate for righteousness and piety and do not cooperate for sin and transgression. (Quran 5:2)

عَنِ ابْنِ عُمَرَ قَالَ: سمعت رسول الله صلى الله عليه وسلم يقول "من خلع يداً من طاعة لقي الله يوم القيامة ولا حجة له، ومن مات وليس في عنقه بيعة مات ميتة جاهلية" (صحيح مسلم)

Ibn Umar reported: the Messenger of Allah (peace be upon him) said, "One who withdraws his hand from obedience (to the Amir) will find no argument (in his defense) when he stands before Allah on the Day of Resurrection; and one who dies without having sworn allegiance will die the death of one belonging to the Days of Ignorance." (Muslim - Sahih)

عَنْ أَبِي هُرَيْرَةَ، قَالَ قَالَ رَسُولُ اللَّهِ صلى الله عليه وسلم "مَنْ نَفَّسَ عَنْ مُؤْمِنٍ كُرْبَةً مِنْ كُرَبِ الدُّنْيَا نَفَّسَ اللَّهُ عَنْهُ كُرْبَةً مِنْ كُرَبِ يَوْمِ الْقِيَامَةِ وَمَنْ يَسَّرَ عَلَى مُعْسِرٍ يَسَّرَ اللَّهُ عَلَيْهِ فِي الدُّنْيَا وَالآخِرَةِ وَمَنْ سَتَرَ مُسْلِمًا سَتَرَهُ اللَّهُ فِي الدُّنْيَا وَالآخِرَةِ وَاللَّهُ فِي عَوْنِ الْعَبْدِ مَا كَانَ الْعَبْدُ فِي عَوْنِ أَخِيهِ وَمَنْ سَلَكَ طَرِيقًا يَلْتَمِسُ فِيهِ عِلْمًا سَهَّلَ اللَّهُ لَهُ بِهِ طَرِيقًا إِلَى الْجَنَّةِ وَمَا اجْتَمَعَ قَوْمٌ فِي بَيْتٍ مِنْ بُيُوتِ اللَّهِ يَتْلُونَ كِتَابَ اللَّهِ وَيَتَدَارَسُونَهُ بَيْنَهُمْ إِلاَّ نَزَلَتْ عَلَيْهِمُ السَّكِينَةُ وَغَشِيَتْهُمُ الرَّحْمَةُ وَحَفَّتْهُمُ الْمَلاَئِكَةُ وَذَكَرَهُمُ اللَّهُ فِيمَنْ عِنْدَهُ وَمَنْ بَطَّأَ بِهِ عَمَلُهُ لَمْ يُسْرِعْ بِهِ نَسَبُهُ" (صحيح مسلم)

Abu Huraira reported: The Messenger of Allah (peace be upon him) said: "Whoever removes a worldly grief from a believer, Allah will remove from him one of the griefs of the Day of Judgment, whoever alleviates [the condition] a needy person, Allah will alleviate [his condition] in this world and the next, whoever shields a Muslim, Allah will shield him in this world and the next, Allah will aid a servant [of His] so long as the servant aids his brother, whoever follows a path to seek knowledge, Allah will make easy for him a path to Paradise, no people gather together in one of the houses of Allah, reciting the Book of Allah and studying it among themselves, without tranquility descending upon them, mercy enveloping them, the angels surrounding them, and Allah making mention of them amongst those who are with Him, whoever is slowed down by his actions will not be hastened forward by his lineage." (Muslim - Sahih)

Comprehensiveness (شُمُولِيَة)

Islam is a complete way of life. It is universal in nature, comprehensive in scope and gradual in its approach. Allah the Exalted has provided us guidance in every aspect of our lives. Thus every area of Islamic work is within our scope. Due to the gradual approach of Islam, we focus on our priorities, addressing higher priorities before tackling lower priorities.

مَّا فَرَّطْنَا فِى ٱلْكِتَبِ مِن شَىْءٍ ثُمَّ إِلَىٰ رَبِّهِمْ يُحْشَرُونَ (القرآن ٦:٣٨)

We have neglected nothing in the Book, then unto their Lord they (all) shall be gathered. (Quran 6:38)

وَنَزَّلْنَا عَلَيْكَ ٱلْكِتَبَ تِبْيَنًا لِّكُلِّ شَىْءٍ وَهُدًى وَرَحْمَةً وَبُشْرَىٰ لِلْمُسْلِمِينَ (القرآن ١٦:٨٩)

And we have sent down to you the Book as a clear exposition of all things and a guidance and mercy and glad tidings for those who submit. (Quran 16:89)

مَا كَانَ حَدِيثًا يُفْتَرَىٰ وَلَـٰكِن تَصْدِيقَ ٱلَّذِى بَيْنَ يَدَيْهِ وَتَفْصِيلَ كُلِّ شَىْءٍ وَهُدًى وَرَحْمَةً لِّقَوْمٍ يُؤْمِنُونَ (القرآن ١٢:١١١)

This is not a narration invented, but a confirmation of what was before it and a detailed explanation of all things and guidance and mercy for a people who believe. (Quran 12:111)

قَالَ رَسُولُ اللَّهِ صلى الله عليه وسلم "ما تركت من شيءٍ يقرّبكم إلى الجنةِ إلا وقد حدثتكم به ، ولا تركتُ من شيءٍ يبعدكم عن النارِ إلا وقد حدثتكم به" (رواه الألباني – صحيح)

The Prophet said (peace be upon him) said: "I have not left anything to bring you closer to Paradise except I have told you about it, and I have not left anything that will keep you away from the hell fire except I have told you about it." (Albani - Sahih)

أَفَتُؤْمِنُونَ بِبَعْضِ ٱلْكِتَٰبِ وَتَكْفُرُونَ بِبَعْضٍ ۚ فَمَا جَزَآءُ مَن يَفْعَلُ ذَٰلِكَ مِنكُمْ إِلَّا خِزْىٌ فِى ٱلْحَيَوٰةِ ٱلدُّنْيَا ۖ وَيَوْمَ ٱلْقِيَٰمَةِ يُرَدُّونَ إِلَىٰٓ أَشَدِّ ٱلْعَذَابِ ۗ وَمَا ٱللَّهُ بِغَٰفِلٍ عَمَّا تَعْمَلُونَ (القرآن ٢:٨٥)

So do you believe in part of the Scripture and disbelieve in part? Then what is the recompense for those who do that among you except disgrace in worldly life; and on the Day of Resurrection they will be sent back to the severest of punishment. And Allah is not unaware of what you do. (Quran 2:85)

يَٰٓأَيُّهَا ٱلَّذِينَ ءَامَنُوا۟ ٱدْخُلُوا۟ فِى ٱلسِّلْمِ كَآفَّةً (القرآن ٢:٢٠٨)

O believers, enter into Islam completely. (Quran 2:208)

عَنْ عَائِشَةَ، قَالَتْ قَالَ رَسُولُ اللَّهِ صلى الله عليه وسلم "مَنْ أَحْدَثَ فِي أَمْرِنَا هَذَا مَا لَيْسَ مِنْهُ فَهُوَ رَدٌّ" (رواه مسلم والبخاري وأبو داود وابن ماجه – صحيح)

Aisha reported: The Messenger of Allah (peace be upon him) said: "Anyone who brings something new to this matter of ours (Islam) will have it rejected". (Muslim, Bukhari, Abu Dawud, Ibn Majah - Sahih)

ٱلْيَوْمَ أَكْمَلْتُ لَكُمْ دِينَكُمْ وَأَتْمَمْتُ عَلَيْكُمْ نِعْمَتِى وَرَضِيتُ لَكُمُ ٱلْإِسْلَٰمَ دِينًا (القرآن ٣:٥)

This day I have perfected for you your religion and completed My favor upon you and have approved for you Islam as religion. (Quran 5:3)

إِنِ ٱلْحُكْمُ إِلَّا لِلَّهِ (القرآن ١٢:٤٠)

Legislation is not except for Allah. (Quran 12:40)

أَفَغَيْرَ ٱللَّهِ أَبْتَغِى حَكَمًا وَهُوَ ٱلَّذِى أَنزَلَ إِلَيْكُمُ ٱلْكِتَٰبَ مُفَصَّلًا (القرآن ٦:١١٤)

Shall I seek other than Allah as a source of law, when He has revealed to you this book which is fully detailed? (Quran 6:114)

Constructive (بِنَاء)

We seek to be constructive. Our goal is to build the society. We are in the business of benefiting people, even if they hurt us. We support the constructive efforts of anyone who seeks to genuinely serve the community.

وَلَا تَسْتَوِى ٱلْحَسَنَةُ وَلَا ٱلسَّيِّئَةُ ٱدْفَعْ بِٱلَّتِى هِىَ أَحْسَنُ فَإِذَا ٱلَّذِى بَيْنَكَ وَبَيْنَهُۥ عَدَاوَةٌ كَأَنَّهُۥ وَلِىٌّ حَمِيمٌ ۝ (القرآن ٣٤:٤١)

And not equal are the good deed and the bad. Repel evil by an action which is better; and thereupon the one whom between you and him is enmity will become like a devoted friend. (Quran 41:34)

ٱدْفَعْ بِٱلَّتِى هِىَ أَحْسَنُ ٱلسَّيِّئَةَ نَحْنُ أَعْلَمُ بِمَا يَصِفُونَ ۝ (القرآن ٢٣:٩٦)

Repel, by means of what is better than their evil. We are most knowing of what they describe. (Quran 23:96)

عَنْ أَنَسٍ، قَالَ خَدَمْتُ رَسُولَ اللهِ صلى الله عليه وسلم تِسْعَ سِنِينَ فَمَا أَعْلَمُهُ قَالَ لِي قَطُّ لِمَ فَعَلْتَ كَذَا وَكَذَا وَلاَ عَابَ عَلَىَّ شَيْئًا قَطُّ (صحيح مسلم)

Anas reported: I served the Messenger of Allah (peace be upon him) for nine years, and I do not know (of any instance) when he said to me: Why you have done this and that, and he never found fault with me in anything. (Muslim - Sahih)

أَلَمْ تَرَ كَيْفَ ضَرَبَ ٱللَّهُ مَثَلًا كَلِمَةً طَيِّبَةً كَشَجَرَةٍ طَيِّبَةٍ أَصْلُهَا ثَابِتٌ وَفَرْعُهَا فِي ٱلسَّمَاءِ ۝ تُؤْتِي أُكُلَهَا كُلَّ حِينٍ بِإِذْنِ رَبِّهَا ۗ وَيَضْرِبُ ٱللَّهُ ٱلْأَمْثَالَ لِلنَّاسِ لَعَلَّهُمْ يَتَذَكَّرُونَ ۝ وَمَثَلُ كَلِمَةٍ خَبِيثَةٍ كَشَجَرَةٍ خَبِيثَةٍ ٱجْتُثَّتْ مِن فَوْقِ ٱلْأَرْضِ مَا لَهَا مِن قَرَارٍ ۝ (القرآن ١٤: ٢٤-٢٦)

Have you not considered how Allah presents an example? A good word is like a good tree, whose root is firmly fixed and its branches reaching the sky. It produces its fruit all the time, by permission of its Lord. And Allah presents examples for the people that perhaps they will be reminded. And the example of a bad word is like a bad tree, uprooted from the surface of the earth, not having any stability. (Quran 14:24-26)

وَٱلصُّلْحُ خَيْرٌ (القرآن ٤: ١٢٨)

Reconciliation is best. (Quran 4:128)

عَنْ أَبِي هُرَيْرَةَ، عَنِ النَّبِيِّ صلى الله عليه وسلم قَالَ "مَنْ كَانَ يُؤْمِنُ بِاللَّهِ وَالْيَوْمِ الآخِرِ فَلاَ يُؤْذِ جَارَهُ، وَمَنْ كَانَ يُؤْمِنُ بِاللَّهِ وَالْيَوْمِ الآخِرِ فَلْيُكْرِمْ ضَيْفَهُ، وَمَنْ كَانَ يُؤْمِنُ بِاللَّهِ وَالْيَوْمِ الآخِرِ فَلْيَقُلْ خَيْرًا أَوْ لِيَصْمُتْ" (صحيح البخاري)

Narrated Abu Huraira: The Prophet (peace be upon him) said, "Whoever believes in Allah and the Last Day, should not hurt his neighbor and whoever believes in Allah and the Last Day, should serve his guest generously and whoever believes in Allah and the Last Day, should speak what is good or keep silent." (Bukhari - Sahih)

Imam Ibn Rajab al Hanbali recorded in his famous book, Jami al-Ulum wal-Hikam.

Some of the righteous predecessors said: *"The people who love Allah look by the light of Allah, and they are compassionate with those who disobey Allah. They find their deeds reprehensible but show mercy to them so that through their admonitions they might leave their actions"*.

Universality (عَالَمِيَة)

Our religion is universal. For all times and all peoples. Our message is not restricted to any tribe, ethnicity or nationality. It is valid and viable until the end of time.

وَإِنَّ هَـٰذِهِۦٓ أُمَّتُكُمْ أُمَّةً وَٰحِدَةً وَأَنَا۠ رَبُّكُمْ فَٱتَّقُونِ ۝ (القرآن ٢٣:٥٢)

Indeed this your community is one community and I am your Lord, therefore be mindful of your duty to Me. (Quran 23:52)

قُلْ يَـٰٓأَيُّهَا ٱلنَّاسُ إِنِّى رَسُولُ ٱللَّهِ إِلَيْكُمْ جَمِيعًا (القرآن ٧:١٥٨)

Say, [O Muhammad], "O humanity, indeed I am the Messenger of Allah to all of you. (Quran 7:158)

أَخْبَرَنَا جَابِرُ بْنُ عَبْدِ اللَّهِ، أَنَّ النَّبِيَّ صلى الله عليه وسلم قَالَ "كَانَ النَّبِيُّ يُبْعَثُ إِلَى قَوْمِهِ خَاصَّةً، وَبُعِثْتُ إِلَى النَّاسِ عَامَّةً" (صحيح البخاري)

Narrated Jabir bin Abdullah: The Prophet (peace be upon him) said, "Every Prophet used to be sent to his nation only but I have been sent to all of humanity." (Bukhari - Sahih)

عن جابر بن عبد الله عن رسول الله - صلى الله عليه وسلم - يقول "لا فضل لعربي على أعجمي إلا بالتقوى" (رواه الألباني – صحيح)

Narrated Jabir bin Abdullah: The Messenger of Allah (peace be upon him) said, "No arab has superiority over a non arab except in God consciousness". (Albani – Sahih)

Gradualism (تَدَرُّج)

Islam is a religion for human beings, not robots or angels. Human beings naturally resist being controlled. Thus a wise implementation of Islam gives people breathing room to see the wisdom of the Divine commands and agree to follow them.

Allah the Exalted has the ability to create instantaneously, but He choose to create the universe and human beings in stages, in part to teach us the value of gradualism. In His mercy, He chose to reveal commands to His servants in stages, easing their implementation upon this ummah.

Our beloved Prophet (peace be upon him) taught people based on their level of understanding. Khalifah Umar bin Abdul Aziz said to his son, "*Do not deal with matters hastily, son. Allah Almighty [Himself] discouraged drinking alcohol twice in the Quran and did not declare it forbidden except in the third time. I am afraid that if I enjoined the right on people at one stroke, they would give it up all at once, which might lead to sedition.*" (Ash-Shatibī's Al-Muwafaqat 2:94)

This concept oif gradualism is not to be used as a justification for declaring permitted anything Allah has forbidden. This principle merely sets the focus on the final goal rather than the first step.

وَقُرْءَانًا فَرَقْنَٰهُ لِتَقْرَأَهُۥ عَلَى ٱلنَّاسِ عَلَىٰ مُكْثٍ وَنَزَّلْنَٰهُ تَنزِيلًا ۝ (القرآن ١٧:١٠٦)

And the Quran We have divided (into parts), so that you might recite it to people at intervals. And We have revealed it by stages. (Quran 17:106)

وَقَالَ ٱلَّذِينَ كَفَرُوا۟ لَوْلَا نُزِّلَ عَلَيْهِ ٱلْقُرْءَانُ جُمْلَةً وَٰحِدَةً ۚ كَذَٰلِكَ لِنُثَبِّتَ بِهِۦ فُؤَادَكَ ۖ وَرَتَّلْنَٰهُ تَرْتِيلًا ۝ (القرآن ٢٥:٣٢)

And those who disbelieve say, "Why was the Quran not revealed to him all at once?" Thus so We may strengthen thereby your heart. And We have spaced it distinctly. (Quran 25:32)

عَنْ يُوسُفَ بْنِ مَاهَكَ، قَالَ إِنِّي عِنْدَ عَائِشَةَ أُمِّ الْمُؤْمِنِينَ ـ رضى الله عنها ـ إِذْ جَاءَهَا عِرَاقِيٌّ فَقَالَ أَيُّ الْكَفَنِ خَيْرٌ قَالَتْ وَيْحَكَ وَمَا يَضُرُّكَ قَالَ يَا أُمَّ الْمُؤْمِنِينَ أَرِينِي مُصْحَفَكِ. قَالَتْ لِمَ قَالَ لَعَلِّي أُؤَلِّفُ الْقُرْآنَ عَلَيْهِ فَإِنَّهُ يُقْرَأُ غَيْرَ مُؤَلَّفٍ. قَالَتْ وَمَا يَضُرُّكَ أَيَّهُ قَرَأْتَ قَبْلُ، إِنَّمَا نَزَلَ أَوَّلَ مَا نَزَلَ مِنْهُ سُورَةٌ مِنَ الْمُفَصَّلِ فِيهَا ذِكْرُ الْجَنَّةِ وَالنَّارِ حَتَّى إِذَا ثَابَ النَّاسُ إِلَى الإِسْلاَمِ نَزَلَ الْحَلاَلُ وَالْحَرَامُ، وَلَوْ نَزَلَ أَوَّلَ شَىْءٍ لاَ تَشْرَبُوا الْخَمْرَ. لَقَالُوا لاَ نَدَعُ الْخَمْرَ أَبَدًا. وَلَوْ نَزَلَ. لاَ تَزْنُوا. لَقَالُوا لاَ نَدَعُ الزِّنَا أَبَدًا. لَقَدْ نَزَلَ بِمَكَّةَ عَلَى مُحَمَّدٍ صلى الله عليه وسلم وَإِنِّي لَجَارِيَةٌ أَلْعَبُ {بَلِ السَّاعَةُ مَوْعِدُهُمْ وَالسَّاعَةُ أَدْهَى وَأَمَرُّ} وَمَا نَزَلَتْ سُورَةُ الْبَقَرَةِ وَالنِّسَاءِ إِلاَّ وَأَنَا عِنْدَهُ. قَالَ فَأَخْرَجَتْ لَهُ الْمُصْحَفَ فَأَمْلَتْ عَلَيْهِ آىَ السُّوَرِ. (صحيح البخاري)

Narrated Yusuf bin Mahk: While I was with Aisha, the mother of the Believers, a person from Iraq came and asked, "What type of shroud is the best?" Aisha said, "May Allah be merciful to you! What does it matter?" He said, "O mother of the Believers! Show me your Quran," She said, "Why?" He said, "In order to compile and arrange the Quran according to it, for people recite it with its Suras not in proper order." Aisha said, "What does it matter which part of it you read first? The first portion revealed was a short Sura, and in it was mentioned Paradise and the Fire. When the people embraced Islam, the verses regarding legal and illegal things were revealed. If the first thing to be revealed was: 'Do not drink alcohol.' people would have said, 'We will never leave alcohol,' and if there had been revealed, 'Do not commit adultery,' they would have said, 'We will never give up adultery.' While I was a young girl of playing age, the following verse was revealed to Muhammad (peace be upon him) in Makkah: 'Indeed the Hour is their appointed time and it shall be grievous and bitter' (54:46). Chapters containing regulations (Sura Al-Baqara and Surat An-Nisa) were revealed after I was married to him." Then Aisha took out the copy of the Quran for the man and dictated to him the order of the Suras. (Bukhari - Sahih)

$$\text{وَمَآ أَمۡرُ ٱلسَّاعَةِ إِلَّا كَلَمۡحِ ٱلۡبَصَرِ} \quad (القرآن ١٦:٧٧)$$

And the command for the Hour is not but as a glance of the eye. (Quran 16:77)

$$\text{إِنَّمَآ أَمۡرُهُۥ إِذَآ أَرَادَ شَيۡـًٔا أَن يَقُولَ لَهُۥ كُن فَيَكُونُ} \quad (القرآن ٣٦:٨٢)$$

His command is only when He intends a thing that He says to it, "Be," and it is. (Quran 36:82)

$$\text{كَذَٰلِكِ ٱللَّهُ يَخۡلُقُ مَا يَشَآءُ ۚ إِذَا قَضَىٰٓ أَمۡرًا فَإِنَّمَا يَقُولُ لَهُۥ كُن فَيَكُونُ} \quad (القرآن ٣:٤٧)$$

Such is Allah; He creates what He wills. When He decrees a matter, He only says to it, 'Be,' and it is. (Quran 3:47)

$$\text{إِنَّ رَبَّكُمُ ٱللَّهُ ٱلَّذِى خَلَقَ ٱلسَّمَٰوَٰتِ وَٱلۡأَرۡضَ فِى سِتَّةِ أَيَّامٍ ثُمَّ ٱسۡتَوَىٰ عَلَى ٱلۡعَرۡشِ ۖ يُدَبِّرُ ٱلۡأَمۡرَ} \quad (القرآن ١٠:٣)$$

Indeed, your Lord is Allah, who created the heavens and the earth in six days and then established Himself above the Throne, arranging the matter. (Quran 10:3)

وَلَقَدْ خَلَقْنَا ٱلْإِنسَٰنَ مِن سُلَٰلَةٍ مِّن طِينٍ ۝ ثُمَّ جَعَلْنَٰهُ نُطْفَةً فِى قَرَارٍ مَّكِينٍ ۝ ثُمَّ خَلَقْنَا ٱلنُّطْفَةَ عَلَقَةً فَخَلَقْنَا ٱلْعَلَقَةَ مُضْغَةً فَخَلَقْنَا ٱلْمُضْغَةَ عِظَٰمًا فَكَسَوْنَا ٱلْعِظَٰمَ لَحْمًا ثُمَّ أَنشَأْنَٰهُ خَلْقًا ءَاخَرَ ۚ فَتَبَارَكَ ٱللَّهُ أَحْسَنُ ٱلْخَٰلِقِينَ ۝ (القرآن ٢٣: ١٢-١٤)

Verily We created man from a product of wet earth; then placed him as a drop (of seed) in a safe lodging; then We fashioned the drop into a clot, then We fashioned the clot into a little lump, then We fashioned the little lump into bones, then clothed the bones with flesh, and then produced it another creation. So blessed be Allah, the Best of Creators! (Quran 23:12-14)

Balance & Moderation (تَوَازُنٌ وَ وَسَطِيَةٌ)

Islam is a perfectly balanced system as revealed by Allah the Exalted and as practiced by the Messenger (peace be upon him). Exaggerating or abandoning any aspect of this perfectly balanced system results in an unstable outcome. We adhere to the balanced understanding and application of Islam as practiced by the Messenger (peace be upon him).

وَكَذَٰلِكَ جَعَلْنَٰكُمْ أُمَّةً وَسَطًا لِّتَكُونُوا۟ شُهَدَآءَ عَلَى ٱلنَّاسِ وَيَكُونَ ٱلرَّسُولُ عَلَيْكُمْ شَهِيدًا (القرآن ٢:١٤٣)

And thus we have made you a justly balanced community so that you may be witnesses upon mankind and the Messenger be a witness upon you. (Quran 2:143)

إِنَّ هَٰذَا ٱلْقُرْءَانَ يَهْدِى لِلَّتِى هِىَ أَقْوَمُ وَيُبَشِّرُ ٱلْمُؤْمِنِينَ ٱلَّذِينَ يَعْمَلُونَ ٱلصَّٰلِحَٰتِ أَنَّ لَهُمْ أَجْرًا كَبِيرًا (القرآن ١٧:٩)

Verily this Quran guides to that which is most upright and gives glad tidings to the believers who works deeds of righteousness that they shall have a great reward. (Quran 17:9)

عَنْ أَبِي هُرَيْرَةَ، عَنِ النَّبِيِّ صلى الله عليه وسلم قَالَ "إِنَّ الدِّينَ يُسْرٌ، وَلَنْ يُشَادَّ الدِّينَ أَحَدٌ إِلاَّ غَلَبَهُ، فَسَدِّدُوا وَقَارِبُوا وَأَبْشِرُوا، وَاسْتَعِينُوا بِالْغَدْوَةِ وَالرَّوْحَةِ وَشَىْءٍ مِنَ الدُّلْجَةِ" (صحيح البخاري)

Narrated Abu Huraira: The Prophet (peace be upon him) said: "The religion is easy and whoever overburdens himself in his religion will not be able to continue in that way. So you should not be extremists, but try to be near to perfection and receive the good tidings that you will be rewarded; and gain strength by worshipping in the mornings, the afternoons, and during the last hours of the nights." (Bukhari – Sahih)

يَٰأَهْلَ ٱلْكِتَٰبِ لَا تَغْلُوا۟ فِى دِينِكُمْ (القرآن ٤:١٧١)

O People of the Scripture, do not commit excess in your religion. (Quran 4:171)

يَٰبَنِىٓ ءَادَمَ خُذُوا۟ زِينَتَكُمْ عِندَ كُلِّ مَسْجِدٍ وَكُلُوا۟ وَٱشْرَبُوا۟ وَلَا تُسْرِفُوٓا۟ إِنَّهُۥ لَا يُحِبُّ ٱلْمُسْرِفِينَ (القرآن ٧:٣١)

O children of Adam, take your adornment at every masjid, and eat and drink, but be not excessive. Indeed, He likes not those who commit excess. (Quran 7:31)

عَنْ أَنَسِ بْنِ مَالِكٍ ـ رضى الله عنه ـ يَقُولُ جَاءَ ثَلاَثَةُ رَهْطٍ إِلَى بُيُوتِ أَزْوَاجِ النَّبِيِّ صلى الله عليه وسلم يَسْأَلُونَ عَنْ عِبَادَةِ النَّبِيِّ صلى الله عليه وسلم فَلَمَّا أُخْبِرُوا كَأَنَّهُمْ تَقَالُّوهَا فَقَالُوا وَأَيْنَ نَحْنُ مِنَ النَّبِيِّ صلى الله عليه وسلم قَدْ غُفِرَ لَهُ مَا تَقَدَّمَ مِنْ ذَنْبِهِ وَمَا تَأَخَّرَ‏.‏ قَالَ أَحَدُهُمْ أَمَّا أَنَا فَإِنِّي أُصَلِّي اللَّيْلَ أَبَدًا‏.‏ وَقَالَ آخَرُ أَنَا أَصُومُ الدَّهْرَ وَلاَ أُفْطِرُ‏.‏ وَقَالَ آخَرُ أَنَا أَعْتَزِلُ النِّسَاءَ فَلاَ أَتَزَوَّجُ أَبَدًا‏.‏ فَجَاءَ رَسُولُ اللَّهِ صلى الله عليه وسلم فَقَالَ ‏"‏ أَنْتُمُ الَّذِينَ قُلْتُمْ كَذَا وَكَذَا أَمَا وَاللَّهِ إِنِّي لأَخْشَاكُمْ لِلَّهِ وَأَتْقَاكُمْ لَهُ، لَكِنِّي أَصُومُ وَأُفْطِرُ، وَأُصَلِّي وَأَرْقُدُ وَأَتَزَوَّجُ النِّسَاءَ، فَمَنْ رَغِبَ عَنْ سُنَّتِي فَلَيْسَ مِنِّي‏"‏ (متفق عليه)

Narrated Anas bin Malik: A group of three men came to the houses of the wives of the Prophet (peace be upon him) asking how the Prophet (peace be upon him) worshipped, and when they were informed, they considered their worship insufficient and said, "Where are we from the Prophet (peace be upon him) as his past and future sins have been forgiven." Then one of them said, "I will offer the prayer throughout the night forever." The other said, "I will fast throughout the year and will not break my fast." The third said, "*I will keep away from the women and will not marry forever.*" Prophet (peace be upon him) came to them and said, "*Are you the people who said so-and-so? By Allah, I am more submissive to Allah and more afraid of Him than you; yet I fast and break my fast, I do sleep and I also marry women. So he who does not follow my tradition in religion, is not from me.*" (Bukhari, Muslim – Sahih)

لَقَدْ أَرْسَلْنَا رُسُلَنَا بِٱلْبَيِّنَٰتِ وَأَنزَلْنَا مَعَهُمُ ٱلْكِتَٰبَ وَٱلْمِيزَانَ لِيَقُومَ ٱلنَّاسُ بِٱلْقِسْطِ (القرآن ٥٧:٢٥)

We have sent Our messengers with clear evidences and sent down with them the Scripture and the balance that the people may maintain [their affairs] in justice. (Quran 57:25)

وَٱلَّذِينَ إِذَآ أَنفَقُواْ لَمْ يُسْرِفُواْ وَلَمْ يَقْتُرُواْ وَكَانَ بَيْنَ ذَٰلِكَ قَوَامًا (القرآن ٢٥:٦٧)

And those who, when they spend, do so not excessively or stingily but are always between them moderately balanced. (Quran 25:67)

عَنْ عَائِشَةَ ـ رضى الله عنها ـ أَنَّهَا قَالَتْ سُئِلَ النَّبِيُّ صلى الله عليه وسلم أَيُّ الأَعْمَالِ أَحَبُّ إِلَى اللَّهِ قَالَ "أَدْوَمُهَا وَإِنْ قَلَّ". وَقَالَ "اكْلَفُوا مِنَ الأَعْمَالِ مَا تُطِيقُونَ". (صحيح البخاري)

Narrated Aisha: The Prophet (peace be upon him) was asked, "*What deeds are loved most by Allah?*" He said, "*The most regular constant deeds even though they may be few.*" He added, "*Don't take upon yourselves, except the deeds which are within your ability.*" (Bukhari – Sahih)

وَلَا تَجْعَلْ يَدَكَ مَغْلُولَةً إِلَىٰ عُنُقِكَ وَلَا تَبْسُطْهَا كُلَّ ٱلْبَسْطِ فَتَقْعُدَ مَلُومًا مَّحْسُورًا ۝ (القرآن ١٧:٢٩)

Do not chain your hand to your neck (in stinginess), nor stretch it out to the utmost limit (sin extravagance). (Quran 17:29)

عَنْ أَبِي هُرَيْرَةَ، أَنَّ رَسُولَ اللهِ صلى الله عليه وسلم قَالَ "إِذَا صَلَّى أَحَدُكُمْ لِلنَّاسِ فَلْيُخَفِّفْ، فَإِنَّ مِنْهُمُ الضَّعِيفَ وَالسَّقِيمَ وَالْكَبِيرَ، وَإِذَا صَلَّى أَحَدُكُمْ لِنَفْسِهِ فَلْيُطَوِّلْ مَا شَاءَ" (صحيح البخاري)

Narrated Abu Huraira: The Messenger of Allah (peace be upon him) said, "If anyone of you leads the people in the prayer, he should shorten it for amongst them are the weak, the sick and the old; and if anyone among you prays alone then he may prolong (the prayer) as much as he wishes." (Bukhari - Sahih)

Realism (وَاقِعِيَة)

Islam is a pragmatic way of life. Allah the Exalted has not commanded us anything that is unnatural for human beings. Our jurisprudence (fiqh) takes into account the situation of the society it is to be implemented in.

$$\text{يُرِيدُ اللَّهُ بِكُمُ الْيُسْرَ وَلَا يُرِيدُ بِكُمُ الْعُسْرَ (القرآن ٢:١٨٥)}$$

Allah wishes for you ease and does not wish for you hardship. (Quran 2:185)

$$\text{فَمَنِ اضْطُرَّ غَيْرَ بَاغٍ وَلَا عَادٍ فَلَا إِثْمَ عَلَيْهِ (القرآن ٢:١٧٣)}$$

But whoever is forced [by necessity], neither desiring [it] nor transgressing [its limit], there is no sin upon him. (Quran 2:173)

قَالَ أَبُو سَعِيدٍ سَمِعْتُ رَسُولَ اللهِ صلى الله عليه وسلم قَالَ "مَنْ رَأَى مُنْكَرًا فَلْيُغَيِّرْهُ بِيَدِهِ فَإِنْ لَمْ يَسْتَطِعْ فَبِلِسَانِهِ فَإِنْ لَمْ يَسْتَطِعْ فَبِقَلْبِهِ وَذَلِكَ أَضْعَفُ الْإِيمَانِ" (رواه النّسائي – صحيح)

Abu Saeed said: I heard the Messenger of Allah (peace be upon him) say: "Whoever among you sees an evil, let him change it with his hand; if he cannot, then with his tongue; if he cannot, then with his heart- and that is the weakest of Faith." (Nasai - Sahih)

عَنْ عَائِشَةَ ـ رضي الله عنها ـ أَنَّهَا قَالَتْ مَا خُيِّرَ رَسُولُ اللهِ صلى الله عليه وسلم بَيْنَ أَمْرَيْنِ إِلَّا أَخَذَ أَيْسَرَهُمَا، مَا لَمْ يَكُنْ إِثْمًا، فَإِنْ كَانَ إِثْمًا كَانَ أَبْعَدَ النَّاسِ مِنْهُ. (صحيح البخاري)

Narrated Aisha: Whenever the Messenger of Allah (peace be upon him) was given the choice of one of two matters, he would choose the easier of the two, as long as it was not sinful to do so, but if it was sinful to do so, he would not approach it. (Bukhari - Sahih)

Key Ingredients Of Successful Teams

Successful teams exist to serve a higher purpose. And what purpose could be loftier than Tawhid (Oneness of Allah), the objective of the Prophets (peace be upon them) and all those loved and honored by Allah the Exalted?

The most successful teams have several key ingredients in common. They create a proactive environment, pursue justice, focus on continuous learning and growth, cherish diversity and demonstrate rigorous commitment to their goals.

يَٰٓأَيُّهَا ٱلَّذِينَ ءَامَنُوا۟ ٱتَّقُوا۟ ٱللَّهَ وَٱبْتَغُوٓا۟ إِلَيْهِ ٱلْوَسِيلَةَ وَجَٰهِدُوا۟ فِى سَبِيلِهِۦ لَعَلَّكُمْ تُفْلِحُونَ ۝ (القرآن ٥:٣٥)

O believers, be mindful of Allah and seek the means of nearness to Him and strive in His cause that you may succeed. (Quran 5:35)

قُلْ يَٰقَوْمِ ٱعْمَلُوا۟ عَلَىٰ مَكَانَتِكُمْ إِنِّى عَامِلٌ ۖ فَسَوْفَ تَعْلَمُونَ مَن تَكُونُ لَهُۥ عَٰقِبَةُ ٱلدَّارِ ۗ إِنَّهُۥ لَا يُفْلِحُ ٱلظَّٰلِمُونَ ۝ (القرآن ٦:١٣٥)

Say, "O my people, work according to your ability; indeed, I am also working. And you are going to know who will have destination in the end. Indeed, the wrongdoers will not be successful. (Quran 6:135)

قُل لَّا يَسْتَوِى ٱلْخَبِيثُ وَٱلطَّيِّبُ وَلَوْ أَعْجَبَكَ كَثْرَةُ ٱلْخَبِيثِ ۚ فَٱتَّقُوا۟ ٱللَّهَ يَـٰٓأُو۟لِى ٱلْأَلْبَـٰبِ لَعَلَّكُمْ تُفْلِحُونَ ۝ (القرآن ٥:١٠٠)

Say, "Not equal are the evil and the good, although the abundance of evil might impress you." So be mindful of Allah, O you of understanding, that you may be successful. (Quran 5:100)

Proactiveness (إِيجَابِيَة)

Our compassion for humanity drives us to care for all people, Muslims and people of other faiths. We are full participants in the dynamics of our American society where we positively contribute. We work together to serve our community, our country and all of humanity; we serve the Creator by serving His creation.

Our activism compels us to promote the good, wherever we find it and to oppose the evil, regardless of who performs it. We don't ignore the bigger picture. We are not passive.

وَلْتَكُن مِّنكُمْ أُمَّةٌ يَدْعُونَ إِلَى ٱلْخَيْرِ وَيَأْمُرُونَ بِٱلْمَعْرُوفِ وَيَنْهَوْنَ عَنِ ٱلْمُنكَرِ وَأُوْلَٰٓئِكَ هُمُ ٱلْمُفْلِحُونَ ۞ (القرآن ٣:١٠٤)

Let there continue to arise out of you a community who call to all that is good, promote what is right and forbid what is wrong, and those are the successful. (Quran 3:104)

عَنْ أَبِي ذَرٍّ، قَالَ قَالَ رَسُولُ اللهِ صلى الله عليه وسلم "تَبَسُّمُكَ فِي وَجْهِ أَخِيكَ لَكَ صَدَقَةٌ وَأَمْرُكَ بِالْمَعْرُوفِ وَنَهْيُكَ عَنِ الْمُنْكَرِ صَدَقَةٌ وَإِرْشَادُكَ الرَّجُلَ فِي أَرْضِ الضَّلاَلِ لَكَ صَدَقَةٌ وَبَصَرُكَ لِلرَّجُلِ الرَّدِيءِ الْبَصَرِ لَكَ صَدَقَةٌ وَإِمَاطَتُكَ الْحَجَرَ وَالشَّوْكَةَ وَالْعَظْمَ عَنِ الطَّرِيقِ لَكَ صَدَقَةٌ وَإِفْرَاغُكَ مِنْ دَلْوِكَ فِي دَلْوِ أَخِيكَ لَكَ صَدَقَةٌ" (رواه الترمذي – حسن)

Abu Dharr narrated: The Messenger of Allah (peace be upon him) said: "Your smiling in the face of your brother is charity, commanding good and forbidding evil is charity, your giving directions to a man lost in the land is charity for you. Your seeing for a man with bad sight is a charity for you, your removal of a rock, a thorn or a bone from the road is charity for you. Your pouring what remains from your bucket into the bucket of your brother is charity for you." (Tirmidhi – Hassan)

$$\text{إِنَّ ٱللَّهَ لَا يُغَيِّرُ مَا بِقَوْمٍ حَتَّىٰ يُغَيِّرُوا۟ مَا بِأَنفُسِهِمْ} \quad (\text{القرآن } 13:11)$$

Indeed, Allah will not change the condition of a people until they change what is in themselves. (Quran 13:11)

$$\text{وَمَآ أَرْسَلْنَا مِن رَّسُولٍ إِلَّا بِلِسَانِ قَوْمِهِۦ لِيُبَيِّنَ لَهُمْ} \quad (\text{القرآن } 14:4)$$

And We did not send any messenger except in the language of his people to make clear for them. (Quran 14:4)

$$\text{وَمَن يَتَّقِ ٱللَّهَ يَجْعَل لَّهُۥ مَخْرَجًا وَيَرْزُقْهُ مِنْ حَيْثُ لَا يَحْتَسِبُ وَمَن يَتَوَكَّلْ عَلَى ٱللَّهِ فَهُوَ حَسْبُهُۥٓ} \quad (\text{القرآن } 65: 2-3)$$

And whoever is mindful of Allah, He will make for him a way out and will provide for him from where he does not expect. And whoever relies upon Allah – then He is sufficient for him. (Quran 65:2-3)

$$\text{وَٱتَّقُوا۟ فِتْنَةً لَّا تُصِيبَنَّ ٱلَّذِينَ ظَلَمُوا۟ مِنكُمْ خَآصَّةً وَٱعْلَمُوٓا۟ أَنَّ ٱللَّهَ شَدِيدُ ٱلْعِقَابِ} \quad (\text{القرآن } 8:25)$$

And fear an affliction which may not strike only those of you who are unjust; and know that Allah is severe in retribution. (Quran 8:25)

أَتَأْمُرُونَ ٱلنَّاسَ بِٱلْبِرِّ وَتَنسَوْنَ أَنفُسَكُمْ وَأَنتُمْ تَتْلُونَ ٱلْكِتَٰبَ ۚ أَفَلَا تَعْقِلُونَ ۝ (القرآن ٢:٤٤)

Do you command people to be good and neglect yourselves while you read the Book; have you then no sense? (Quran 2:44)

وَأَنفِقُوا۟ فِى سَبِيلِ ٱللَّهِ وَلَا تُلْقُوا۟ بِأَيْدِيكُمْ إِلَى ٱلتَّهْلُكَةِ ۛ وَأَحْسِنُوٓا۟ ۛ إِنَّ ٱللَّهَ يُحِبُّ ٱلْمُحْسِنِينَ ۝ (القرآن ٢:١٩٥)

And spend in the way of Allah and do not destroy yourselves with your own hands. And do good; indeed, Allah loves the doers of good. (Quran 2:195)

يَٰٓأَيُّهَا ٱلَّذِينَ ءَامَنُوا۟ ٱرْكَعُوا۟ وَٱسْجُدُوا۟ وَٱعْبُدُوا۟ رَبَّكُمْ وَٱفْعَلُوا۟ ٱلْخَيْرَ لَعَلَّكُمْ تُفْلِحُونَ ۩ ۝ (القرآن ٢٢:٧٧)

O believers! Bow and prostrate yourselves and serve your Lord, and do good that you may succeed. (Quran 22:77)

وَإِذْ أَخَذْنَا مِيثَٰقَكُمْ وَرَفَعْنَا فَوْقَكُمُ ٱلطُّورَ خُذُوا۟ مَآ ءَاتَيْنَٰكُم بِقُوَّةٍ وَٱذْكُرُوا۟ مَا فِيهِ لَعَلَّكُمْ تَتَّقُونَ ۝ (القرآن ٢:٦٣)

And when We took a promise from you and lifted the mountain over you saying: Take hold of the law We have given you with firmness and remember what is in it, so that you may be vigilant. (Quran 2:63)

عَنْ أَبِي سَعِيدٍ الْخُدْرِيِّ، قَالَ دَخَلَ رَسُولُ اللهِ صلى الله عليه وسلم ذَاتَ يَوْمٍ الْمَسْجِدَ فَإِذَا هُوَ بِرَجُلٍ مِنَ الْأَنْصَارِ يُقَالُ لَهُ أَبُو أُمَامَةَ فَقَالَ "يَا أَبَا أُمَامَةَ مَا لِي أَرَاكَ جَالِسًا فِي الْمَسْجِدِ فِي غَيْرِ وَقْتِ الصَّلَاةِ". قَالَ هُمُومٌ لَزِمَتْنِي وَدُيُونٌ يَا رَسُولَ اللهِ. قَالَ "أَفَلَا أُعَلِّمُكَ كَلَامًا إِذَا أَنْتَ قُلْتَهُ أَذْهَبَ اللهُ عَزَّ وَجَلَّ هَمَّكَ وَقَضَى عَنْكَ دَيْنَكَ". قَالَ قُلْتُ بَلَى يَا رَسُولَ اللهِ. قَالَ "قُلْ إِذَا أَصْبَحْتَ وَإِذَا أَمْسَيْتَ اللَّهُمَّ إِنِّي أَعُوذُ بِكَ مِنَ الْهَمِّ وَالْحَزَنِ وَأَعُوذُ بِكَ مِنَ الْعَجْزِ وَالْكَسَلِ وَأَعُوذُ بِكَ مِنَ الْجُبْنِ وَالْبُخْلِ وَأَعُوذُ بِكَ مِنْ غَلَبَةِ الدَّيْنِ وَقَهْرِ الرِّجَالِ". قَالَ فَفَعَلْتُ ذَلِكَ فَأَذْهَبَ اللهُ عَزَّ وَجَلَّ هَمِّي وَقَضَى عَنِّي دَيْنِي. (رواه أبو داود والبخاري — صحيح)

Narrated AbuSaid al-Khudri: One day the Messenger of Allah (peace be upon him) entered the mosque. He saw there a man from the Ansar called Abu Umamah. He said: "What is the matter that I am seeing you sitting in the mosque when there is no time of prayer?" He said: I am entangled in cares and debts, O Messenger of Allah. He replied: "Shall I not teach you words by which, when you say them, Allah will remove your care, and settle your debt?" He said: Why not, Messenger of Allah? He said: "Say in the morning and evening: <u>O Allah, I seek refuge in You from anxiety and grief, I seek refuge in You from incapacity and laziness, I seek refuge in You from cowardice and stinginess, and I seek in You from being overcome by debt and being put in subjection by men</u>." He said: When I did that Allah removed my care and settled my debt. (Abu Dawud, Bukhari - Sahih)

Justice (عَدَالَة)

Justice is an attribute of Allah the Exalted and is among the highest Islamic values. We uphold and advocate justice for everyone out of our deep commitment to it, even under difficult circumstances and even against ourselves. We insist on the highest levels of integrity in everything we do.

The minimum standard in Islam is that goodness is returned with goodness, and evil is returned with justice. If this limit is transgressed, it becomes oppression.

عَنْ أَبِي ذَرٍّ، قَالَ قَالَ رَسُولُ اللَّهِ صلى الله عليه وسلم فِيمَا يَرْوِي عَنْ رَبِّهِ تَبَارَكَ وَتَعَالَى "إِنِّي حَرَّمْتُ عَلَى نَفْسِي الظُّلْمَ وَعَلَى عِبَادِي فَلاَ تَظَالَمُوا"
(صحيح مسلم)

Abu Dharr reported: The Messenger of Allah (peace be upon him) said that he reported it from his Lord, the Exalted and Glorious: "Verily I have made oppression unlawful for Me and for My servants too, so do not commit oppression." (Muslim - Sahih)

إِنَّ ٱللَّهَ يَأْمُرُ بِٱلْعَدْلِ وَٱلْإِحْسَٰنِ وَإِيتَآئِ ذِى ٱلْقُرْبَىٰ وَيَنْهَىٰ عَنِ ٱلْفَحْشَآءِ وَٱلْمُنكَرِ وَٱلْبَغْىِ ۚ يَعِظُكُمْ لَعَلَّكُمْ تَذَكَّرُونَ (القرآن ١٦:٩٠)

Indeed, Allah commands justice and good conduct and giving to relatives and forbids immorality and bad conduct and oppression. He admonishes you that perhaps you will be reminded. (Quran 16:90)

وَأَقْسِطُوٓا۟ إِنَّ ٱللَّهَ يُحِبُّ ٱلْمُقْسِطِينَ ۝ (القرآن ٤٩:٩)

Be just, for Allah loves those who are just. (Quran 49:9)

عَنْ عَبْدِ اللهِ بْنِ عَمْروٍ، قَالَ رَسُولُ اللهِ صلى الله عليه وسلم "إِنَّ الْمُقْسِطِينَ عِنْدَ اللهِ عَلَى مَنَابِرَ مِنْ نُورٍ عَنْ يَمِينِ الرَّحْمَنِ عَزَّ وَجَلَّ وَكِلْتَا يَدَيْهِ يَمِينٌ الَّذِينَ يَعْدِلُونَ فِي حُكْمِهِمْ وَأَهْلِيهِمْ وَمَا وَلُوا" (رواه مسلم والنسائي – صحيح)

On the authority of Abdullah bin Umar that the Messenger of Allah (peace be upon him) said: "Indeed the dispensers of justice will be seated on the pulpits of light beside Allah, on the right side of the Merciful, Exalted and Glorious. And both His hands are right hands. Those who do justice in their rules, in matters relating to their families and in all that they undertake to do." (Muslim, Nasai - Sahih)

يَـٰٓأَيُّهَا ٱلَّذِينَ ءَامَنُوا۟ كُونُوا۟ قَوَّٰمِينَ بِٱلْقِسْطِ شُهَدَآءَ لِلَّهِ وَلَوْ عَلَىٰٓ أَنفُسِكُمْ أَوِ ٱلْوَٰلِدَيْنِ وَٱلْأَقْرَبِينَ (القرآن ٤:١٣٥)

O believers, stand up firmly for justice, as witnesses to Allah, even against yourselves or your parents or kin. (Quran 4:135)

وَجَزَٰٓؤُا۟ سَيِّئَةٍ سَيِّئَةٌ مِّثْلُهَا ۖ فَمَنْ عَفَا وَأَصْلَحَ فَأَجْرُهُۥ عَلَى ٱللَّهِ ۚ إِنَّهُۥ لَا يُحِبُّ ٱلظَّـٰلِمِينَ ۝ (القرآن ٤٢:٤٠)

The retribution for a harm is an equivalent harm, but whoever pardons and reconciles his reward is from Allah. Indeed, He does not love the wrongdoers. (Quran 42:40)

فَأَصْلِحُوا۟ بَيْنَهُمَا بِٱلْعَدْلِ وَأَقْسِطُوٓا۟ ۖ إِنَّ ٱللَّهَ يُحِبُّ ٱلْمُقْسِطِينَ ۞ (القرآن ٩:٤٩)

Make reconciliation between opposing parties with justice, and be equitable. Indeed Allah loves those who are equitable. (Quran 49:9)

وَإِذَا قُلْتُمْ فَٱعْدِلُوا۟ وَلَوْ كَانَ ذَا قُرْبَىٰ ۖ (القرآن ٦:١٥٢)

And when you speak, be just, even if it concerns a near relative. (Quran 6:152)

Personal Development (تَرْبِيَة)

To achieve our mission we must continually develop as individuals and as a society of people dedicated to working in the way of Allah the Exalted. This development is spiritual, intellectual and physical. We must be ambitious, yet practical, never losing focus of our objectives. This was the topic of the first revelation.

اقْرَأْ بِاسْمِ رَبِّكَ الَّذِى خَلَقَ ۝ خَلَقَ الْإِنسَـٰنَ مِنْ عَلَقٍ ۝ اقْرَأْ وَرَبُّكَ الْأَكْرَمُ ۝ الَّذِى عَلَّمَ بِالْقَلَمِ ۝ عَلَّمَ الْإِنسَـٰنَ مَا لَمْ يَعْلَمْ ۝ (القرآن ٩٦: ١-٥)

Read in the name of your Lord Who has created, He created man from a clump. Read and your Lord is the Most Honorable, Who has taught by the pen. He taught man what he did not know. (Quran 96:1-5)

وَنَفْسٍ وَمَا سَوَّىٰهَا ۝ فَأَلْهَمَهَا فُجُورَهَا وَتَقْوَىٰهَا ۝ قَدْ أَفْلَحَ مَن زَكَّىٰهَا ۝ وَقَدْ خَابَ مَن دَسَّىٰهَا ۝ (القرآن ٩١: ٧-١٠)

And by the soul and He who proportioned it. And inspired it [with discernment of] its wickedness and its righteousness. Indeed He has succeeded who purifies it, And he has failed who debases it. (Quran 91:7-10)

عَنِ النَّوَّاسِ بْنِ سَمْعَانَ الْأَنْصَارِيِّ، قَالَ سَأَلْتُ رَسُولَ اللهِ صلى الله عليه وسلم عَنِ الْبِرِّ وَالْإِثْمِ فَقَالَ "الْبِرُّ حُسْنُ الْخُلُقِ وَالْإِثْمُ مَا حَاكَ فِي صَدْرِكَ وَكَرِهْتَ أَنْ يَطَّلِعَ عَلَيْهِ النَّاسُ" (صحيح مسلم)

Nawwas bin Saman al-Ansari reported: I asked the Messenger of Allah (peace be upon him) about virtue and vice. He said: "Virtue is a kind disposition and vice is what rankles in your heart and that you disapprove that people should come to know of it". (Muslim - Sahih)

$$\text{لَقَدْ مَنَّ اللَّهُ عَلَى الْمُؤْمِنِينَ إِذْ بَعَثَ فِيهِمْ رَسُولًا مِّنْ أَنفُسِهِمْ يَتْلُو عَلَيْهِمْ ءَايَاتِهِ وَيُزَكِّيهِمْ وَيُعَلِّمُهُمُ الْكِتَابَ وَالْحِكْمَةَ وَإِن كَانُوا مِن قَبْلُ لَفِى ضَلَالٍ مُّبِينٍ}$$ (القرآن ٣:١٦٤)

Certainly did Allah confer favor upon the believers when He sent among them a Messenger from themselves, reciting to them His verses and purifying them and teaching them the Book and wisdom, although they had been before in manifest error. (Quran 3:164)

$$\text{كَمَا أَرْسَلْنَا فِيكُمْ رَسُولًا مِّنكُمْ يَتْلُو عَلَيْكُمْ ءَايَاتِنَا وَيُزَكِّيكُمْ وَيُعَلِّمُكُمُ الْكِتَابَ وَالْحِكْمَةَ وَيُعَلِّمُكُم مَّا لَمْ تَكُونُوا تَعْلَمُونَ}$$ (القرآن ٢:١٥١)

Thus We have sent among you a messenger from yourselves reciting to you Our verses and purifying you and teaching you the Book and wisdom and teaching you that which you did not know. (Quran 2:151)

$$\text{هُوَ الَّذِى بَعَثَ فِى الْأُمِّيِّنَ رَسُولًا مِّنْهُمْ يَتْلُو عَلَيْهِمْ ءَايَاتِهِ وَيُزَكِّيهِمْ وَيُعَلِّمُهُمُ الْكِتَابَ وَالْحِكْمَةَ وَإِن كَانُوا مِن قَبْلُ لَفِى ضَلَالٍ مُّبِينٍ}$$ (القرآن ٦٢:٢)

It is He who has sent among the unlettered a Messenger from themselves reciting to them His verses and purifying them and teaching them the Book and wisdom; although they were before in clear error. (Quran 62:2)

عَنِ ابْنِ مَسْعُودٍ ـ رضي الله عنه ـ قَالَ سَمِعْتُ النَّبِيَّ صلى الله عليه وسلم يَقُولُ "لَا حَسَدَ إِلَّا فِي اثْنَتَيْنِ رَجُلٌ آتَاهُ اللَّهُ مَالًا فَسَلَّطَهُ عَلَى هَلَكَتِهِ فِي الْحَقِّ، وَرَجُلٌ آتَاهُ اللَّهُ حِكْمَةً فَهُوَ يَقْضِي بِهَا وَيُعَلِّمُهَا" (صحيح البخاري)

Narrated Ibn Masud: I heard the Prophet (peace be upon him) say, "There is no envy except in two: a person whom Allah has given wealth and he spends it in the right way, and a person whom Allah has given wisdom and he gives his decisions accordingly and teaches it to the others." (Bukhari - Sahih)

لَقَدْ خَلَقْنَا ٱلْإِنسَـٰنَ فِىٓ أَحْسَنِ تَقْوِيمٍ ۝ ثُمَّ رَدَدْنَـٰهُ أَسْفَلَ سَـٰفِلِينَ ۝ إِلَّا ٱلَّذِينَ ءَامَنُوا۟ وَعَمِلُوا۟ ٱلصَّـٰلِحَـٰتِ فَلَهُمْ أَجْرٌ غَيْرُ مَمْنُونٍ ۝ (القرآن ٩٥: ٤-٦)

We have certainly created man in the best of forms; then We return him to the lowest of the low, except for those who believe and do righteous deeds, for they will have a reward uninterrupted. (Quran 95:4-6)

وَقُل رَّبِّ زِدْنِى عِلْمًا ۝ (القرآن ٢٠:١١٤)

And say, "My Lord, increase me in knowledge." (Quran 20:114)

وَوَصَّىٰ بِهَآ إِبْرَٰهِـۧمُ بَنِيهِ وَيَعْقُوبُ يَـٰبَنِىَّ إِنَّ ٱللَّهَ ٱصْطَفَىٰ لَكُمُ ٱلدِّينَ فَلَا تَمُوتُنَّ إِلَّا وَأَنتُم مُّسْلِمُونَ ۝ (القرآن ٢:١٣٢)

And Ibrahim instructed his sons and so did Yakub, "O my sons, indeed Allah has chosen for you this religion, so do not die except while you are Muslims." (Quran 2:132)

عَنْ أَنَسِ بْنِ مَالِكٍ، قَالَ قَالَ رَسُولُ اللَّهِ ـ صلى الله عليه وسلم ـ "يَخْرُجُ قَوْمٌ فِي آخِرِ الزَّمَانِ ـ أَوْ فِي هَذِهِ الأُمَّةِ ـ يَقْرَءُونَ الْقُرْآنَ لاَ يُجَاوِزُ تَرَاقِيَهُمْ" (رواه ابن ماجه – صحيح)

Narrated Anas bin Malik: The Messenger of Allah said (peace be upon him): "At the end of time or among this nation (Ummah) there will appear people who will recite the Quran but it will not go any deeper than their collarbones or their throats." (Ibn Majah - Sahih)

وَلَقَدْ ذَرَأْنَا لِجَهَنَّمَ كَثِيرًا مِّنَ ٱلْجِنِّ وَٱلْإِنسِ ۖ لَهُمْ قُلُوبٌ لَّا يَفْقَهُونَ بِهَا وَلَهُمْ أَعْيُنٌ لَّا يُبْصِرُونَ بِهَا وَلَهُمْ ءَاذَانٌ لَّا يَسْمَعُونَ بِهَا ۚ أُوْلَٰٓئِكَ كَٱلْأَنْعَٰمِ بَلْ هُمْ أَضَلُّ ۚ أُوْلَٰٓئِكَ هُمُ ٱلْغَٰفِلُونَ ۝ (القرآن ٧:١٧٩)

And We have certainly created for Hell many of the jinn and mankind. They have hearts with which they do not understand, they have eyes with which they do not see, and they have ears with which they do not hear. Those are like livestock; rather, they are more astray. It is they who are the heedless. (Quran 7:179)

A Classical Approach To Tarbiyah

One day Shaqiq al-Balkhi asked his student Hatim al-Asamm, "How long have you kept my company?" "Thirty-three years," he replied.

"And what have you learned from me in all this time?"

"Eight things," he said.

"**We belong to Allah and we return to him**!" (Quran 2:156) exclaimed Shaqiq. "You have spent your whole life with me and only learned eight things! What are they?"

"Firstly," replied Hatim, "I looked at mankind and I saw that everyone loves something and continues to do so. However, when he goes to his grave, whatever he loved leaves him behind. Therefore I made my good deeds beloved to me, so that when I enter the grave they will enter it along with me."

"You have done well," said Shaqiq. "What is the second?"

The second is that I examined the words of the Almighty, **'But as for him who feared the Station of his Lord and forbade his soul its desires, the Garden shall be his destination**.' (Quran 79:40-41) Knowing that the words of the Almighty are true, I struggled to control my desires until I was firm in the sight of Allah Almighty.

The third is that I looked at people and saw that everyone has something of worth which they value and protect. Then I looked at the words of the Almighty, **'What is with you comes to an end. But what is with Allah is everlasting**.' (Quran 16:96) Therefore whenever something of value comes to me, I send it to Allah Almighty so that it may remain with Him for me.

The fourth is that I looked at Allah's creatures and saw that all of them set much store by property, reputation, honor, and lineage. I examined those things and found them to be nothing. Then I looked at the words of the Almighty, **'The noblest among you in Allah's sight is the one most aware of God among you.'** (Quran 49:13) Therefore I decided to value the awareness of Allah so that I might be noble in His sight.

The fifth is that I looked at people and I found that some of them attacked others and some of them cursed others; and I realized that the reason they did that was envy. Then I looked at the words of the Almighty, **'We have allotted among them their livelihood in the life of this world**.' (Quran 43:32) Therefore I abandoned envy and enmity towards created beings, knowing that what is allotted to me will and must reach me.

The sixth is that I saw that people fought and were hostile to one another. I looked for my true enemy and found it to be Shaytan and indeed Allah Almighty says, **'Shaytan is an enemy to you, so treat him as an enemy**.' (Quran 35:6) Thus I made Shaytan my enemy and loved everyone else.

The seventh is that I looked at mankind and found them seeking excessive wealth and humiliating themselves because of it. I looked at the words of the Almighty, **'There is no creature on the earth whose provision is not with Allah alone**.' (Quran 11:6) I realized that I am one of those who are provided for and so I busied myself with Allah Almighty and abandoned everything else besides Him.

The eighth is that I looked at people and I saw that they relied on different things: one on his commerce, another on his profession, and yet another on his health. Every creature was relying on another creature! I looked at the words of the

Almighty, **'And whoever puts his trust in Allah, He is enough for him**.' (Quran 65:3) Therefore I put my trust in Allah Almighty.

"Hatim, Allah has given you success, and you have left nothing out. He gives wisdom to whomever He wishes.'" said Shaqiq.

Source: *Mukhtasar Minhaj Alqasidin* (Path of the Seekers - Abridged)

Diversity (تَنَوُّع)

People were created by Allah the Exalted with similarities and differences. This wonderful diversity enriches our community. All people are honored by Allah the Exalted. We believe that there is intrinsic value in every person.

We do not only tolerate, but rather appreciate and value diversity. Unity becomes all the more important and beautiful in the light of the wide ranges of difference in social status, gender, age, personality, culture, race, talent and perspective.

وَلَقَدْ كَرَّمْنَا بَنِي ءَادَمَ (القرآن ١٧:٧٠)

We have certainly honored the children of Adam. (Quran 17:70)

يَٰٓأَيُّهَا ٱلنَّاسُ إِنَّا خَلَقْنَٰكُم مِّن ذَكَرٍ وَأُنثَىٰ وَجَعَلْنَٰكُمْ شُعُوبًا وَقَبَآئِلَ لِتَعَارَفُوٓا۟ إِنَّ أَكْرَمَكُمْ عِندَ ٱللَّهِ أَتْقَىٰكُمْ (القرآن ٤٩:١٣)

O humanity, indeed We created you from male and female and made you into peoples and tribes so that you may know one another. Indeed the most honorable among you in with Allah is the most God-conscious. (Quran 49:13)

وَمِنْ ءَايَٰتِهِۦ خَلْقُ ٱلسَّمَٰوَٰتِ وَٱلْأَرْضِ وَٱخْتِلَٰفُ أَلْسِنَتِكُمْ وَأَلْوَٰنِكُمْ ۚ إِنَّ فِى ذَٰلِكَ لَءَايَٰتٍ لِّلْعَٰلِمِينَ ۝ (القرآن ٣٠:٢٢)

And of His signs is the creation of the heavens and the earth and the diversity of your languages and your colors. Indeed in that are signs for those of knowledge. (Quran 30:22)

لَا يَسْخَرْ قَوْمٌ مِّن قَوْمٍ عَسَىٰٓ أَن يَكُونُوا۟ خَيْرًا مِّنْهُمْ وَلَا نِسَآءٌ مِّن نِّسَآءٍ عَسَىٰٓ أَن يَكُنَّ خَيْرًا مِّنْهُنَّ ۖ وَلَا تَلْمِزُوٓا۟ أَنفُسَكُمْ وَلَا تَنَابَزُوا۟ بِٱلْأَلْقَٰبِ ۖ (القرآن ٤٩:١١)

Let not a people ridicule another people; perhaps they may be better than them; nor let some women ridicule other women; perhaps they may be better than them. And do not insult one another and do not call each other by offensive nicknames. (Quran 49:11)

وَلَوْ شَآءَ ٱللَّهُ لَجَعَلَكُمْ أُمَّةً وَٰحِدَةً وَلَٰكِن لِّيَبْلُوَكُمْ فِى مَآ ءَاتَىٰكُمْ ۖ فَٱسْتَبِقُوا۟ ٱلْخَيْرَٰتِ ۚ إِلَى ٱللَّهِ مَرْجِعُكُمْ جَمِيعًا فَيُنَبِّئُكُم بِمَا كُنتُمْ فِيهِ تَخْتَلِفُونَ ۝ (القرآن ٥:٤٨)

Had Allah willed, He would have made you one community, instead He tests you in what He has given you; so compete in good deeds. To Allah is your return all together, and He will inform you concerning that over which you used to differ. (Quran 5:48)

أَلَمْ تَرَ أَنَّ ٱللَّهَ أَنزَلَ مِنَ ٱلسَّمَآءِ مَآءً فَأَخْرَجْنَا بِهِۦ ثَمَرَٰتٍ مُّخْتَلِفًا أَلْوَٰنُهَا ۚ وَمِنَ ٱلْجِبَالِ جُدَدٌۢ بِيضٌ وَحُمْرٌ مُّخْتَلِفٌ أَلْوَٰنُهَا وَغَرَابِيبُ سُودٌ ۝ وَمِنَ ٱلنَّاسِ وَٱلدَّوَآبِّ وَٱلْأَنْعَٰمِ مُخْتَلِفٌ أَلْوَٰنُهُۥ كَذَٰلِكَ ۗ إِنَّمَا يَخْشَى ٱللَّهَ مِنْ عِبَادِهِ ٱلْعُلَمَٰٓؤُاْ ۗ إِنَّ ٱللَّهَ عَزِيزٌ غَفُورٌ ۝ (القرآن ٣٥: ٢٧-٢٨)

Do you not see that Allah sends down rain from the sky? With it We then bring out produce of various colors. And in the mountains are tracts white and red, of various shades of color, and black intense in hue. And also among people and crawling creatures and cattle, they are of various colors. Only they truly fear Allah, among His Servants, who have knowledge, for Allah is Exalted in Might, Oft-Forgiving. (Quran 35:27-28)

Commitment (إِلْتِزَام)

Great goals require great effort. Success in this world and the next world requires steadfastness of purpose, discipline, compliance and perseverance. The road is long and challenging, it is the way of the Messengers and those who follow them, it is the path of excellence, Ihsaan, which is most pleasing to Allah the Exalted.

يَٰٓأَيُّهَا ٱلَّذِينَ ءَامَنُواْ ٱسْتَجِيبُواْ لِلَّهِ وَلِلرَّسُولِ إِذَا دَعَاكُمْ لِمَا يُحْيِيكُمْ (القرآن ٨:٢٤)

O believers, respond to Allah and to the Messenger when he calls you to that which gives you life. (Quran 8:24)

عَنْ سُفْيَانَ بْنِ عَبْدِ اللهِ الثَّقَفِيِّ، قَالَ قُلْتُ يَا رَسُولَ اللهِ قُلْ لِي فِي الإِسْلَامِ قَوْلاً لاَ أَسْأَلُ عَنْهُ أَحَدًا بَعْدَكَ - وَفِي حَدِيثِ أَبِي أُسَامَةَ غَيْرَكَ - قَالَ "قُلْ آمَنْتُ بِاللهِ فَاسْتَقِمْ" (صحيح مسلم)

Narrated Sufyan bin Abdulla al-Thaqafi: I asked the Messenger of Allah (peace be upon him) to tell me about Islam a thing which might dispense with the necessity of my asking anybody after you. He (peace be upon him) said: "Say I affirm my faith in Allah and then remain steadfast to it." (Muslim - Sahih)

ٱلَّذِينَ ٱسْتَجَابُواْ لِلَّهِ وَٱلرَّسُولِ مِنۢ بَعْدِ مَآ أَصَابَهُمُ ٱلْقَرْحُ ۚ لِلَّذِينَ أَحْسَنُواْ مِنْهُمْ وَٱتَّقَوْاْ أَجْرٌ عَظِيمٌ ۝ (القرآن ٣:١٧٢)

Those who responded to Allah and the Messenger after injury had struck them. For those who did good among them and feared Allah is a great reward. (Quran 3:172)

$$\text{لِلَّذِينَ ٱسْتَجَابُوا۟ لِرَبِّهِمُ ٱلْحُسْنَىٰ ۚ وَٱلَّذِينَ لَمْ يَسْتَجِيبُوا۟ لَهُۥ لَوْ أَنَّ لَهُم مَّا فِى ٱلْأَرْضِ جَمِيعًا وَمِثْلَهُۥ مَعَهُۥ لَٱفْتَدَوْا۟ بِهِۦٓ ۚ أُو۟لَـٰٓئِكَ لَهُمْ سُوٓءُ ٱلْحِسَابِ وَمَأْوَىٰهُمْ جَهَنَّمُ ۖ وَبِئْسَ ٱلْمِهَادُ (القرآن ١٣:١٨)}$$

For those who have responded to their Lord is the best [reward], but those who did not respond to Him - if they had all that is in the earth entirely and the like of it with it, they would [attempt to] ransom themselves thereby. Those will have the worst account, and their refuge is Hell, and wretched is the destination. (Quran 13:18)

$$\text{عَنْ أَبِي ثَعْلَبَةَ الْخُشَنِيِّ قَالَ قَالَ رَسُولُ اللهِ ـ صلى الله عليه وسلم "فَإِنَّ مِنْ وَرَائِكُمْ أَيَّامَ الصَّبْرِ، الصَّبْرُ فِيهِنَّ مِثْلُ قَبْضٍ عَلَى الْجَمْرِ لِلْعَامِلِ فِيهِنَّ مِثْلُ أَجْرِ خَمْسِينَ رَجُلاً يَعْمَلُونَ بِمِثْلِ عَمَلِهِ" (رواه ابن ماجه – حسن)}$$

Abu Thalabah Al-Khushani narrated: The Messenger of Allah (peace be upon him) said: "After you will come days of patience, during which patience will be like grasping a burning ember, and one who does good deeds will have a reward like that of fifty men doing the same deed." (Ibn Majah - Hasan)

$$\text{مِّنَ ٱلْمُؤْمِنِينَ رِجَالٌ صَدَقُوا۟ مَا عَـٰهَدُوا۟ ٱللَّهَ عَلَيْهِ ۖ فَمِنْهُم مَّن قَضَىٰ نَحْبَهُۥ وَمِنْهُم مَّن يَنتَظِرُ ۖ وَمَا بَدَّلُوا۟ تَبْدِيلًا (القرآن ٣٣:٢٣)}$$

Among the believers are men true to what they promised Allah. Among them is he who has fulfilled his vow, and among them is he who remains waiting. And they did not alter their commitment in the least. (Quran 33:23)

$$\text{لِّكَيْلَا تَأْسَوْا۟ عَلَىٰ مَا فَاتَكُمْ وَلَا تَفْرَحُوا۟ بِمَآ ءَاتَىٰكُمْ ۗ (القرآن ٥٧:٢٣)}$$

In order that you not despair over what has eluded you and not exult [in pride] over what He has given you. (Quran 57:23)

Dimensions Of Commitment

The Messenger of Allah (peace be upon him) took an oath of commitment (Bayah) from his companions. The committed Muslim takes an oath pledging allegiance to work continuously for the pleasure of Allah the Exalted.

Scholars of Tarbiyah and Tazkiyah have identified ten dimensions of commitment for this pledge, namely: Understanding, Sincerity, Activism, Struggle, Sacrifice, Obedience, Perseverance, Steadfastness, Fraternity & Confidence in the leadership.

لَقَدْ رَضِيَ ٱللَّهُ عَنِ ٱلْمُؤْمِنِينَ إِذْ يُبَايِعُونَكَ تَحْتَ ٱلشَّجَرَةِ فَعَلِمَ مَا فِي قُلُوبِهِمْ فَأَنزَلَ ٱلسَّكِينَةَ عَلَيْهِمْ وَأَثَٰبَهُمْ فَتْحًا قَرِيبًا ۝ (القرآن ٤٨:١٨)

Certainly Allah was pleased with the believers when they pledged allegiance to you, under the tree, and He knew what was in their hearts, so He sent down tranquility upon them and rewarded them with an imminent victory. (Quran 48:18)

عَنِ ابْنِ عُمَرَ قَالَ: سمعت رسول الله صلى الله عليه وسلم يقول "من خلع يداً من طاعةٍ لقي الله يوم القيامة ولا حجة له، ومن مات وليس في عنقه بيعة مات مِيتةً جاهليةً" (صحيح مسلم)

Ibn Umar reported: The Messenger of Allah (peace be upon him) said, "One who withdraws his hand from obedience will find no argument (in his defense) when he stands before Allah on the Day of Resurrection; and one who dies without having sworn allegiance will die the death of one belonging to the Days of Ignorance." (Muslim - Sahih)

Understanding (فَهْم)

Classical Islamic scholars held that the first obligation the servant owes to his Lord, the Exalted, is to acquire knowledge of his Creator.

The knowledge of what to believe is called Akidah (creed). The root word is "knot". In Islam, we call our creed Akidah because it is strongly tied to our hearts. Akidah are things that must be believed in our hearts, without the slightest hesitation, that bring tranquility to our soul.

By definition humans have no knowledge of the unseen. Mere intellectual excercises cannot reliably lead us to what we must believe about our Lord the Exalted. Thus, everything in the science of Akidah is based entirely upon Divine revelation (wahy).

وَكَذَٰلِكَ أَوْحَيْنَآ إِلَيْكَ رُوحًا مِّنْ أَمْرِنَا ۚ مَا كُنتَ تَدْرِى مَا ٱلْكِتَـٰبُ وَلَا ٱلْإِيمَـٰنُ وَلَـٰكِن جَعَلْنَـٰهُ نُورًا نَّهْدِى بِهِۦ مَن نَّشَآءُ مِنْ عِبَادِنَا ۚ وَإِنَّكَ لَتَهْدِىٓ إِلَىٰ صِرَٰطٍ مُّسْتَقِيمٍ ۝ (القرآن ٤٢:٥٢)

And thus We have revealed to you an inspiration of Our command. You did not know what is the book or what is faith, but We have made it a light by which We guide whom We will of Our servants. And indeed, you guide to a straight path. (Quran 42:52)

وعن معاوية رضي الله عنه قال: قال رسول الله صلى الله عليه وسلم: "من يرد الله به خيرًا يفقّهه في الدين" (متفق عليه)

Muawiyah reported: The Messenger of Allah (peace be upon him) said, "When Allah wishes good for someone, He bestows upon him the understanding of Deen." (Bukhari, Muslim - Sahih)

إِنَّا أَنزَلْنَـٰهُ قُرْءَٰنًا عَرَبِيًّا لَّعَلَّكُمْ تَعْقِلُونَ ۝ (القرآن ١٢:٢)

We have sent it down as an Arabic Quran, in order that you may gain understanding. (Quran 12:2)

عَنْ أَبِي هُرَيْرَةَ، قَالَ كَانَ مِنْ دُعَاءِ النَّبِيِّ ـ صلى الله عليه وسلم ـ "اللَّهُمَّ إِنِّي أَعُوذُ بِكَ مِنْ عِلْمٍ لاَ يَنْفَعُ وَمِنْ دُعَاءٍ لاَ يُسْمَعُ وَمِنْ قَلْبٍ لاَ يَخْشَعُ وَمِنْ نَفْسٍ لاَ تَشْبَعُ" (رواه ابن ماجه)

Abu Hurairah said: One of the supplications that the Prophet (peace be upon him) used to say was: "O Allah, I seek refuge with You from knowledge that is of no benefit, from a supplication that is not heard, from a heart that does not fear (You) and from a soul that is not satisfied." (Ibn Majah - Sahih)

وَلَقَدْ أُوحِىَ إِلَيْكَ وَإِلَى ٱلَّذِينَ مِن قَبْلِكَ لَئِنْ أَشْرَكْتَ لَيَحْبَطَنَّ عَمَلُكَ وَلَتَكُونَنَّ مِنَ ٱلْخَـٰسِرِينَ ۝ (القرآن ٣٩:٦٥)

And it was already revealed to you and to those before you that if you should associate [partners] with Allah, your work would surely become worthless, and you would surely be among the losers." (Quran 39:65)

مَّثَلُ ٱلَّذِينَ كَفَرُوا۟ بِرَبِّهِمْ ۖ أَعْمَٰلُهُمْ كَرَمَادٍ ٱشْتَدَّتْ بِهِ ٱلرِّيحُ فِى يَوْمٍ عَاصِفٍ ۖ لَّا يَقْدِرُونَ مِمَّا كَسَبُوا۟ عَلَىٰ شَىْءٍ ۚ ذَٰلِكَ هُوَ ٱلضَّلَٰلُ ٱلْبَعِيدُ ﴿١٨﴾
(القرآن ١٤:١٨)

The example of those who disbelieve in their Lord is their deeds are like ashes which the wind blows forcefully on a stormy day; they are unable [to keep] from what they earned anything. That is extreme error. (Quran 14:18)

The Twenty Principles of Understanding

Many voluminous encyclopedias have been written on the topic of Akidah. They delve into finer points and technicalities and are written by specialists in this topic. Most of them are difficult for the average Muslim to benefit from.

One of the earliest books on Akidah from the Ahl al Sunnah wal Jamaah (Sunni Scholars) is called Al Fiqh Al Akbar which is attributed to Imam Abu Haneefah. Imam Ibn Qudaamah, Imam Ibn Taymiyah, Imam Ibn al-Qayyim and Imam adh-Dhahabi have quoted extensively from this book in their works.

By most accounts, the most famous book on Akidah is popularly called Akidah al Tahawiyyah which was compiled by Imam Abu Jafar Ahmad at-Tahawi. Over 500 different commentaries of this work have been produced by Islamic scholars.

Of all the works on Akidah, the easiest to understand for the average Muslim is perhaps to be found in the Twenty Principles of Understanding in the Majmuat al Rasail. In addition to being easy to understand, it serves as a guideline for Muslims on how to deal with significant current issues from the Akidah perspective. The twenty principles of proper understanding of Islam are presented below:

1. Islam is a comprehensive system that deals with all spheres of life. It is a government and an ummah. It is mercy and justice. It is a culture and jurisprudence. It is gain and prosperity. It is struggle and a call. And finally, it is true belief and worship.

2. The glorious Quran and the purified tradition (Sunnah) of the Prophet (peace be upon him) are the references of every Muslim for the realization of the rules of Islam. The Quran can be understood according to the principles of the Arabic language without affectation or controversy, and the Sunnah can be acquired by reference to the trustworthy transmitters of Hadith.

3. True belief, proper worship, and striving in the path of Allah have light and warmth that Allah casts in the hearts of whomever He chooses from among His servants. But inspirations, notions, revelations, and visions are not authentic references for Islamic Law, and therefore should not be given any consideration except when they do not conflict with the authentic references and established principles of Islam.

4. Talismans, incantations, geomancy, gnosis, fortune telling, claiming knowledge of the unseen, and similar practices are all detested atrocities that must be actively opposed, except what is mentioned in the Quran or transmitted to us as an authentic incantation of the Prophet (peace be upon him).

5. The opinion of the leadership or their deputies are acceptable in matters which are of proven benefit to the public, provided that his opinion does not conflict with any established principle of Islam. In this regard, the opinion of the leader is allowed to marginally differ from similar preceding rulings by virtue of changing circumstances, customs, and conventions of the society.

6. The opinion of everyone except the infallible Prophet (peace be upon him), is liable to changes and modifications. All that has reached us of the opinions

and rulings of the righteous early Muslims is acceptable to us as long as it is in agreement with the Quran and the Sunnah. In case of disagreement, the Book of Allah and the practice of His Apostle are more deserving of our adherence. However, we do not criticize or attack any of those individuals who were in disagreement, since we do not know what their intentions were nor the circumstances that necessitated their decision.

7. Every Muslim who reaches the level of understanding the arguments of legal deduction and jurisprudence is encouraged to investigate the works of the four great Imams of Islamic jurisprudence and see which of them attracts him most. With the help of the arguments of that Imam and the proven opinions of trustworthy workers of his own age, he should be able to increase his knowledge of Islamic Law and find the Islamic solutions to the contemporary problems of his society. Those Muslims who are unable to do so are advised to exert the necessary efforts to acquire such a level of understanding.

8. Differences in opinion regarding secondary matters should not be allowed to cause division, contention, or hatred within the ranks of the Muslims. To every seeker of knowledge is a reward. In cases of disagreement, however, there is no harm in objective scientific investigation in an atmosphere of love for the sake of Allah and cooperation with the aim of realizing the truth. Fanaticism, obstinacy, and controversy have no place among true Muslims.

9. Wasting time and effort in investigating trivial matters that will not lead to action is prohibited in Islam. This category includes debating minute aspects of rulings in cases which have never occurred, investigating the meaning of the Quranic verses which are still beyond

the scope of human knowledge (the allegorical verses), and differentiating between the companions of the Prophet (peace be upon him) or investigating the instances of disagreement that took place among them. Every companion, may Allah be pleased with them all, has the honor and distinction of being a companion of the Messenger of Allah (peace be upon him), and to each is the recompense of his motives.

10. Recognizing the existence of Allah the Exalted, believing in His oneness, and glorifying Him are the most sublime beliefs of Islam. We believe in the Quranic verses and authentic traditions of the Prophet (peace be upon him) which describe the exalted attributes of Allah and glorify His name. We also believe in the allegorical (mutashabihat) Quranic verses, which serve this same purpose, without rejecting any part of them or attempting to interpret them on our own. We stand aloof from the disagreement which exists among the scholars concerning these verses; we are satisfied with adopting the attitude of the Prophet (peace be upon him) and his companions: "**And those who are established in knowledge say: We believe in the Book; the whole of it is from our Lord.**" (Quran 3:7)

11. Every innovation introduced by the people into the religion of Allah on the grounds of their whims and without authentic foundation, whether by adding to the principles of Islam or taking from them, is considered a serious deviation from the path of truth and must therefore be opposed vigorously and abolished by the best means which do not lead to worse deviations.

12. There is a difference of opinion regarding innovations which do not contradict established Islamic principles, such as praising Imams and religious figures with

pronouncements of their credibility and binding people to acts of worship left open to one's choice. We adopt what can be confirmed by sound evidence.

13. Love of pious people, respecting them, and honoring their righteous achievements brings one closer to Allah the Exalted. However, one should not extend this to other than the favorites of Allah who are described in the Quranic verse: "those who believed and were fearful of Allah". Honor and prestige are due to them with the conditions prescribed in the Islamic Law, but we must firmly believe that they (may Allah be pleased with them) had no power over their own fates and, thereby, cannot avail or harm anyone after their death.

14. Visiting grave sites and cemeteries is an authentic Sunnah if done in the manner prescribed by the Prophet (peace be upon him). But seeking the help of the dead, whomever they may be, appealing to them, asking them to fulfill certain requests, vowing to them, and swearing with their names instead of the name of Allah are all gross atrocities that must be fought, no matter what the excuses are. Building high tombs, covering them with curtains, illuminating them, and throwing one's body on them are evil innovations that are equally prohibited.

15. There is a difference of opinion regarding the use of the names of the favorites of Allah in supplication. However, this is a matter of secondary importance and does not pertain to the fundamentals of the Islamic beliefs.

16. Erroneous practices of the people should be restrained irrespective of the names or titles under which they may be disguised. If something contradicts an Islamic principle in its essence, it should be opposed without

regard to what people call it. In Islam, consideration is given to the significance and meaning of names and not to the names themselves.

17. Belief is the basis of action. Sincere intentions are more important than good actions with bad or no intentions. However, the Muslim is urged to attain improvement in both spheres: purification of the heart and performance of righteous deeds.

18. Islam liberates the mind, urges contemplation of the universe, honors science and scientists, and welcomes all that is good and beneficial to mankind: *"Wisdom is the lost wealth of the believer. Wherever he finds it, he is more deserving to it."*

19. Islamic principles may be evident or uncertain, as are pure scientific principles. The evident principles of the two classes will never conflict; that is, it is impossible for an established scientific fact to contradict an authentic Islamic principle. However, this may happen if one or both of them are uncertain. If one of them is uncertain, then it should be reinterpreted so as to remove the contradiction. If both are uncertain, then the uncertain Islamic principle should be given precedence over the uncertain scientific notion until the latter is proven.

20. Never label as an unbeliever (kafir) any Muslim who has adopted the two declarations (shahadah) of faith, acts accordingly and performs the obligatory (fard) duties of Islam unless he clearly professes the word of unbelief, refuses to acknowledge a fundamental principle of Islam, rejects the verses of the Quran, or commits an evident act of unbelief.

Source: *Majmuat Ar Rasail* (The Compiled Letters)

Sincerity (إِخْلَاص)

Soundness of heart is the ultimate standard. All human endeavor boils down to this accomplishment. Cultivating sincerity was the main preoccupation of the noble companions. Their great accomplishments were merely byproducts of their sincerity.

قُلْ إِنَّ صَلَاتِي وَنُسُكِي وَمَحْيَايَ وَمَمَاتِي لِلَّهِ رَبِّ ٱلْعَالَمِينَ ۝ لَا شَرِيكَ لَهُ وَبِذَٰلِكَ أُمِرْتُ وَأَنَا۠ أَوَّلُ ٱلْمُسْلِمِينَ ۝ (القرآن ٦: ١٦٢-١٦٣)

Say. Surely my prayers and my sacrifices and my life and my death are all for Allah, the Lord of the worlds; He has no associate; and this am I commanded, and I am the first of those who submit. (Quran 6:162-163)

عَنْ النُّعْمَانَ بْنَ بَشِيرٍ، يَقُولُ سَمِعْتُ رَسُولَ اللَّهِ صلى الله عليه وسلم يَقُولُ "أَلاَ وَإِنَّ فِي الْجَسَدِ مُضْغَةً إِذَا صَلَحَتْ صَلَحَ الْجَسَدُ كُلُّهُ، وَإِذَا فَسَدَتْ فَسَدَ الْجَسَدُ كُلُّهُ. أَلاَ وَهِيَ الْقَلْبُ" (متفق عليه)

Narrated An-Numan bin Bashir: I heard the Messenger of Allah (peace be upon him) saying: "Indeed in the body is a piece of flesh, If it is correct the entire body will be correct, and if it is corrupt the entire body will be corrupt, listen! This is the heart." (Bukhari, Muslim - Sahih)

فَاعْبُدِ ٱللَّهَ مُخْلِصًا لَّهُ ٱلدِّينَ ۝ أَلَا لِلَّهِ ٱلدِّينُ ٱلْخَالِصُ (القرآن ٣٩: ٢-٣)

Therefore worship Allah, sincerely to Him. Indeed to Allah alone is the sincere religion. (Quran 39:2-3)

قُلْ إِن تُخْفُوا۟ مَا فِي صُدُورِكُمْ أَوْ تُبْدُوهُ يَعْلَمْهُ ٱللَّهُ (القرآن ٣:٢٩)

Say, "Whether you conceal what is in your breasts or reveal it, Allah knows it." (Quran 3:29)

$$\text{وَمَا أُمِرُوا إِلَّا لِيَعْبُدُوا اللَّهَ مُخْلِصِينَ لَهُ الدِّينَ حُنَفَاءَ وَيُقِيمُوا الصَّلَاةَ وَيُؤْتُوا الزَّكَاةَ ۚ وَذَٰلِكَ دِينُ الْقَيِّمَةِ ۝ (القرآن ٩٨: ٥)}$$

And they were not commanded anything except that they should serve Allah, being sincere to Him in obedience, upright, and establish the prayer and pay the charity, and that is the right religion. (Quran 98:5)

$$\text{عَنْ أَبِي هُرَيْرَةَ، قَالَ قَالَ رَسُولُ اللَّهِ صلى الله عليه وسلم "إِنَّ اللَّهَ لاَ يَنْظُرُ إِلَى صُوَرِكُمْ وَأَمْوَالِكُمْ وَلَكِنْ يَنْظُرُ إِلَى قُلُوبِكُمْ وَأَعْمَالِكُمْ" (صحيح مسلم)}$$

Abu Huraira reported: The Messenger of Allah (peace be upon him) as saying: "Indeed, Allah does not look at your appearance or wealth, but rather he looks at your hearts and actions." (Muslim - Sahih)

$$\text{يَا أَيُّهَا الَّذِينَ آمَنُوا لِمَ تَقُولُونَ مَا لَا تَفْعَلُونَ ۝ كَبُرَ مَقْتًا عِنْدَ اللَّهِ أَنْ تَقُولُوا مَا لَا تَفْعَلُونَ ۝ (القرآن ٦١: ٣)}$$

O believers, why do you say what you do not do? It is most hateful in the sight of Allah that you say what you do not do. (Quran 61:2-3)

$$\text{قُلِ اللَّهَ أَعْبُدُ مُخْلِصًا لَهُ (القرآن ٣٩: ١٤)}$$

Say: Allah I serve, sincerely in submission. (Quran 39:14)

$$\text{فَوَيْلٌ لِلْمُصَلِّينَ ۝ الَّذِينَ هُمْ عَن صَلَاتِهِمْ سَاهُونَ ۝ الَّذِينَ هُمْ يُرَاءُونَ ۝ (القرآن ١٠٧: ٤-٦)}$$

So woe to those who pray. But are heedless of their prayer. Those who make show (of their deeds). (Quran 107:4-6)

Activism (عَمَل)

Our faith is dynamic, not static. Good deeds help bring our faith to life. They include ritual acts of worship such as prayer and fasting. They also include generic good deeds such as feeding poor people and helping the homeless. All these are acts of worship for a Muslim.

وَبَشِّرِ ٱلَّذِينَ ءَامَنُواْ وَعَمِلُواْ ٱلصَّٰلِحَٰتِ أَنَّ لَهُمْ جَنَّٰتٍ تَجْرِى مِن تَحْتِهَا ٱلْأَنْهَٰرُ (القرآن ٢:٢٥)

And give good tidings to those who believe and do righteous deeds that they will have gardens beneath which rivers flow. (Quran 2:25)

عَنْ أَبِي هُرَيْرَةَ، أَنَّ رَسُولَ اللَّهِ صلى الله عليه وسلم قَالَ "بَادِرُوا بِالْأَعْمَالِ" (صحيح مسلم)

Narrated Abu Huraira: The Messenger of Allah (peace be upon him) said: "Be prompt in doing good deeds." (Muslim – Sahih)

وَعَدَ ٱللَّهُ ٱلَّذِينَ ءَامَنُواْ وَعَمِلُواْ ٱلصَّٰلِحَٰتِ ۙ لَهُم مَّغْفِرَةٌ وَأَجْرٌ عَظِيمٌ (القرآن ٥:٩)

Allah has promised those who believe and do righteous deeds that for them there is forgiveness and great reward. (Quran 5:9)

عَنْ أَبِي هُرَيْرَةَ قَالَ قَالَ رَسُولُ اللَّهِ ـ صلى الله عليه وسلم ـ : "اكْلَفُوا مِنَ الْعَمَلِ مَا تُطِيقُونَ فَإِنَّ خَيْرَ الْعَمَلِ أَدْوَمُهُ وَإِنْ قَلَّ" (رواه ابن ماجه – صحيح)

Abu Hurairah narrated: The Messenger of Allah (peace be upon him) said: "Take on only as much as you can do of good deeds, for the best of deeds is that which is done consistently, even if it is little." (Ibn Majah – Sahih)

وَٱلَّذِينَ ءَامَنُوا۟ وَعَمِلُوا۟ ٱلصَّٰلِحَٰتِ لَنُكَفِّرَنَّ عَنْهُمْ سَيِّـَٔاتِهِمْ وَلَنَجْزِيَنَّهُمْ أَحْسَنَ ٱلَّذِى كَانُوا۟ يَعْمَلُونَ ۩ (القرآن ٧:٢٩)

And those who believe and do righteous deeds, We will surely remove from them their misdeeds and will surely reward them according to the best of what they used to do. (Quran 29:7)

عَنْ أَبِي ذَرٍّ، قَالَ قَالَ لِي رَسُولُ اللَّهِ صلى الله عليه وسلم "اتَّقِ اللَّهَ حَيْثُمَا كُنْتَ وَأَتْبِعِ السَّيِّئَةَ الْحَسَنَةَ تَمْحُهَا وَخَالِقِ النَّاسَ بِخُلُقٍ حَسَنٍ" (رواه الترمذي – حسن)

Abu Dharr naratted: The Messenger of Allah (peace be upon him) said to me: "Be mindful of Allah wherever you are, and follow an evil deed with a good one to wipe it out, and treat the people with good behavior." (Tirmidhi - Hasan)

إِنَّ ٱلَّذِينَ ءَامَنُوا۟ وَعَمِلُوا۟ ٱلصَّٰلِحَٰتِ سَيَجْعَلُ لَهُمُ ٱلرَّحْمَٰنُ وُدًّا ۩ (القرآن ١٩:٩٦)

Indeed, those who have believed and done righteous deeds - the Most Merciful will appoint for them affection. (Quran 19:96)

عَنْ أَبِي هُرَيْرَةَ، عَنْ رَسُولِ اللَّهِ صلى الله عليه وسلم قَالَ "قَالَ اللَّهُ عَزَّ وَجَلَّ إِذَا هَمَّ عَبْدِي بِحَسَنَةٍ وَلَمْ يَعْمَلْهَا كَتَبْتُهَا لَهُ حَسَنَةً فَإِنْ عَمِلَهَا كَتَبْتُهَا عَشْرَ حَسَنَاتٍ إِلَى سَبْعِمِائَةِ ضِعْفٍ وَإِذَا هَمَّ بِسَيِّئَةٍ وَلَمْ يَعْمَلْهَا لَمْ أَكْتُبْهَا عَلَيْهِ فَإِنْ عَمِلَهَا كَتَبْتُهَا سَيِّئَةً وَاحِدَةً" (صحيح مسلم)

Narrated Abu Huraira: The Messenger of Allah (peace be upon him) said: "Allah, the Great and Glorious, said: Whenever my bondsman intends to do good, but does not do it, I write one good act for him, but if he puts it into practice I wrote from ten to seven hundred good deeds in favor of him. When he intends to commit an evil, but does not actually do it, do not record it. But if he does it, I write only one evil." (Muslim - Sahih)

لَّيْسَ ٱلْبِرَّ أَن تُوَلُّواْ وُجُوهَكُمْ قِبَلَ ٱلْمَشْرِقِ وَٱلْمَغْرِبِ وَلَٰكِنَّ ٱلْبِرَّ مَنْ ءَامَنَ بِٱللَّهِ وَٱلْيَوْمِ ٱلْأَخِرِ وَٱلْمَلَٰٓئِكَةِ وَٱلْكِتَٰبِ وَٱلنَّبِيِّۦنَ وَءَاتَى ٱلْمَالَ عَلَىٰ حُبِّهِۦ ذَوِى ٱلْقُرْبَىٰ وَٱلْيَتَٰمَىٰ وَٱلْمَسَٰكِينَ وَٱبْنَ ٱلسَّبِيلِ وَٱلسَّآئِلِينَ وَفِى ٱلرِّقَابِ وَأَقَامَ ٱلصَّلَوٰةَ وَءَاتَى ٱلزَّكَوٰةَ وَٱلْمُوفُونَ بِعَهْدِهِمْ إِذَا عَٰهَدُواْ ۖ وَٱلصَّٰبِرِينَ فِى ٱلْبَأْسَآءِ وَٱلضَّرَّآءِ وَحِينَ ٱلْبَأْسِ ۗ أُوْلَٰٓئِكَ ٱلَّذِينَ صَدَقُواْ ۖ وَأُوْلَٰٓئِكَ هُمُ ٱلْمُتَّقُونَ (القرآن ٢: ١٧٧)

Righteousness is not that you turn your faces toward the east or the west, but [true] righteousness is [in] one who believes in Allah , the Last Day, the angels, the Book, and the prophets and gives wealth, in spite of love for it, to relatives, orphans, the needy, the traveler, those who ask [for help], and for freeing slaves; [and who] establishes prayer and gives charity; fulfill their promise when they promise; and are patient in poverty and hardship and during battle. Those are the ones who have been true, and it is those who are the righteous. (Quran 2:177)

عَنْ أَبِي هُرَيْرَةَ، قَالَ قَالَ رَسُولُ اللهِ صلى الله عليه وسلم "الإِيمَانُ بِضْعٌ وَسَبْعُونَ أَوْ بِضْعٌ وَسِتُّونَ شُعْبَةً فَأَفْضَلُهَا قَوْلُ لاَ إِلَهَ إِلاَّ اللَّهُ وَأَدْنَاهَا إِمَاطَةُ الأَذَى عَنِ الطَّرِيقِ وَالْحَيَاءُ شُعْبَةٌ مِنَ الإِيمَانِ" (صحيح مسلم)

Narrated Abu Huraira: The Messenger of Allah (peace be upon him) said: "Faith has over seventy branches or over sixty branches, the most excellent of which is the declaration that there is no god but Allah, and the humblest of which is the, removal of what is injurious from the path: and modesty is the branch of faith." (Muslim - Sahih)

عَنْ عَائِشَةَ، أَنَّ رَسُولَ اللَّهِ صلى الله عليه وسلم قَالَ "سَدِّدُوا وَقَارِبُوا، وَاعْلَمُوا أَنْ لَنْ يُدْخِلَ أَحَدَكُمْ عَمَلُهُ الْجَنَّةَ، وَأَنَّ أَحَبَّ الأَعْمَالِ أَدْوَمُهَا إِلَى اللَّهِ، وَإِنْ قَلَّ" (صحيح البخاري)

Narrated Aisha: The Messenger of Allah (peace be upon him) said, "Do good deeds properly, sincerely and moderately and know that your deeds will not make you enter Paradise, and that the most beloved deed to Allah is the most regular and constant even if it were little." (Bukhari - Sahih)

Struggle (الجِهَاد)

Those who care for truth and justice have no choice but to struggle. Truth and falsehood are bound to clash. The struggle is inevitable. It stated with the creation of our father Adam (peace be upon him), and continues to this day.

We struggle against evil impulses in our soul. We exert significant effort to the deeds that please Allah the Exalted. We struggle against the evil actions we encounter. The good news is that Allah the Exalted has promised us His support in this struggle.

أَحَسِبَ ٱلنَّاسُ أَن يُتْرَكُوٓا۟ أَن يَقُولُوٓا۟ ءَامَنَّا وَهُمْ لَا يُفْتَنُونَ ۝ وَلَقَدْ فَتَنَّا ٱلَّذِينَ مِن قَبْلِهِمْ ۖ فَلَيَعْلَمَنَّ ٱللَّهُ ٱلَّذِينَ صَدَقُوا۟ وَلَيَعْلَمَنَّ ٱلْكَٰذِبِينَ ۝

(القرآن ٢٩: ٢-٣)

Do the people think that they will be left to say, "We believe" and they will not be tested? But We have certainly tried those before them, and Allah will surely make evident those who are truthful, and He will surely make evident the liars. (Quran 29:2-3)

فَلَا ٱقْتَحَمَ ٱلْعَقَبَةَ ۝ (القرآن ٩٠:١١)

He has not attempted to ascend the steep path. (Quran 90:11)

إِنَّمَا ٱلْمُؤْمِنُونَ ٱلَّذِينَ ءَامَنُوا بِٱللَّهِ وَرَسُولِهِ ثُمَّ لَمْ يَرْتَابُوا وَجَـٰهَدُوا بِأَمْوَٰلِهِمْ وَأَنفُسِهِمْ فِى سَبِيلِ ٱللَّهِ ۚ أُو۟لَـٰٓئِكَ هُمُ ٱلصَّـٰدِقُونَ ۝ (القرآن ٤٩:١٥)

The believers are only those who believe in Allah and His Messenger then they doubt not and struggle hard with their wealth and their lives in the way of Allah; they are the truthful ones. (Quran 49:15)

إِنَّ ٱللَّهَ ٱشْتَرَىٰ مِنَ ٱلْمُؤْمِنِينَ أَنفُسَهُمْ وَأَمْوَٰلَهُم بِأَنَّ لَهُمُ ٱلْجَنَّةَ ۚ يُقَـٰتِلُونَ فِى سَبِيلِ ٱللَّهِ فَيَقْتُلُونَ وَيُقْتَلُونَ ۖ وَعْدًا عَلَيْهِ حَقًّا فِى ٱلتَّوْرَىٰةِ وَٱلْإِنجِيلِ وَٱلْقُرْءَانِ ۚ وَمَنْ أَوْفَىٰ بِعَهْدِهِۦ مِنَ ٱللَّهِ ۚ فَٱسْتَبْشِرُوا بِبَيْعِكُمُ ٱلَّذِى بَايَعْتُم بِهِۦ ۚ وَذَٰلِكَ هُوَ ٱلْفَوْزُ ٱلْعَظِيمُ ۝ (القرآن ٩:١١١)

Surely Allah has purchased from the believers their persons and their property for this, that they shall have the garden; they fight in Allah's way, they slay and are slain; a promise which is binding on Him in the Taurat and the Injeel and the Quran; and who is more faithful to his covenant than Allah? Rejoice therefore in the pledge which you have made; and that is the mighty achievement. (Quran 9:111)

قَالَ فَضَالَةُ بْنُ عُبَيْدٍ سَمِعْتُ رَسُولَ اللهِ صلى الله عليه وسلم يَقُولُ "الْمُجَاهِدُ مَنْ جَاهَدَ نَفْسَهُ" (رواه الترمذي – صحيح)

Narrated Fadalah bin Ubaid: I heard the Messenger of Allah (peace be upon him) saying: "The Mujahid is one who strives against his own soul." (Tirmidhi - Sahih)

ٱنفِرُواْ خِفَافًا وَثِقَالًا وَجَٰهِدُواْ بِأَمْوَٰلِكُمْ وَأَنفُسِكُمْ فِى سَبِيلِ ٱللَّهِ ۚ ذَٰلِكُمْ خَيْرٌ لَّكُمْ إِن كُنتُمْ تَعْلَمُونَ ۝ (القرآن ٩:٤١)

Go forth light and heavy, and struggle in Allah's way with your wealth and your persons; this is better for you, if you know. (Quran 9:41)

وَٱلَّذِينَ جَٰهَدُواْ فِينَا لَنَهْدِيَنَّهُمْ سُبُلَنَا ۚ وَإِنَّ ٱللَّهَ لَمَعَ ٱلْمُحْسِنِينَ ۝ (القرآن ٢٩:٦٩)

And those who strive for Us - We will surely guide them to Our ways. And indeed, Allah is with the doers of good. (Quran 29:69)

Sacrifice (تَضْحِيَة)

Believers are happy to sacrifice for the pleasure of the Lord. An essential component of our relationship with Allah the Exalted is our willingness to sacrifice in obedience to Him. The best example of sacrifice is the example of our father Ibrahim (peace be upon him), who was willing to sacrifice his life, family and heritage for Allah the Exalted.

قُلْ إِنَّ صَلَاتِي وَنُسُكِي وَمَحْيَايَ وَمَمَاتِي لِلَّهِ رَبِّ ٱلْعَالَمِينَ ۝ (القرآن ٦:١٦٢)

Say: Surely my prayers and my sacrifices and my life and my death are all for Allah, the Lord of the worlds. (Quran 6:162)

وَٱتْلُ عَلَيْهِمْ نَبَأَ ٱبْنَىْ ءَادَمَ بِٱلْحَقِّ إِذْ قَرَّبَا قُرْبَانًا فَتُقُبِّلَ مِنْ أَحَدِهِمَا وَلَمْ يُتَقَبَّلْ مِنَ ٱلْآخَرِ (القرآن ٥:٢٧)

And recite the true story of Adam's two sons when they both offered a sacrifice, and it was accepted from one of them but was not accepted from the other. (Quran 5:27)

لَن تَنَالُوا۟ ٱلْبِرَّ حَتَّىٰ تُنفِقُوا۟ مِمَّا تُحِبُّونَ ۚ وَمَا تُنفِقُوا۟ مِن شَىْءٍ فَإِنَّ ٱللَّهَ بِهِۦ عَلِيمٌ ۝ (القرآن ٣:٩٢)

Never will you attain piety until you donate from that which you love. And whatever you spend - indeed, Allah is Knowing of it. (Quran 3:92)

عَنْ أَنَسِ بْنِ مَالِكٍ ـ رضى الله عنه ـ يَقُولُ كَانَ أَبُو طَلْحَةَ أَكْثَرَ أَنْصَارِيٍّ بِالْمَدِينَةِ نَخْلاً، وَكَانَ أَحَبَّ أَمْوَالِهِ إِلَيْهِ بَيْرُحَاءَ، وَكَانَتْ مُسْتَقْبِلَةَ الْمَسْجِدِ، وَكَانَ رَسُولُ اللَّهِ صلى الله عليه وسلم يَدْخُلُهَا وَيَشْرَبُ مِنْ مَاءٍ فِيهَا طَيِّبٍ، فَلَمَّا أُنْزِلَتْ ‏{‏لَنْ تَنَالُوا الْبِرَّ حَتَّى تُنْفِقُوا مِمَّا تُحِبُّونَ‏}‏ قَامَ أَبُو طَلْحَةَ فَقَالَ يَا رَسُولَ اللَّهِ، إِنَّ اللَّهَ يَقُولُ ‏{‏لَنْ تَنَالُوا الْبِرَّ حَتَّى تُنْفِقُوا مِمَّا تُحِبُّونَ‏}‏ وَإِنَّ أَحَبَّ أَمْوَالِي إِلَىَّ بَيْرُحَاءَ وَإِنَّهَا صَدَقَةٌ لِلَّهِ، أَرْجُو بِرَّهَا وَذُخْرَهَا عِنْدَ اللَّهِ، فَضَعْهَا يَا رَسُولَ اللَّهِ حَيْثُ أَرَاكَ اللَّهُ‏.‏ قَالَ رَسُولُ اللَّهِ صلى الله عليه وسلم ‏"‏ بَخٍ، ذَلِكَ مَالٌ رَايِحٌ، ذَلِكَ مَالٌ رَايِحٌ، وَقَدْ سَمِعْتُ مَا قُلْتَ، وَإِنِّي أَرَى أَنْ تَجْعَلَهَا فِي الأَقْرَبِينَ ‏"‏‏.‏ قَالَ أَبُو طَلْحَةَ أَفْعَلُ يَا رَسُولَ اللَّهِ‏.‏ فَقَسَمَهَا أَبُو طَلْحَةَ فِي أَقَارِبِهِ وَبَنِي عَمِّهِ‏.‏ قَالَ عَبْدُ اللَّهِ بْنُ يُوسُفَ وَرَوْحُ بْنُ عُبَادَةَ ‏"‏ ذَلِكَ مَالٌ رَابِحٌ ‏"‏‏.‏ حَدَّثَنِي يَحْيَى بْنُ يَحْيَى قَالَ قَرَأْتُ عَلَى مَالِكٍ ‏"‏ مَالٌ رَايِحٌ ‏"‏ (صحيح البخاري)

Narrated Anas bin Malik: Out of all the Ansar, living in Medina, Abu Talha had the largest number of (date palm trees) gardens, and the most beloved of his property to him was Bairuha garden which was standing opposite the Masjid. The Messenger of Allah (peace be upon him) used to enter it and drink of its sweet water. When the Verse:--"By no means shall you attain righteousness unless you donate of that which you love." (Quran 3:92), Abu Talha got up and said: O Messenger of Allah, Allah says:-"By no means shall you attain righteousness unless you spend (in charity) of that which you love." (3.92) and the most beloved of my property to me is the Bairuha garden, so I donate it in Allah's Cause and hope to receive good out of it, and to have it stored for me with Allah. So, O Messenger of Allah! Utilize it in the way Allah as He orders you to. The Messenger of Allah (peace be upon him) said, "Wonderful! That is a property you have benefited from! That is a property you have benefited from! I have heard what you have said and I think that you should distribute that (garden) amongst your relatives." Then Abu Talha distributed that garden amongst his relatives and his cousins. (Bukhari - Sahih)

فَلَمَّا بَلَغَ مَعَهُ ٱلسَّعْىَ قَالَ يَٰبُنَىَّ إِنِّىٓ أَرَىٰ فِى ٱلْمَنَامِ أَنِّىٓ أَذْبَحُكَ فَٱنظُرْ مَاذَا تَرَىٰ ۚ قَالَ يَٰٓأَبَتِ ٱفْعَلْ مَا تُؤْمَرُ ۖ سَتَجِدُنِىٓ إِن شَآءَ ٱللَّهُ مِنَ ٱلصَّٰبِرِينَ

﴿١٢﴾ فَلَمَّا أَسْلَمَا وَتَلَّهُ لِلْجَبِينِ ﴿١٣﴾ وَنَادَيْنَاهُ أَن يَا إِبْرَاهِيمُ ﴿١٤﴾ قَدْ صَدَّقْتَ الرُّؤْيَا ۚ إِنَّا كَذَٰلِكَ نَجْزِي الْمُحْسِنِينَ ﴿١٥﴾ إِنَّ هَٰذَا لَهُوَ الْبَلَاءُ الْمُبِينُ ﴿١٦﴾ وَفَدَيْنَاهُ بِذِبْحٍ عَظِيمٍ ﴿١٧﴾ وَتَرَكْنَا عَلَيْهِ فِي الْآخِرِينَ ﴿١٨﴾ (القرآن ٣٧: ١٠٢-١٠٨)

And when he came of age, he said: O my son! I have seen in a dream that I should sacrifice you; consider then what you see. He said: O my father! Do as you are commanded; if Allah wills, you will find me of the patient ones. So when they both submitted and he placed him down upon his forehead, and We called out to him: O Ibrahim! You have indeed fulfilled the vision; surely thus do We reward the doers of good. Most surely this was a manifest trial. And We ransomed him with a great sacrifice. And We caused him to be praised among the later generations. (Quran 37:102-108)

قُلْ إِن كَانَ آبَاؤُكُمْ وَأَبْنَاؤُكُمْ وَإِخْوَانُكُمْ وَأَزْوَاجُكُمْ وَعَشِيرَتُكُمْ وَأَمْوَالٌ اقْتَرَفْتُمُوهَا وَتِجَارَةٌ تَخْشَوْنَ كَسَادَهَا وَمَسَاكِنُ تَرْضَوْنَهَا أَحَبَّ إِلَيْكُم مِّنَ اللَّهِ وَرَسُولِهِ وَجِهَادٍ فِي سَبِيلِهِ فَتَرَبَّصُوا حَتَّىٰ يَأْتِيَ اللَّهُ بِأَمْرِهِ ۗ وَاللَّهُ لَا يَهْدِي الْقَوْمَ الْفَاسِقِينَ ﴿٢٤﴾ (القرآن ٩: ٢٤)

Say: If your fathers and your sons and your brothers and your spouses and your relatives and property which you have acquired, and the reduction of commerce which you fear and houses which you desire, are more beloved to you than Allah and His Messenger and striving in His way, then wait till Allah brings about His command: and Allah does not guide the transgressing people. (Quran 9:24)

Obedience (طَاعَة)

Enjoined upon all Muslims is the duty of obedience. Our Lord, the Most High, has commanded us to obey Himself and His Messenger (peace be upon him). Allah the Exalted has also commanded us to obey those in authority, but only within the limits of His commands.

قُلْ أَطِيعُوا۟ ٱللَّهَ وَٱلرَّسُولَ ۖ فَإِن تَوَلَّوْا۟ فَإِنَّ ٱللَّهَ لَا يُحِبُّ ٱلْكَٰفِرِينَ ۝ (القرآن ٣:٣٢)

Say, "Obey Allah and the Messenger." But if they turn away - then indeed, Allah does not like the disbelievers. (Quran 3:32)

وَأَطِيعُوا۟ ٱللَّهَ وَٱلرَّسُولَ لَعَلَّكُمْ تُرْحَمُونَ ۝ (القرآن ٣:١٤٢)

And obey Allah and the Messenger that you may obtain mercy. (Quran 3:132)

عَنْ عَبْدِ اللَّهِ بْنِ عُمَرَ - رضى الله عنهما - قَالَ كُنَّا إِذَا بَايَعْنَا رَسُولَ اللَّهِ صلى الله عليه وسلم عَلَى السَّمْعِ وَالطَّاعَةِ يَقُولُ لَنَا "فِيمَا اسْتَطَعْتَ" (صحيح البخاري)

Narrated Abdullah bin Umar: Whenever we gave the Pledge of allegiance to the Messenger of Allah (peace be upon him) for to listen to and obey, he used to say to us, "for as much as you can." (Bukhari - Sahih)

وَمَا ءَاتَىٰكُمُ ٱلرَّسُولُ فَخُذُوهُ وَمَا نَهَىٰكُمْ عَنْهُ فَٱنتَهُواْ ۚ وَٱتَّقُواْ ٱللَّهَ (القرآن ٥٩:٧)

And whatever the Messenger has given you - take; and what he has forbidden you - refrain from. And fear Allah. (Quran 59:7)

فَلَا وَرَبِّكَ لَا يُؤْمِنُونَ حَتَّىٰ يُحَكِّمُوكَ فِيمَا شَجَرَ بَيْنَهُمْ ثُمَّ لَا يَجِدُواْ فِىٓ أَنفُسِهِمْ حَرَجًا مِّمَّا قَضَيْتَ وَيُسَلِّمُواْ تَسْلِيمًا ۝ (القرآن ٤:٦٥)

But no, by your Lord, they will not believe until they make you, [O Muhammad], judge concerning that over which they dispute among themselves and then find within themselves no reservation from what you have judged and submit in [full, willing] submission. (Quran 4:65)

يَـٰٓأَيُّهَا ٱلَّذِينَ ءَامَنُوٓاْ أَطِيعُواْ ٱللَّهَ وَأَطِيعُواْ ٱلرَّسُولَ وَأُوْلِى ٱلْأَمْرِ مِنكُمْ ۖ فَإِن تَنَـٰزَعْتُمْ فِى شَىْءٍ فَرُدُّوهُ إِلَى ٱللَّهِ وَٱلرَّسُولِ إِن كُنتُمْ تُؤْمِنُونَ بِٱللَّهِ وَٱلْيَوْمِ ٱلْءَاخِرِ ۚ ذَٰلِكَ خَيْرٌ وَأَحْسَنُ تَأْوِيلًا ۝ (القرآن ٤:٥٩)

O believers, obey Allah and obey the Messenger and those in authority among you. And if you disagree over anything, refer it to Allah and the Messenger, if you should believe in Allah and the Last Day. That is the best way and best in result. (Quran 4:59)

عَنِ ابْنِ عَبَّاسٍ ـ رضى الله عنهما ـ {أَطِيعُوا اللَّهَ وَأَطِيعُوا الرَّسُولَ وَأُولِي الأَمْرِ مِنْكُمْ}. قَالَ نَزَلَتْ فِي عَبْدِ اللَّهِ بْنِ حُذَافَةَ بْنِ قَيْسِ بْنِ عَدِيٍّ، إِذْ بَعَثَهُ النَّبِيُّ صلى الله عليه وسلم فِي سَرِيَّةٍ. (صحيح البخاري)

Narrated Ibn Abbas: The Verse: "Obey Allah and Obey the Messenger and those in authority." (4.59) was revealed in connection with Abdullah bin Hudhafa bin Qais bin Adi' when the Prophet (peace be upon him) appointed him as the commander of an army detachment. (Bukhari- Sahih)

عَنْ أَبِي هُرَيْرَةَ ـ رضي الله عنه ـ أَنَّ رَسُولَ اللَّهِ صلى الله عليه وسلم قَالَ "مَنْ أَطَاعَنِي فَقَدْ أَطَاعَ اللَّهَ، وَمَنْ عَصَانِي فَقَدْ عَصَى اللَّهَ، وَمَنْ أَطَاعَ أَمِيرِي فَقَدْ أَطَاعَنِي، وَمَنْ عَصَى أَمِيرِي فَقَدْ عَصَانِي" (رواه البخاري ومسلم والنّسائي وابن ماجه — صحيح)

Narrated Abu Huraira: The Messenger of Allah (peace be upon him) said, "Whoever obeys me, obeys Allah, and whoever disobeys me, disobeys Allah, and whoever obeys the ruler I appoint, obeys me, and whoever disobeys him, disobeys me." (Bukhari, Muslim, Nasai, Ibn Majah - Sahih)

عَنْ عَبْدِ اللَّهِ ـ رضي الله عنه ـ عَنِ النَّبِيِّ صلى الله عليه وسلم قَالَ "السَّمْعُ وَالطَّاعَةُ عَلَى الْمَرْءِ الْمُسْلِمِ، فِيمَا أَحَبَّ وَكَرِهَ، مَا لَمْ يُؤْمَرْ بِمَعْصِيَةٍ، فَإِذَا أُمِرَ بِمَعْصِيَةٍ فَلاَ سَمْعَ وَلاَ طَاعَةَ" (صحيح البخاري)

Narrated Abdullah: The Prophet (peace be upon him) said, "A Muslim has to listen to and obey whether he likes it or not, as long as his orders involve not one in disobedience (to Allah), but if an act of disobedience (to Allah) is imposed one should not listen to it or obey it." (Bukhari - Sahih)

عَنْ أَبِي هُرَيْرَةَ، أَنَّ رَسُولَ اللَّهِ صلى الله عليه وسلم قَالَ "عَلَيْكَ بِالطَّاعَةِ فِي مَنْشَطِكَ وَمَكْرَهِكَ وَعُسْرِكَ وَيُسْرِكَ وَأَثَرَةٍ عَلَيْكَ" (رواه النّسائي — صحيح)

Narrated Abu Hurairah: The Messenger of Allah (peace be upon him) said: "You have to obey when you feel energetic and when you feel tired, during your ease and your hardship, and when others are preferred over you." (Nasai - Sahih)

Perseverance (ثَبَات)

Nothing worthy of achievement in human history has been achieved without perseverance. This is the natural order of things that Allah the Exalted has decreed upon this universe. The prophets (peace be upon them) showed the most perseverance because they were more beloved to Allah the Exalted and because their objective was the most important, namely the pleasure of Allah the Exalted.

The Muslim continues to work and strive to achieve the goal despite his distance to the goal and the length of his journey, until he meets Allah the Exalted in this state of continuous struggle.

مِّنَ ٱلْمُؤْمِنِينَ رِجَالٌ صَدَقُواْ مَا عَـٰهَدُواْ ٱللَّهَ عَلَيْهِ ۖ فَمِنْهُم مَّن قَضَىٰ نَحْبَهُۥ وَمِنْهُم مَّن يَنتَظِرُ ۖ وَمَا بَدَّلُواْ تَبْدِيلًا ۝ (القرآن ٢٣:٣٣)

Among the believers are men who have been true to their covenant with Allah. Of them, some have completed their vow (to the extreme), and some still wait: But they have never changed (their determination) in the least. (Quran 33:23)

$$\text{أَمْ حَسِبْتُمْ أَن تَدْخُلُوا۟ ٱلْجَنَّةَ وَلَمَّا يَأْتِكُم مَّثَلُ ٱلَّذِينَ خَلَوْا۟ مِن قَبْلِكُم ۖ مَّسَّتْهُمُ ٱلْبَأْسَاءُ وَٱلضَّرَّاءُ وَزُلْزِلُوا۟ حَتَّىٰ يَقُولَ ٱلرَّسُولُ وَٱلَّذِينَ ءَامَنُوا۟ مَعَهُۥ مَتَىٰ نَصْرُ ٱللَّهِ ۗ أَلَا إِنَّ نَصْرَ ٱللَّهِ قَرِيبٌ}$$ (القرآن ٢:٢١٤)

Do you think that you will enter Paradise while such [trial] has not yet come to you as came to those who passed on before you? They were touched by poverty and hardship and were shaken until even their messenger and those who believed with him said, "When is the help of Allah?" Indeed, the help of Allah is near. (Quran 2:214)

$$\text{كَذَٰلِكَ لِنُثَبِّتَ بِهِۦ فُؤَادَكَ}$$ (القرآن ٢٥:٣٢)

Thus with (the Quran) We strengthened your heart. (Quran 25:32)

$$\text{يُثَبِّتُ ٱللَّهُ ٱلَّذِينَ ءَامَنُوا۟ بِٱلْقَوْلِ ٱلثَّابِتِ فِى ٱلْحَيَوٰةِ ٱلدُّنْيَا وَفِى ٱلْءَاخِرَةِ ۖ وَيُضِلُّ ٱللَّهُ ٱلظَّٰلِمِينَ ۚ وَيَفْعَلُ ٱللَّهُ مَا يَشَاءُ}$$ (القرآن ١٤:٢٧)

Allah keeps firm those who believe, with the firm word, in worldly life and in the Hereafter. And Allah sends astray the wrongdoers. And Allah does what He wills. (Quran 14:27)

حَدَّثَنِي النَّوَّاسُ بْنُ سَمْعَانَ الْكِلَابِيُّ، قَالَ سَمِعْتُ رَسُولَ اللهِ ـ صلى الله عليه وسلم ـ يَقُولُ "مَا مِنْ قَلْبٍ إِلاَّ بَيْنَ إِصْبَعَيْنِ مِنْ أَصَابِعِ الرَّحْمَنِ إِنْ شَاءَ أَقَامَهُ وَإِنْ شَاءَ أَزَاغَهُ". وَكَانَ رَسُولُ اللهِ ـ صلى الله عليه وسلم ـ يَقُولُ "يَا مُثَبِّتَ الْقُلُوبِ ثَبِّتْ قُلُوبَنَا عَلَى دِينِكَ" (رواه ابن ماجه – صحيح)

Nawwas bin Saman Al-Kilabi sad: I heard the Messenger of Allah (peace be upon him) say: "There is no heart that is not between two of the Fingers of the Most Merciful. If He wills, He guides it and if He wills, He sends it astray." The Messenger of Allah used to say:

"O You Who makes hearts steadfast make our hearts steadfast in adhering to Your religion." (Ibn Majah - Sahih)

يَٰٓأَيُّهَا ٱلَّذِينَ ءَامَنُواْ ٱصْبِرُواْ وَصَابِرُواْ وَرَابِطُواْ وَٱتَّقُواْ ٱللَّهَ لَعَلَّكُمْ تُفْلِحُونَ ۝ (القرآن ٣: ٢٠٠)

O believers, persevere and outdo all others in perseverance and be ready and observe your duty to Allah in order that you may succeed. (Quran 3:200)

وَكُلًّا نَّقُصُّ عَلَيْكَ مِنْ أَنۢبَآءِ ٱلرُّسُلِ مَا نُثَبِّتُ بِهِۦ فُؤَادَكَ وَجَآءَكَ فِى هَٰذِهِ ٱلْحَقُّ وَمَوْعِظَةٌ وَذِكْرَىٰ لِلْمُؤْمِنِينَ ۝ (القرآن ١١: ١٢٠)

And each [story] We relate to you from the news of the messengers is that by which We make firm your heart. And there has come to you, in this, the truth and an instruction and a reminder for the believers. (Quran 11:120)

Dedication (تَجَرُّد)

We commit ourselves to one goal, Islam itself, and abandon all other competing principles. This is because this goal, Islam, is loftier and more worthy than all other goals. Dedication to Islam will unburden us from competing goals, drives our whole being to a single comprehensive objective.

صِبْغَةَ ٱللَّهِ ۖ وَمَنْ أَحْسَنُ مِنَ ٱللَّهِ صِبْغَةً ۖ وَنَحْنُ لَهُۥ عَٰبِدُونَ ۝ (القرآن ٢:١٣٨)

(Ours is) the color of Allah and which color can be better than Allah's? And we are His worshipers. (Quran 2:138)

يَٰٓأَيُّهَا ٱلَّذِينَ ءَامَنُوا۟ لَا تُلْهِكُمْ أَمْوَٰلُكُمْ وَلَآ أَوْلَٰدُكُمْ عَن ذِكْرِ ٱللَّهِ ۚ وَمَن يَفْعَلْ ذَٰلِكَ فَأُو۟لَٰٓئِكَ هُمُ ٱلْخَٰسِرُونَ ۝ (القرآن ٦٣:٩)

O believers, let not your wealth and your children divert you from remembrance of Allah. And whoever does that, then those are the losers. (Quran 63:9)

أَحَسِبَ ٱلنَّاسُ أَن يُتْرَكُوٓا۟ أَن يَقُولُوٓا۟ ءَامَنَّا وَهُمْ لَا يُفْتَنُونَ ۝ وَلَقَدْ فَتَنَّا ٱلَّذِينَ مِن قَبْلِهِمْ ۖ فَلَيَعْلَمَنَّ ٱللَّهُ ٱلَّذِينَ صَدَقُوا۟ وَلَيَعْلَمَنَّ ٱلْكَٰذِبِينَ ۝ (القرآن ٢٩: ٢-٣)

Do the people think that they will be left to say, "We believe" and they will not be tried? But We have certainly tried those before them, and Allah will surely make evident those who are truthful, and He will surely make evident the liars. (Quran 29:2-3)

$$\text{وَمِنَ ٱلنَّاسِ مَن يَشْرِى نَفْسَهُ ٱبْتِغَآءَ مَرْضَاتِ ٱللَّهِ ۗ وَٱللَّهُ رَءُوفٌ بِٱلْعِبَادِ}$$

(القرآن ٢:٢٠٧)

And among the people is he who gives himself completely to seek the pleasure of Allah; and Allah is affectionate to the servants. (Quran 2:207)

عَنْ خَبَّابِ بْنِ الأَرَتِّ، قَالَ شَكَوْنَا إِلَى رَسُولِ اللهِ صلى الله عليه وسلم وَهُوَ مُتَوَسِّدٌ بُرْدَةً لَهُ فِي ظِلِّ الْكَعْبَةِ، قُلْنَا لَهُ أَلاَ تَسْتَنْصِرُ لَنَا أَلاَ تَدْعُو اللهَ لَنَا قَالَ "كَانَ الرَّجُلُ فِيمَنْ قَبْلَكُمْ يُحْفَرُ لَهُ فِي الأَرْضِ فَيُجْعَلُ فِيهِ، فَيُجَاءُ بِالْمِنْشَارِ، فَيُوضَعُ عَلَى رَأْسِهِ فَيُشَقُّ بِاثْنَتَيْنِ، وَمَا يَصُدُّهُ ذَلِكَ عَنْ دِينِهِ، وَيُمْشَطُ بِأَمْشَاطِ الْحَدِيدِ، مَا دُونَ لَحْمِهِ مِنْ عَظْمٍ أَوْ عَصَبٍ، وَمَا يَصُدُّهُ ذَلِكَ عَنْ دِينِهِ، وَاللَّهِ لَيُتِمَّنَّ هَذَا الأَمْرَ حَتَّى يَسِيرَ الرَّاكِبُ مِنْ صَنْعَاءَ إِلَى حَضْرَمَوْتَ، لاَ يَخَافُ إِلاَّ اللَّهَ أَوِ الذِّئْبَ عَلَى غَنَمِهِ، وَلَكِنَّكُمْ تَسْتَعْجِلُونَ" (صحيح البخاري)

Narrated Khabbab bin Al-Arat: We complained to the Messenger of Allah (peace be upon him) while he was sitting in the shade of the Kaba, leaning over his claok. We said to him: Would you seek help for us? Would you pray to Allah for us? He said: "Among the nations before you a (believing) man would be put in a ditch that was dug for him, and a saw would be put over his head and he would be cut into two pieces; yet that would not make him give up his religion. His body would be combed with iron combs that would remove his flesh from the bones and nerves, yet that would not make him abandon his religion. By Allah, this religion will prevail until a traveler from Sana to Hadrarmaut will fear none but Allah, or a wolf as regards his sheep, but you people are hasty. (Bukhari – Sahih)

$$\text{ٱلَّذِينَ يُبَلِّغُونَ رِسَٰلَٰتِ ٱللَّهِ وَيَخْشَوْنَهُۥ وَلَا يَخْشَوْنَ أَحَدًا إِلَّا ٱللَّهَ ۗ وَكَفَىٰ بِٱللَّهِ حَسِيبًا}$$

(القرآن ٣٣:٣٩)

Those who deliver the messages of Allah and fear Him, and fear no one except Allah, and Allah suffices as reckoner. (Quran 33:39)

Fraternity (أُخُوَّة)

Wonderful indeed is our membership in the Ummat Muhammad (peace be upon him)! A community whose leader is the most noble human to ever walk on Earth. The largest club. The community of believers, united in brotherhood through worship and love to Allah the Exalted.

إِنَّمَا ٱلْمُؤْمِنُونَ إِخْوَةٌ (القرآن ٤٩:١٠)

The believers are but brothers. (Quran 49:10)

عَنِ النُّعْمَانِ بْنِ بَشِيرٍ، قَالَ قَالَ رَسُولُ اللَّهِ صلى الله عليه وسلم "مَثَلُ الْمُؤْمِنِينَ فِي تَوَادِّهِمْ وَتَرَاحُمِهِمْ وَتَعَاطُفِهِمْ مَثَلُ الْجَسَدِ إِذَا اشْتَكَى مِنْهُ عُضْوٌ تَدَاعَى لَهُ سَائِرُ الْجَسَدِ بِالسَّهَرِ وَالْحُمَّى" (متفق عليه)

Numan bin Bashir reported that the Messenger of Allah (peace be upon him) said: "The example of believers in regard to their mutual love, affection, fellow-feeling is that of one body; when any limb of it aches, the whole body aches, because of sleeplessness and fever." (Muslim, Bukhari - Sahih)

وَٱلْمُؤْمِنُونَ وَٱلْمُؤْمِنَٰتُ بَعْضُهُمْ أَوْلِيَآءُ بَعْضٍ (القرآن ٩:٧١)

The believing men and believing women are allies of one another. (Quran 9:71)

عَنْ أَنَسِ بْنِ مَالِكٍ، أَنَّ رَسُولَ اللهِ صلى الله عليه وسلم قَالَ "لاَ تَبَاغَضُوا وَلاَ تَحَاسَدُوا وَلاَ تَدَابَرُوا وَكُونُوا عِبَادَ اللهِ إِخْوَانًا وَلاَ يَحِلُّ لِمُسْلِمٍ أَنْ يَهْجُرَ أَخَاهُ فَوْقَ ثَلاَثٍ" (صحيح مسلم)

Anas bin Malik reported: The Messenger of Allah (peace be upon him) said: "Don't harbor mutual hatred, or jealousy, or enmity, and become as brothers and servants of Allah. It is not lawful for a Muslim to keep his relations estranged with his brother beyond three days." (Muslim - Sahih)

وَالَّذِينَ جَاءُو مِنْ بَعْدِهِمْ يَقُولُونَ رَبَّنَا اغْفِرْ لَنَا وَلِإِخْوَانِنَا الَّذِينَ سَبَقُونَا بِالْإِيمَانِ وَلَا تَجْعَلْ فِي قُلُوبِنَا غِلًّا لِلَّذِينَ آمَنُوا رَبَّنَا إِنَّكَ رَءُوفٌ رَحِيمٌ ۝ (القرآن ١٠:٥٩)

And those who came after them, saying, "Our Lord, forgive us and our brothers who preceded us in faith and put not in our hearts resentment toward those who have believed. Our Lord, indeed You are Kind and Merciful." (Quran 59:10)

عَنْ أَبِي الدَّرْدَاءِ، قَالَ قَالَ رَسُولُ اللهِ صلى الله عليه وسلم "مَا مِنْ عَبْدٍ مُسْلِمٍ يَدْعُو لِأَخِيهِ بِظَهْرِ الْغَيْبِ إِلاَّ قَالَ الْمَلَكُ وَلَكَ بِمِثْلٍ" (صحيح مسلم)

Abu Darda reported: The Messenger of Allah (peace be upon him) said: "There is no believing servant who supplicates for his brother in his absence except that the angels say: The same be for you too." (Muslim - Sahih)

عَنْ عَلِيٍّ، قَالَ قَالَ رَسُولُ اللهِ ـ صلى الله عليه وسلم ـ "لِلْمُسْلِمِ عَلَى الْمُسْلِمِ سِتَّةٌ بِالْمَعْرُوفِ يُسَلِّمُ عَلَيْهِ إِذَا لَقِيَهُ وَيُجِيبُهُ إِذَا دَعَاهُ وَيُشَمِّتُهُ إِذَا عَطَسَ وَيَعُودُهُ إِذَا مَرِضَ وَيَتْبَعُ جِنَازَتَهُ إِذَا مَاتَ وَيُحِبُّ لَهُ مَا يُحِبُّ لِنَفْسِهِ" (رواه ابن ماجه ــ صحيح)

Narrated Ali: The Messenger of Allah (peace be upon him) said: "The Muslim has six rights from the Muslim: He should greet him when he meets him; he should accept his invitation if he invites him; he should answer his sneeze (by invoking the mercy of Allah upon him); he should visit him if he becomes sick; he should follow his funeral if he dies; and he should love for him what he loves for himself." (Ibn Majah - Sahih)

عَنْ أَنَسٍ ـ رضي الله عنه ـ قَالَ قَالَ رَسُولُ اللَّهِ صلى الله عليه وسلم "انْصُرْ أَخَاكَ ظَالِمًا أَوْ مَظْلُومًا". فَقَالَ رَجُلٌ يَا رَسُولَ اللَّهِ أَنْصُرُهُ إِذَا كَانَ مَظْلُومًا، أَفَرَأَيْتَ إِذَا كَانَ ظَالِمًا كَيْفَ أَنْصُرُهُ قَالَ "تَحْجُزُهُ أَوْ تَمْنَعُهُ مِنَ الظُّلْمِ، فَإِنَّ ذَلِكَ نَصْرُهُ" (صحيح البخاري)

Narrated Anas: The Messenger of Allah (peace be upon him) said, "Help your brother whether he is an oppressor or an oppressed," A man said: O Messenger of Allah! I will help him if he is oppressed, but if he is an oppressor, how shall I help him?" The Prophet (peace be upon him) said, "By preventing him from oppressing (others), for that is how to help him." (Bukhari - Sahih)

Confidence in Leadership (الثِّقَةُ فِي القِيَادَةِ)

The Messenger of Allah (peace be upon him) has commanded us to perform Islamic work in a team and he (peace be upon him) has also commanded us to appoint leadership for our teams.

Every Muslim has a right and an obligation to participate in a team organized for Islamic work where they are able to trust, obey and advise their leaders.

Thus each Islamic activist should have confidence that the leadership is (i) working towards what please Allah the Exalted, (ii) qualified for their leadership role, (iii) has their best interests at heart.

The Islamic activist should be able to turn to their leadership for comfort, advice and guidance. Their relationship with their spiritual guide or mentor should ideally be like that of a brother.

If an Islamic activist is unable to attain confidence in these matters, then either there is a defect in themselves which they need to fix or the leadership does not meet this standard, then they should leave their current team and go to a team that better meets the highest of Islamic ideals.

وَإِذَا جَآءَهُمْ أَمْرٌ مِّنَ ٱلْأَمْنِ أَوِ ٱلْخَوْفِ أَذَاعُوا۟ بِهِۦ ۖ وَلَوْ رَدُّوهُ إِلَى ٱلرَّسُولِ وَإِلَىٰٓ أُو۟لِى ٱلْأَمْرِ مِنْهُمْ لَعَلِمَهُ ٱلَّذِينَ يَسْتَنۢبِطُونَهُۥ مِنْهُمْ ۗ وَلَوْلَا فَضْلُ ٱللَّهِ عَلَيْكُمْ وَرَحْمَتُهُۥ لَٱتَّبَعْتُمُ ٱلشَّيْطَـٰنَ إِلَّا قَلِيلًا (القرآن ٤:٨٣)

And when there comes to them information about [public] security or fear, they spread it around. But if they had referred it back to the Messenger or to those of authority among them, then the ones who [can] draw correct conclusions from it would have known about it. And if not for the favor of Allah upon you and His mercy, you would have followed Shaytan, except for a few. (Quran 4:83)

عَنْ عَبْدِ اللهِ بْنِ عَمْرٍو، أَنَّ النَّبِيَّ صلى الله عليه وسلم قَالَ "مَنْ بَايَعَ إِمَامًا فَأَعْطَاهُ صَفْقَةَ يَدِهِ وَثَمَرَةَ قَلْبِهِ فَلْيُطِعْهُ مَا اسْتَطَاعَ" (رواه أبو داود والنَّسائي وابن ماجه ومسلم — صحيح)

Narrated Abdullah bin Amr: The Prophet (peace be upon him) said: "If a man takes an oath of allegiance to a leader, and puts his hand on his hand and does it with the sincerity of his heart, he should obey him as much as possible." (Abu Dawud, Nasai, Ibn Majah, Muslim - Sahih)

عَن ابْنِ عَبَّاسٍ، عَنِ النَّبِيِّ صلى الله عليه وسلم قَالَ "مَنْ كَرِهَ مِنْ أَمِيرِهِ شَيْئًا فَلْيَصْبِرْ، فَإِنَّهُ مَنْ خَرَجَ مِنَ السُّلْطَانِ شِبْرًا مَاتَ مِيتَةً جَاهِلِيَّةً" (متفق عليه)

Narrated Ibn Abbas: The Prophet (peace be upon him) said, "Whoever disapproves of something done by his Amir then he should be patient, for whoever disobeys the ruler even a little will die as those who died in the Period of Ignorance." (Bukhari, Muslim - Sahih)

Shall the reward of excellence be other than excellent?

Made in the USA
Columbia, SC
17 April 2018